THE
12 PILLARS
OF
BUSINESS
SUCCESS

THE
12 PILLARS
OF
BUSINESS
SUCCESS

How to Achieve
Extraordinary Results
from Ordinary People

RON SEWELL

KOGAN
PAGE

YOURS TO HAVE AND TO HOLD
BUT NOT TO COPY

First published in 1996
Reprinted 1997
Paperback edition published in 1997

Kogan Page Limited
120 Pentonville Road
London N1 9JN

© Ron Sewell, 1996

British Library Cataloguing in Publication Data
A CIP record for this book is available from the British Library.
ISBN 0 7494 2005 7 (Hardback) ISBN 0 7494 2476 1 (Paperback)

Typeset by Saxon Graphics Ltd, Derby
Printed and bound in Great Britain by Biddles Ltd, Guildford and King's Lynn

CONTENTS

Advisory Team

Professor Jonathan Brown

Brian Coolahan, Former Managing Director, GE Capital Finance

Professor Stephane Garelli, IMD and Lausanne University

Bryan Gourlay, Sewells International Ltd

David Heslop, Managing Director, Mazda Cars (GB) Ltd

Daniel Jones, Professor of Manufacturing, Cardiff Business School

Richard Whipp, Professor of Human Resources, Cardiff Business School

Martin Wibberley, Personnel and Organisation Director, Sun Valley

Production Team

Aubrey McILrath
Julia Howarth
Kathy Luscombe
Gabi Facer – Kogan Page Publishers
Jennifer Gubbay – Kogan Page Publishers
Deborah Dawson – Kogan Page Publishers

FOREWORD

I feel very honoured to have been invited to contribute the Foreword to this important book which I believe is a helpful extension of the views I have been trying to proselytise for so long. All of us know that our businesses will only succeed if we create an environment in which the entire company is working together to a predetermined destination. Moreover, all of us can recognise when every individual is contributing and when the leadership of the team is moving effortlessly from individual to individual, dependent only on the relevance of their skills and background, in order to deal effectively with whatever problem the team as a whole is facing. The difficulty lies not in describing the end result but, as so often in management and business, in actually the steps which need to be taken in order to achieve that result. I have long believed that one of the reasons business tends to be regarded so poorly as a way of life is that despite the fact that the general objectives are usually quite simple (indeed they have to be because they involve the wholehearted collaboration of a large number of people) the actual achievement of these objectives can be immeasurably difficult.

Ron Sewell's book seems to me to answer a number of these questions and it actually does show some of the things to which I believe any business leader should be turning his attention. Leadership in business is like so many other things in life. Positive investment is needed if you are to achieve the pay off and positive investment means devoting very large amounts of time to the processes through which business can be improved. One of the difficulties is that we confuse dealing with the limitless number of immediate and fascinating tangible problems, with which we are comfortable and familiar, with the actual management of the business. The reality is that the job of the Chief Executive, manager of a department or leader of any group of people is to create the conditions under which they can perform extraordinarily. If you are successful in creating such conditions you will be constantly surprised, not only by the capability of your people, but by their commitment, enthusiasm and sheer ability to achieve the apparently unachievable.

When the goal is so clear and the pay off so large is it not extraordinary that so few business leaders are actually prepared to study what is needed and then devote a proportion of their time to trying to manage the processes of the whole organisation? Ron Sewell draws upon a vast gallery of business people, academics and others who have contributed to this crusade – indeed it truly is a crusade. There is no way in which Britain will obtain competitive advantage over the peoples of the Far East, Europe or America by being more Japanese, Chinese or whatever it may be than our competitors. We have to find and devise ways in which we can release the capability of our people and these capabilities are based almost entirely upon their individualism, creativity and ingenuity. These are priceless national advantages which in the past have stood us in good stead. The enormous range of British inventions and innovations in political systems, trade unions, academia and so on have all contributed to moving the world ahead. What are needed are ways in which we can create a new initiative and emphasis on business leadership which will enable our people to achieve the world leadership which alone will meet the overwhelming needs of our country and of the new generations of our children coming along. I believe that Ron Sewell's book will be a real assistance in this quest.

Sir John Harvey-Jones MBE

AUTHOR'S INTRODUCTION

For the past 30 years I have acted as a 'personal coach' to senior executives of companies, large and small, throughout Britain and overseas. To ensure that my 'coaching' was well-informed, I have spent the past 30 years in studying books and articles on outstandingly successful business executives and the leading management 'gurus' of the day.

Thirty years ago I started my own business from scratch and built it into an integrated consultancy, training and strategic information service. So, when 'coaching' my clients, I was able to talk to them from the first-hand experience I was gaining of building and running my own business.

To find the most cost-effective way of helping my clients, I progressively developed a three-day 'Workshop' at which a dozen or so senior executives could discuss the issues confronting them with their peers, while I acted as the facilitator. From time to time I invited a leading 'guru' to give them fresh insights. To provide a framework for these 'Workshops' I developed a 'Management Consultancy Workbook' which, with case studies and examples of best practice, could aid them in their syndicate discussions.

Arising from this, I have been invited to speak at conferences and seminars from which has evolved a demand for me to set out in book form, the concepts about which I talk. Hence this book, which I hope you will find interesting to read, and helpful as you strive to develop your career, or to grow your own successful business.

May I close by apologising to the females who read this book. My wife and I built our business in partnership. We have had many women as clients, and I respect the many outstanding females who hold senior positions in business. But it can get tedious to keep writing him/her, he/she, so I hope you can accept that though I have kept to the masculine throughout the book, everything I say applies equally well to both sexes. In fact, part of the reason for the success of many women in business is that they have the empathy, the natural aptitude, to build *The Twelve Pillars*.

Ron Sewell

'There is tremendous unused potential in our people. Our organisations are constructed so that most of our employees are asked to use 5 to 10 per cent of their capacity at work. It is only when these same individuals go home that they can engage the other 90 to 95 per cent – to run their households, lead a Boy Scout troop, or build a summer home. We have to be able to recognise and employ that untapped ability that each individual brings to work every day.'

Percy Barnevik – ABB

Asea Brown Boveri has been judged Europe's most successful company.

THE MOST IMPORTANT BOOK YOU WILL EVER READ

If you are an executive, at any level, in any organisation, *your success will depend on your people.* This is such a trite truism that you may be tempted to say, *'I know, so what?'*

The reality is that you are likely to be working far too hard, far too long, trying to keep on top of all the conflicting pressures of business today that, with the best will in the world, you are unable to spend enough time on your most important asset: your people.

It is *not* a question of adopting one technique; however good that technique may be. Over the past decades we have seen one technique after another come and go. Research published in *Management Today* shows that companies who have embraced 're-engineering' have largely been disappointed by its impact. As gardeners will know, no plant, however healthy, will thrive if planted in the wrong environment. Similarly, no technique will thrive unless the overall environment is right.

This is the simple message of this book. Your success depends on creating an environment in which every single member of your team will feel totally committed to your success.

The figure missing in most organisations is their *team commitment index:* the extent to which each member of the team is fully committed to achieving the goals needed for the overall success of *their organisation.* This does not depend on *them:* it depends on *us.* All too often we, as senior executives, are to blame. Percy Barnevik has created one of Europe's most successful organisations. He suggests that many organisations are only using five to ten per cent of their people's true capacity. As he says, *'we have to be able to recognise and employ that untapped ability'.*

This book sets out the 12 ingredients, which I have called 'pillars', which have to be present in your organisation to enable you to do this. It is based on five years' intensive research into the ingredients of success behind outstandingly successful organisations, backed by the conclusions of the world's leading 'gurus'.

It is important to bear in mind that although each chapter is dedicated to one 'pillar', each is totally interdependent and, particularly when looking at issues of motivation and communication, it is vital to take into account the impact of the other 11 pillars.

If you can apply the 12 pillars, it will be the most important book you have ever read.

THERE HAS TO BE AN EASIER WAY

You want to win: to have a successful organisation or business. To this end, you probably work far too hard, far too long and under some considerable degree of stress; particularly if you own your own business and are guaranteeing its overdraft!

You do not need me to spell out all the pressures of running an organisation but the end result is that there are never enough hours in the day.

In many organisations there is an underlying sense of tension. The boss is working far too hard to spend enough time on team development and people related issues. Even if his 'door is always open' people are reluctant to interrupt because they can see the stress under which he is working. Lacking guidance from the top, executives compound the problem by being far too busy to spend time with their immediate subordinates who are frustrated by their 'powerlessness'.

There is no one 'big idea' likely to provide a miracle cure with little or no effort. The latest 'fad' by itself will not have lasting impact. (Many senior executives have destroyed their credibility by chasing after the current 'flavour of the month' technique, often without being willing to devote the time and resources needed to create the culture within which the technique might stand a reasonable chance of success.)

We have two options. The first is to continue with the frustration of seeking to *drive* the business with the stresses equivalent to seeking to 'brushing water uphill'.

The second option, *The Easier Way,* is to transform your organisation into a team of individuals who, working together, can run the organisation,

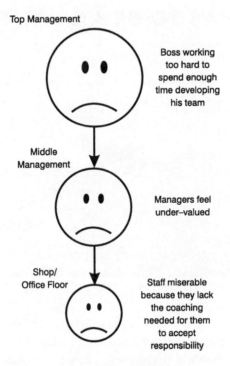

Top Management

Boss working
too hard to
spend enough
time developing
his team

Middle
Management

Managers feel
under–valued

Shop/
Office Floor

Staff miserable
because they lack
the coaching
needed for them
to accept
responsibility

Figure I.1   Managing

often achieving significantly improved results, provided you create the culture within which they can be successful on your behalf.

Ralph Stayer[1] was a very successful business man. He had started his organisation from scratch and built it into a very profitable organisation, producing meat pies and related products. He grew to the point of employing nearly 400 people but by then he was experiencing the type of frustrations we are discussing.

He concluded that he had created an organisation which was the equivalent of a herd of buffaloes. Everyone took their lead from him: when he turned, they turned. He decided that his only option was to transform his organisation into the equivalent of a flock of geese. When geese fly in formation, taking turns to fly 'point', they complete the journey 70 per cent faster than any goose flying by itself. So, *The Easier Way* is to turn your organisation into the equivalent of a flight of geese.

Hard results

The sheer competitiveness of business today means you cannot take risks. You need hard results. Let's learn from Ralph Stayer.

As he admits, Ralph Stayer built his business by being an autocrat. When he realised that he had to change his style for the company to progress, *he ordered his staff to take responsibility; he abdicated.* Obviously, the approach failed. He then realised that he had to create the conditions under which his workers would start to demand responsibility. Once he started to focus on the issues we will be discussing, the climate began to change.

A turning point came when his workers said that they did not want to work at weekends. He passed the problem back to them. They realised that during

One chief executive had an organisation that behaved
like 'buffaloes'. His staff took their lead from him. When he turned:
they turned. He decided to get them to behave more like a
'flock of geese' with his colleagues each taking their turn to lead.

Geese fly in formation, taking turns to fly 'point'.
They complete their journey 70% faster
than any goose flying by itself.

Figure I.2 Fly with the GEESE

the week they had a machine downtime of between 30–40 per cent for which they were responsible. They got downtime to below 10 per cent and did not need to work at weekends.

Line workers took responsibility for the quality of their products. The team gathered data, identified problems, worked with suppliers and with other line workers to develop and implement solutions, even visited retail stores to find out how retailers handled the product. They took responsibility for measuring quality and then used these measurements to improve production processes.

They owned and expected to own all the problems; rejects fell from 5 per cent to less than 0.5 per cent. They asked for information about costs and customer reactions and started to implement improvements. They came to own and expect responsibility for correcting the problems that customers raised.

They took responsibility for selecting and training their own colleagues and for dealing with performance problems. They fired individuals who would not come up to the standards of their team. They developed a self-appraisal scheme linked to a profit sharing scheme based on their performance which was administered by a volunteer team of production workers from various departments.

Progressively, the team began to make all decisions about schedules, performance standards, assignments, budgets, quality measures, and capital expenditures.

The crucial point is that as teams progressively took over the supervisors' functions the supervisors' jobs disappeared. Ralph Stayer did not cut out levels of management. He progressively developed his front-line 'members' until the supervisory levels of management became unnecessary. In passing, supervisors who could only function in an authoritarian way left the company. Most went into other jobs at Johnsonville, such as technical positions.

The second crucial point is that as front line 'members' began to take more responsibility, the need for staff functions changed. Thus quality control stopped checking quality and began providing positive support by developing monitoring techniques and customer panels. The traditional personnel department disappeared and was replaced by a 'learning and personal development team'.

Do you agree that to achieve such transformation would be well worth while and is *The Easier Way* to achieve hard results?

BENEFITS OF FLYING WITH THE GEESE

Turning our organisations into the equivalent of a 'flight of geese' depends on one person, you and I as chief executives. It will add a totally different dimension to our work which will require extra effort on our part and possibly extra stress. It will certainly require a long-term commitment. So, is it going to be worthwhile? The answer must be a resounding *yes,* for four reasons:

- Health
- Happiness
- Performance
- Survival.

Health

Having had a quadruple by-pass, I know only too well that 'driving' a business, with all the stresses involved, including lying awake in the early hours worried stiff on occasions, can damage one's health. The *Financial Times* once ran a feature on the increasing problems of 'executive burnout'. The style of life is no good for us, our families, or our organisations.

Happiness

Most of the executives agree that the 'fun' has gone out of business. We all spend such a significant portion of our lives at work that it is vital to reintroduce fun. *The Easier Way* does this. For senior executives, being carried along by a team of committed people is not only more enjoyable for us, but an essential factor in gaining their commitment. Performance in every area of your organisation will improve, which in turn will reduce stress and increase happiness as everyone starts to feel involved as a member of a 'winning team'.

Survival

Finally, we have no option. In today's highly competitive environment companies will not survive if they employ a 'herd of buffaloes'. Every trade and industry is facing increased direct and indirect competition. High Street banks are faced with the loss of 95,000 jobs, according to one estimate, as people like Direct Line Insurance start to provide lower cost banking services via the phone. Customers are demanding more for less.

As a result, margins are under pressure and, to survive, we need to run very lean organisations. Cutting staff is both negative and often counter-productive as the remaining staff become demotivated. The only answer is to seek vastly improved performance from a committed team of colleagues, our 'flight of geese'. Easier if we have an expanding organisation. Not so easy if we are in a stagnant or declining market – but still the only effective approach.

Performance

Let's come back to improved performance.

We shut our small company down for half a day a month and hire a temporary telephonist, so that everyone can discuss the progress and future of our company. Every member of the team in turn has to stand up to give a short presentation on how they are contributing to the company's success. When Alf, our lovable 70 year old 'post boy' gave his presentation, he came up with ideas that saved us at least £10,000 a year on postage.

Peter Nathan employs just over 100 people at his Abbeyvale Bakery in Devon. Having invested heavily to improve production, his packing department became a bottleneck. Peter did not become involved. He put the issue to Sue Stevens, the packing team leader. Her kitchen table became their 'boardroom'. She and her team researched the different options, including different equipment, and came up with recommendations that not only solved the problem but achieved initial savings of at least £15,000 and enabled one of the team to be transferred to other essential work. These savings are expected to increase as their ideas are developed still further.

One of Unipart's 'My Contribution Counts' forums saved £86,000 on its own while the total savings arising from all the forums in the group is now £2 million.

At Premier Exhaust in Coventry, £300,000 was saved when front-line workers designed and implemented procedures that made a third shift unnecessary.

In one of his Annual Reports, Jack Welch of General Electric commented 'Teams of hourly employees now run, without supervision, $20 million worth of milling machines that *they specified, tested and approved for purchase.* The cycle time for the operation has dropped 80 per cent. It is embarrassing to reflect that for 80 or 90 years we have been dictating equipment needs and managing people who knew how to do things much better and faster than we did.'

At another GE Division, when senior management explained the seriousness of the downturn in business due to the recession, the workers came up with ideas which reduced production costs by 45 per cent. When they were asked why they had not put these ideas forward earlier, they pointed out that they had never previously been involved nor asked for their help.

It comes back to deeply ingrained attitudes. The manager of one Tarmac plant, which had increased production by 40 per cent in six months, admitted that he felt uncomfortable asking his front-line people for help. He thought it was his job to know what was best. But as his Chief Operating Officer commented:

> Those working closest to problems have the best idea of how to resolve them. As one example, innovative solutions from front-line colleagues helped to cut the cost of a £10m tunnel at Heathrow by more than £500,000; a 5 per cent saving which probably went straight down to the bottom line.

The Easier Way is to treat the people doing the job as the experts, and not only give them responsibility for resolving problems but get them totally committed to a continuous search for improvements. Nissan in Sunderland have achieved world-class levels of productivity. Everyone is totally committed to the process of Kaizen, or continuous improvements.

Before we discuss how we achieve this level of commitment, let us stop to consider why people react as they do.

Switching people off

In one of his books[2], Sir John Harvey Jones wrote of the way in which large organisations can, so easily, 'switch people off'. Executives running smaller organisations may delude themselves into thinking that, because they are closely involved with their workforce, this does not happen to them.

Ralph Stayer's medium-sized company was successful but he was unhappy about his workers' reaction so he had an attitude study carried out. He regarded himself as a caring, benevolent employer, involved with his people. He was shattered when the results of the survey showed that his rankings were no better than some of the industrial giants in his area.

He did not want to believe the results. He looked for excuses. The methodology was wrong. The questions were poorly worded. He did not want to believe that he had an employee motivation problem. The survey told him that his people saw nothing for themselves in his organisation. It was merely a job. He wanted them to commit to his company's goals. They saw little to commit to. The very things that had brought him success were creating a counter-productive environment. As he admitted:

> I had been Johnsonville Sausage, assisted by some hired hands who, to my annoyance, lacked commitment. The survey told me that people saw nothing for themselves at Johnsonville. It was a job, a means to some end that lay outside the company. I wanted them to commit themselves to a company goal. They saw little to commit to and, at that stage, I still could not see that the biggest obstacle to changing their point of view was me.

At my seminars, I often ask people to complete the questionnaire overleaf. The reality is that when we are so busy 'chasing our tails' to the point where we have little or no time for people-related issues, we do 'switch people off'.

There's an old story about some stonemasons who were asked what they were doing. One said that he was trying to get even with the bastard of a supervisor. One was so disinterested that he didn't bother to reply. One replied that he was there to earn a living. The fourth explained that he was a skilled stonemason responsible for dressing and shaping stone. The fifth said, very proudly, 'I am helping to build this cathedral!'

At my seminars I ask those present to estimate how many of each category they have within their own organisations. Typical responses are:

		%	%
■	I'll get even	0–10	
■	Couldn't care less	10–20	
■	Only work here	25–40	
■	Feel involved	15–30	
■	Truly committed	5–10	

What percentages would you apply to your own organisation?

The challenge is to get to the point where the majority of our people feel truly involved or enthusiastically committed. This depends on the style of management or leadership we, and our team of executives, display. This, in turn, depends on our fundamental beliefs about people which fall into two categories:

■ **Transactional:** This is the traditional view that the employee is being paid to do a job, should do it when he is told, without challenge, and without concerning himself with the how or why. It is often reinforced by the strongly held belief that 'rank has its privileges'.

■ **Transformational:** This is based on the belief that we are making an important investment in people which we need to optimise by transforming their performance. So, our fundamental attitude to those with whom we work is to say to them, 'We have trust and confidence in your expertise and commitment. We will share information on our vision, goals and performance, to enable you to gain satisfaction and recognition for making a meaningful contribution to our joint success.' The underlying belief, as at Honda, is that *'to lead is to serve'*.

Let me tell you two true stories.

In one traditionally transactionally managed factory, only the Production Director had authority to stop the line. This had to be kept going at all cost. Inspectors at the end of the line rejected products not up to standard. (On occasions this resulted in large areas of products waiting rectification.)

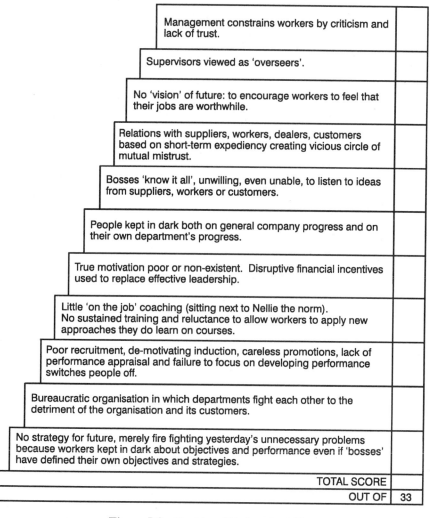

Traditional 'transactional' management. 'You are paid to do what you are told, without challenge and it's not up to you to concern yourself with the how and why.'

Marking	
Untrue	3
Partially True	2
True	1

Management constrains workers by criticism and lack of trust.

Supervisors viewed as 'overseers'.

No 'vision' of future: to encourage workers to feel that their jobs are worthwhile.

Relations with suppliers, workers, dealers, customers based on short-term expediency creating vicious circle of mutual mistrust.

Bosses 'know it all', unwilling, even unable, to listen to ideas from suppliers, workers or customers.

People kept in dark both on general company progress and on their own department's progress.

True motivation poor or non-existent. Disruptive financial incentives used to replace effective leadership.

Little 'on the job' coaching (sitting next to Nellie the norm). No sustained training and reluctance to allow workers to apply new approaches they do learn on courses.

Poor recruitment, de-motivating induction, careless promotions, lack of performance appraisal and failure to focus on developing performance switches people off.

Bureaucratic organisation in which departments fight each other to the detriment of the organisation and its customers.

No strategy for future, merely fire fighting yesterday's unnecessary problems because workers kept in dark about objectives and performance even if 'bosses' have defined their own objectives and strategies.

TOTAL SCORE

OUT OF 33

Figure I.3 Pushing 'Workers' uphill

One day the line stopped. The Chargehand called the Supervisor, who called the Foreman, who called the Manager, who called the Senior Manager, who called the appropriate Engineer. Since many were tucked away in offices, 'paper-pushing' or in meetings, this took time.

While they were waiting, one of the men on the line had the temerity to suggest a solution. Not only was his idea shot down, he was told in no uncertain terms to leave his brains at the factory gate in future. Eventually the expert came along, recommended the idea put forward by the worker, and the line restarted with the workers seething with resentment at the treatment given to their colleague.

At another factory, every worker has the responsibility to stop the line if they spot a problem which would result in a lack of quality. One day one of the workers stopped the line to point out a problem. Immediately, every manager in the area arrived to see what they could do to help. They were there within minutes. Firstly they apologised to the workers for the fact that the problem had arisen. Second, they asked the workers how they thought it could be resolved. One gave a suggestion. It was tried. It worked. He was praised and congratulated for stopping the line and for putting forward the solution.

The line resumed with a highly motivated team of workers, enthused that their views had been taken into account. In passing, no inspection is needed at the end of the line, because every line worker is his own inspector and, on the odd occasion that something does slip through, the product is returned to the workers responsible to rectify.

The five levels of reaction by the stonemasons previously referred to, are typical of any worker, and will be a direct reflection of five different styles of management or leadership (see Table I.1 overleaf).

There are some bloody-minded managers. Some, particularly those promoted because of their technical skills, find refuge in pushing paper: they become bureaucrats. If a manager takes a view that the workers are paid to work, it is not surprising if the workers react accordingly. The fourth level, where workers feel involved, is often created by executives who have an underlying transactional style but demonstrate empathy and have some charisma to get results from their people. The fifth level will only be achieved by those who take the transformational approach of recognising that 'to lead is to serve' and that is their responsibility to optimise the investment that has been made in their major asset, their people.

You might like to use Table I.1 to record the number of your executives who fall under each heading.

Hardest problem

The biggest problem you are going to face lies in changing the deep-seated attitude of you, your executives, and of everyone within your organisation. These influence the 'culture' of your organisation and they can be so deeply entrenched as to create a real barrier to any process of change. These deeply held values and beliefs are often described as the 'mindset' or, as the paradigm (pronounced *paradime*) which is defined as a core set of beliefs and assumptions which fashion an organisation's view of itself and its environment.

Table I.1 *Five styles of management or leadership*

The five levels of reaction of our colleagues will be a direct reflection of the styles of management or leadership we, and our team of executives, display.	Number of executives adopting approach
I'll Get Even	First level reaction is created by **bloody minded managers.**
I Couldn't Care Less	Second level reaction is created by **bureaucratic,** or **preoccupied management.**
I Only Work Here	Third level reaction is caused by **traditional, transactional management.**
I'm Involved	Fourth level reaction is caused by **transactional leaders.**
I'm Committed	Fifth level reaction is generated by **transformational leaders.**
In short, the level of reaction we generate is a direct reflection of our style of management or our style of leadership.	Total no. of executives

Changing the paradigm of your organisation will be your biggest challenge. It is a point we will come back to. Is it worth making the effort?

Hard results

The hard reality is that at a time when senior executives are worried about increased competition and decreased margins, they are failing to optimise on their major investment in people, whose direct and indirect costs are often more than 50 per cent of total operating costs. Research projects continue to show that the majority of people, often more than 75 per cent of those questioned, do not feel that their organisation is using their talents to the full. A significant percentage, frequently as high as 50 per cent, admit that they merely do just enough to keep their jobs.

Even people who their supervisors regard as good, loyal, hard working, conscientious, committed people, are probably performing at only 50 per cent of their potential. Any businessperson who only used half the space of his expensive offices: only used half of his equipment and used only half of his stocks, would, quite rightly, be regarded as a lunatic. Yet, through sheer pressure of transactionally based work, many organisations *are* only using half the potential of the people in their organisation.

Even a 5 or 10 per cent improvement would have a tremendous impact on your business. There is no option. *The Easier Way* of unlocking the potential of your people is the only way forward.

Upturning your organisation

The way to transform your organisation's productivity is to upturn it in the way shown in Figure I.4. Everyone is smiling. Your front-line colleagues are happy at being empowered. Your middle-line executives are happy to revert to having a 'hands-on' approach of using their expertise to act as coaches and facilitators; not paper pushing bureaucrats. Once the transformation is achieved, you will be a lot happier, healthier in yourself and healthier in terms of the improved performance of your organisation.

Leadership

One thing you may notice throughout this book is that I do not refer to *employees*. I think it sounds derogatory. I recommend all my clients to abolish the term. I like 'colleagues', a term which Asda also uses. One client uses 'member'. Honda, at Swindon, use the term 'associate'. We must also get away from the term 'manager', as I will explain later. My clients have been encouraged to use terms such as leaders, coaches or facilitators.

Let's look in more detail at what's involved by looking at Figure I.5 overleaf.

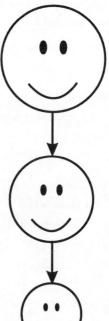

Front Line team members happy to be trusted with the responsibility of making a meaningful contribution to their organisation's success.

Coaches and Facilitators. Much happier to use their original 'practical' skills to help by coaching their teams and to facilitate their successes.

Leaders, relieved of much of their mundane work, happy to be able to focus on providing a sense of direction, and in communicating their vision.

Figure I.4 Leadership

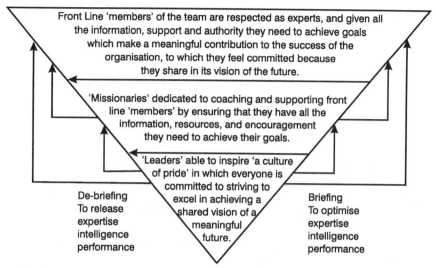

Upturning both the way in which you project your organisation AND the philosophy you adopt towards each level; particularly in regard to their contribution to the success of THEIR organisation.

Figure I.5 Upturning your Organisation

At my seminars I ask those present to underline words they believe to be significant. You may like to do this. The words frequently underlined in respect to the first triangle are:

- Respected as experts
- Given all the information
- Authority to achieve goals
- Meaningful contributions

Words commonly underlined in the second triangle are:

- Dedicated
- Supporting
- Resources
- Achieves
- Coaching
- Information
- Encouragement
- Goals

When it comes to the last triangle the words typically underlined are:

- Inspire
- Culture
- Pride
- Everyone is committed
- Striving to excel
- Achieving shared vision
- A meaningful future

These words touch on the all important issues of values, beliefs and attitude which we'll discuss later.

Twelve crucial ingredients requiring a totally new mindset if performance is to be transformed

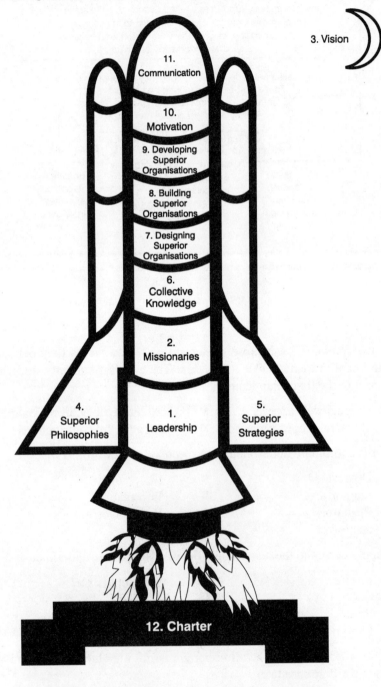

Figure I.6 Your space shuttle to achieve your vision

THE PILLARS FOR SUCCESS

Jack Welch, Chairman of GE, was once asked, 'What do executives have to get right if they want to revise and re-structure their businesses?' He suggested that the question ought to be geared to asking, 'What ingredients do you think people need to win?'

I like his word 'ingredients'. Throughout this book I have substituted the word 'Pillars' to represent the concept that every pillar has to be in place. I have identified the 12 ingredients I believe to be essential. In Figure I.6 my colleague Kathy has shown them in the form of a space rocket on the basis that each section has to work effectively for the rocket to be successful.

Mixing my metaphors, if you want to bake a cake successfully, you have to use all the ingredients in the right proportions. Similarly, if we want to transform our businesses, we have to use all twelve ingredients in a totally integrated manner. We are going to look at each ingredient but, before we do so, let's touch on three important issues.

CHANGING 'MINDSET'

Earlier we discussed the need to change the culture of the organisation, to change our mindset or paradigm. In Table I.2 I have set out the twelve pillars of our transformational approach, and compared them with the typical transactional approach. I hope you can recognise that we are talking about a fundamental difference of approach in every area of the business.

Table I.2

TRANSFORMATIONAL APPROACH	TRANSACTIONAL APPROACH
1. Leadership	1. Scientific management
2. Effective followers and missionaries	2. Managers and controllers
3. Vision	3. Budgets
4. Superior philosophies	4. Expediency
5. Superior strategies, cascaded throughout organisation	5. Confidential business plans
6. Collective knowledge	6. Managers paid to think: workers to work
7. Designing superior organisation	7. Protection of 'territories'
8. Building superior organisation	8. Delegated to personnel department
9. Developing superior organisation	9. Delegated to training department
10. Goal-related motivation	10. Bonuses and commissions
11. Communication of vision	11. Directives on performance
12. Culture (Charter) of change	12. Reluctance to change: 'This is the way we've always done things.'

THE STRATEGIC DIMENSION

But it is more than this. There is a strategic dimension to the 12 ingredients. In the transactional approach, all 12 ingredients may be present but they are not coordinated: there is no cohesive strategy (Figure I.7).

If most of your competitors are doing much the same as yourself, in much the same way, then the only way of gaining a competitive advantage is to get extraordinary performance from teams of ordinary people. The only way to achieve this, is by ensuring that every one of the 12 ingredients is perceived to be an essential, integral element of your overall strategy.

Figure I.7 The uncoordinated approach

The power of the new approach is shown in Figure I.8 overleaf. The strategic holistic approach generates increasing power as each step reinforces the next.

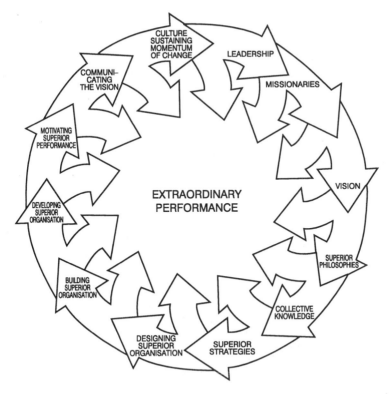

Figure I.8   The strategic, holistic approach

BRAINSTORMING EXERCISES OR PROJECTS

Need to upturn organisation

■ Do you agree on the need to move progressively from traditional, transactional management to a transformational style leadership? If so, what are the most important, immediate things you need to do?

■ Are you 'pushing workers uphill'? Looking at how you have marked yourself on the charts on pages 23 and 25, what are the most important things you need to do to take the brakes off your team?

■ If you accept the concept of 'upturning' your organisation, what do you and your executive team need to do to start easing your own workload by giving far more responsibility to your front-line, customer-facing colleagues? Should you ask every executive to produce an action plan showing the tasks they plan to delegate more effectively, and those they intend to retrain?

1
LEADERSHIP

Ralph Stayer believes *'People want to be great. If they aren't, it's because their management won't let them be.'*

Whenever I give a speech, some members of the audience will challenge my emphasis on leadership and my criticism of transactional management. They accuse me of semantics. By so doing, they are demonstrating their own deeply ingrained 'mindset'. There is a significant difference between transformational leadership and transactional management.

These differences were summarised brilliantly by John P Kotter[3], whose table is reproduced here (Table 1.1). John Kotter then teamed up with James Heskett to write another book called *Corporate Culture and Performance*[4], which is well worth reading. One of their conclusions was that:

> Excellent management, by its very nature, is somewhat conservative, methodically incremental, and short-term oriented. As a result, the very best management cannot produce major change.

The two professors base their conclusion on extensive research but they may be guilty of overemphasis. What we need are good management practices which help us to optimise our performance by the quality of our leadership.

RE-ENGINEERING THE MANAGER

James Champy, co-author of *Re-Engineering the Corporation*[5], pointed out in the *Financial Times* that for 're-engineering' to work, the role of management has to change significantly.

Table 1.1 The difference between management and leadership

MANAGEMENT	LEADERSHIP
Planning and budgeting – establishing detailed steps and timetables for achieving needed results, and then allocating the resources necessary to make that happen	**Establishing direction** – developing a vision of the future, often the distant future, and strategies for producing the changes needed to achieve that vision
Organising and staffing – establishing some structure for accomplishing plan requirements, staffing that structure with individuals, delegating responsibility and authority for carrying out the plan, providing policies and procedures to help guide people, and creating methods or systems to monitor implementation	**Aligning people** – communicating the direction by words and deeds to all those whose cooperation may be needed so as to influence the creation of teams and coalitions that understand the vision and strategies, and accept their validity
Controlling and problem solving – monitoring results vs. plan in some detail, identifying deviations, and then planning and organising to solve these problems	**Motivating and inspiring** – energising people to overcome major political, bureaucratic and resource barriers to change by satisfying very basic, but often unfulfilled, human needs
Produces a degree of **predictability and order**, and has the potential of consistently producing key results expected by various stakeholders (eg, for customers, always being on time; for stockholders, being on budget)	**Produces change**, often to a dramatic degree, and has the potential of producing extremely useful change (eg, new products that customers want, new approaches to labour relations that help make a firm more competitive)

Source: John P Kotter, *A Force for Change: How Leadership Differs from Management*, Free Press

As workers take on more management tasks, managers must take on more leadership tasks – holding a vision for the business, articulating it to workers and customers, and creating an environment that truly empowers workers. Shedding the traditional 'command and control' model for one of 'lead and enable'. Successful executives will be masters at getting people to work effectively together, managing conflict, and being effective coaches.

In any empowered organisation, what is important is what is measured. Measures must track people's contribution to their team, and the team's contribution to the success [of the organisation].

Paradoxically, quality, practicality and relevance of the information provided to workers will need to improve significantly to measure the processes needed to meet customer needs profitably.

James Champy ended his article by adding:

> I am often asked whether workers will be able to perform in their re-engineered jobs. When enabled and empowered, most of them can. The more serious question is whether managers can make the transition.

The more important question is whether we – as senior executives – can provide the leadership and support they will need.

COMPETITIVE CHALLENGE

As a result of their extensive studies, John Kotter and James Heskett conclude that:

> Without leadership, firms cannot adapt to a fast-moving world. If organisations are going to live up to their potential, we must find, develop and encourage more people to lead in the service of others. Excellent leadership from the top (is) the essential ingredient. This leadership empowers other managers and employees who see the need for change but have been constrained by the old culture. It also helps to win over the hearts and minds of others who have not yet recognised the necessity of major change. In many organisations today, providing this kind of leadership is surely the number one challenge for top executives.

FROM MANAGING TO LEADING

You cannot overturn your organisation overnight. It takes time to change deep-seated attitudes but I hope that you agree that achieving a transformational style of leadership is essential.

A personal friend of mine, John Mantle of Biggleswade, enrolled himself and his entire senior management team on a Dale Carnegie leadership course – one night a week for 12 weeks. He felt it was the best investment he had ever made. The important point was that John, as Managing Director, enrolled himself first and then invited his team to join him.

Bill Cullen, Chairman of Renault Ireland, took himself off for a week's course in Arizona led by Stephen Covey. Interestingly, before Bill went, he had to get six of his colleagues to fill in a questionnaire on their perception of his leadership style!

There is no shortage of leadership courses, videos, cassettes and books. It is often possible to link in to the training activities of other organisations. The Police Training College at Exeter runs a very cost-effective leadership course which other organisations find worthy of support. South Devon College will 'franchise' its courses.

The core issue is to recognise the importance of placing less emphasis on managing and more on leading.

One guru stresses the need for self mastery, which he feels is about being vision driven. The need to dream, to put the dream into a statement and commit oneself to its achievement through the organisation.

Figure 1.1 highlights three key issues: competence, confidence and commitment.

Competence

Every team (normally 25 people) at Nissan Sunderland has their own 'mini boardroom area' in which is displayed the level of competence of every member of the team in all the activities which have to be carried out.

Competence is assessed at four levels: (1) can do the work by referring to the manual: (2) can do the work without referring to the manual: (3) has enough competence to suggest improvements: (4) has the ability to train others. I found it refreshing to see this focus on developing competencies to the point where the team is charged with responsibility for making continuous improvements.

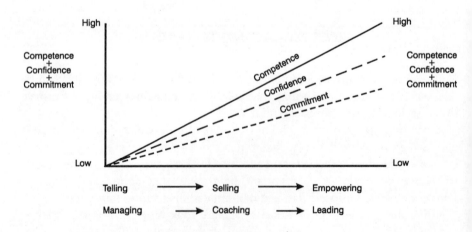

Figure 1.1   Managing to leading

This is the objective: to develop people so that they can run the business with the minimum of supervision. Companies such as GE and Rover set out to give their people the additional competencies that they need to 'manage' themselves: skills such as decision making, inter-personal skills, including assertiveness, and recruitment.

Confidence

It is not merely a question of competence, confidence is just as vital. People need to feel confident if they start making decisions on our behalf; they will be praised for getting them right, and coached and encouraged, not criticised, when they get them wrong. As Tom Peters has said, we must praise people for making mistakes. It is the only way they will gain both experience and confidence.

A very difficult step will be to transform our 'managers' from disciplinarians into coaches.

Commitment

Finally, we have to gain the commitment of those we wish to lead so that they become independent 'entrepreneurs' on our behalf. One client had over 40 'employees'. He was the one who lay awake at night worrying about the business. He has not won over everyone but the majority are now 'colleagues' sharing his concerns and commitment to the success of *their* business. Another client has over 700 employees. He and his top management team used to do all the worrying and driving. Now, they have scores of 'missionaries' helping to transform performance.

Leadership values

Gaining this level of commitment comes down to the standards, the values, we are prepared not only to set but to demonstrate. One of the best set of values I have seen are those set out by Jack Welch of General Electric (GE) (Table 1.2).

What do you think of them? Obviously, the reference to 'global' may not be relevant to you and might be changed to the capacity to developing marketing brains and marketing sensitivity. I will explain 'workout' later. Perhaps point 4 is the biggest challenge, to 'have the self-confidence to empower others'. In GE, Jack Welch will give people a second, third or even fourth chance if they fall down on performance, but people are removed for having the wrong values, with violations of integrity being totally unacceptable.

Table 1.2 GE leadership values

GE LEADERS – ALWAYS WITH UNYIELDING INTEGRITY:

- Create a clear, simple, reality-based, customer-focused vision and are able to communicate it straightforwardly to all constituencies
- Reach – set aggressive targets ...Understand accountability and commitment and are decisive
- Have a passion for excellence ... Hate bureaucracy and all the nonsense that comes with it
- Have the self-confidence to empower others and behave in a boundaryless fashion... Believe in and are committed to 'work out' as a means of empowerment ... Are open to ideas from anywhere
- Have, or have the capacity to develop, global brains and global sensitivity, and are comfortable building diverse global teams
- Stimulate and relish change ... Are not frightened or paralysed by it ... See change as opportunity, not a threat
- Have enormous energy and the ability to energise and invigorate others ... Understand speed as a competitive advantage and see the total organisation benefits that can be derived from a focus on speed

A LIBERATING PHILOSOPHY

Sumantra Ghoshal, Professor of Strategic Leadership at the London Business School, and his colleague Professor Chris Bartlett of Harvard, wrote a brilliant series of three articles for the Harvard Business Review on 'Changing the Role of Top Management'[6], in which they stress the need for a new leadership doctrine.

- **Changing sources of competitive advantage:**
  from assets and resources to knowledge and creativity
- **Changing moral contract with people:**
  from employment security to employability
- **Changing corporate philosophy:**
  from organisation man to the individualised corporation
- **Changing the role of top management:**

from *Strategy*	to *Purpose*
beyond *Structure*	to *Process*
beyond *Systems*	to *People*
from a *Constraining Environment*	to a *Liberating Philosophy*

The objective of all dedicated businessmen should be to thoroughly analyse all situations, anticipate all problems prior to their occurrence, have answers for these problems and move swiftly to solve these problems when called upon.

HOWEVER...
When you are up to your arse in alligators it is difficult to remind yourself your initial objective was to drain the swamp.

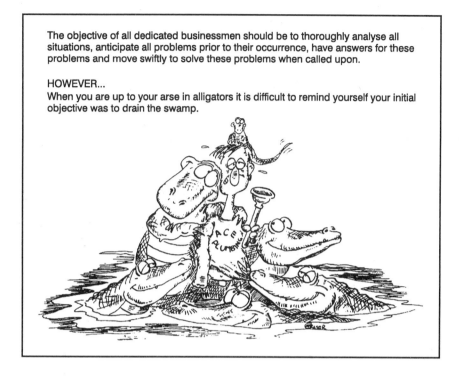

Figure 1.2 When you're up to your arse in alligators

I like my cartoon (Figure 1.2). When you are up to your arse in alligators, it *is* difficult to remember that your objective was to drain the swamp. Let's not get put off by their rhetoric. They make some valid, practical points which we need to reflect upon as we consider our leadership role. They argue that the most basic task of leaders is to unleash the human spirit which makes initiative, creativity and entrepreneurship possible.

The personal effectiveness of a leader

For those of us who have started our own businesses from scratch, it is very difficult. I started as a shy, introverted accountant. Len Lewis, of the successful construction group, MIDAS, started his business having been a Civil Engineer. Many businesses are started by people with a particular area of expertise. Even Chief Executives of larger organisations tend to have risen through the ranks of specialism, be it finance, technical or marketing.

To a very real degree, the success of the businesses we run is a reflection of our ability to transform ourselves into effective leaders.

No company can succeed without a strong leader. What does this mean?

In Japan, senior executives, until now, have ruled their organisations with a 'rod of iron' *but* – an important but – they have always known when to listen and when to delegate. Listening is a crucial element. For many executives, making the time to listen is the biggest problem.

Built to last

Built to Last[7] is a fascinating book by James Collins and Jerry Porras (Century, London) which is based on the research they carried out into why some companies have survived successfully for decades, while their immediate competitors in the same industry have fallen by the wayside.

They describe these successful organisations as *visionary companies*. They say that visionary companies are premier institutions – the crown jewels – in their industries, widely admired by their peers and having a long track record of making a significant impact on the world around them. The key point is that a visionary company is an organisation – an institution. **All individual leaders, no matter how charismatic or visionary, eventually die; and all visionary products and services – all 'great ideas' – eventually become obsolete.** Indeed, entire markets can become obsolete and disappear. Yet the 'visionary companies' they researched prospered over long periods of time, through multiple product life cycles and multiple generations of active leaders.

One of their charts is interesting. It shows the rate of growth of the visionary companies they analysed, against their comparison companies, and against the general stock market (Figure 1.3).

One of the conclusions is that *'A charismatic visionary leader is absolutely NOT required for a visionary company and, in fact, can be detrimental to a company's long-term prospect.'* As an example, they quote the long-term success of 3M, though few people would know the name of its Chief Executive. Their book goes on, in effect, to touch upon many elements of the 12 pillars we will be discussing but their crucial conclusion is that:

> The key difference, we believe, is one of orientation – key people at formative stages of the visionary company have a stronger organisational orientation than in the comparison companies, regardless of their personal leadership style ... in fact, we became increasingly uncomfortable with the term 'leader' and began to embrace the term 'architect' or 'clock builder'. They argue that many senior executives know how to tell the time (by reading management accounts and statistics) but truly successful Chief Executives of visionary companies know how to 'build a clock': by focusing on *building their organisation.*

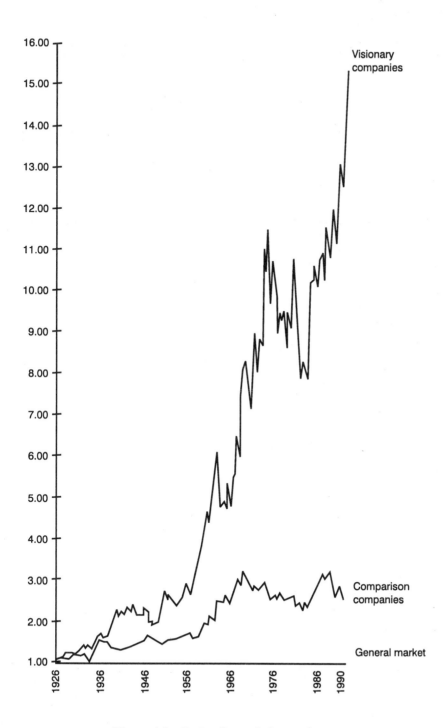

Figure 1.3 Ratio of cumulative stock returns
to general market 1926 -1990

In fact, the theme of *The Easier Way* is for us to refocus our energies, to transform our approach, to recognise that our priority task is to build a 'visionary organisation'. They use the term 'architect' or 'clock builder'. I prefer to use the term 'conductor'. We have to recognise that to be effective we have to be a conductor orchestrating the efforts of every member of our team, by spending time on the 11 pillars we have yet to discuss.

Example

I was very interested to read in the Strategy Plan of the South Devon College that Dr Terry Keen, its Principal and Chief Executive, was expected to:

Measurably demonstrate that he can:

- Provide employees with opportunities to develop their full potential.
- Bring into being, natural, self-motivated work units/teams wherever possible.
- Create 'customer thinking' throughout the organisation.
- Make systems, methods and procedures work for the benefit of employees, customers and suppliers.
- Obtain feedback on performance and practices and communicate these findings.
- Guide the Corporation on strategic goals and targets and to be involved in short and long-term planning.
- Delegate wherever possible.
- Educate and train in order to create a knowledge-based culture.
- Involve people as never before in order to tap ideas, creativity and innovation.
- Plan for future challenges and opportunities.
- Relate to customer needs.
- Share all information in order to create greater efficiency and understanding.
- Support staff and practise an holistic approach to human relations.
- Place the College in a premier position, nationally and internationally, by his continuing involvement in national and international developments.

Later, we will touch on the issue of agreeing in writing the 'key tasks' we expect from the members of our executive team and our colleagues. Our most important task is to define our own 'key tasks' because the care with which we do this will influence the long-term success of our organisation.

BRAINSTORMING EXERCISES OR PROJECTS: 1

From Management to Leadership

■ Do you agree with James Champy that it is 'time to re-engineer the manager'? If so, how would you and your team set about doing this?

■ Do you accept that you should not start this process of transformation unless you are prepared to see it through over whatever time span is needed? What steps do you need to take to ensure that there is a total commitment to such a long-term enterprise?

■ Do you accept that you cannot start to 'upturn' your organisation until you have built the competence, confidence and commitment of your front-line colleagues? If so, what actions do you need to take to ensure that you enhance their competence, build their confidence, and gain their commitment?

■ Do you accept General Electric's leadership values and the way in which they assess leadership qualities? If so, how could you introduce similar concepts into your own organisation?

■ If you are a Chief Executive, do you accept that it is not necessary to be a 'charismatic leader', but to focus your efforts on building an organisation by acting as a *conductor* orchestrating the efforts of every member of your team?

■ If you are a Chief Executive, have you set out in writing your own 'key tasks'?

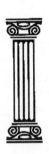
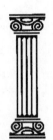

2

EFFECTIVE FOLLOWERS AND MISSIONARIES

I grew up on a diet of 'the charismatic leader'. Hornblower was a prime example of the naval officer always leading from the front, always leading the dangerous missions himself – often to the dismay of his officers. Sadly, too many entrepreneurs seem to model themselves on this style of 'leadership' with all the stresses we mentioned earlier.

We have to create leadership at every level of our organisation.

It is a nonsense to believe that any one man or woman, however gifted, can run a business single-handed. No one individual has all the skills needed, nor a monopoly of good ideas. The only answer is to develop a team of people of complementary skills, who know far more than we can hope to know about their particular areas of expertise.

It comes back to the earlier comment that the people doing the job should be the experts (Figure I.5). Bob Allen, Chief Executive of the American giant, AT&T, once said:

> I have never thought that I could be so knowledgeable and so current in our business and market that I could make the decisions. I have always been an advocate of shared decision making. In fact, I believe this is one of the reasons why I am CEO.

One of the reasons for the outstanding success of the Gulf War was that the correct military forces and the supplies they needed were in the right place, at the right time. General Pagonis, who ran this brilliant logistical operation, says that: *'True leaders create organisations that themselves cultivate leadership.'*

'THE LEADERSHIP CHALLENGE'

It has been pointed out that:

> *Leadership is in the eye of the follower*
> and
> *Followers make leaders powerful.*

Effective followers are defined as being:

Well-balanced and responsible adults who can succeed without leadership; they think for themselves, are energetic and assertive. They are committed, focus their energies, and are courageous, honest and credible because they are risk takers, self starters and independent problem solvers, they get consistently high ratings from peers and any superiors.

I find this thought-provoking. How many of us have really given serious thought to the need to create effective followers, able to provide leadership at every level of our organisation? It comes back to re-thinking the role of Chief Executive.

Leaders in an organisation of 'effective followers' are facilitators of change, conductors of the orchestra, rather than the square-jawed decision makers of the past. They treat followers as co-equals, except in strict line terms. This fits followers for one of their most important (although usually unstated) functions: to keep leadership on the straight and narrow.

MISSIONARIES

In any organisation, people fall into four different groups, in varying proportions:

■ Adventurous, enthusiastic and truly committed people willing to go 'the extra mile', and do anything that is necessary to make their company successful.
■ A core of people who don't see the need for change, but are open to persuasion.
■ You are likely to have your fair share of 'cynics' who have 'seen it all before' (and given the number of companies who have gone off at 'half cock' on various issues, they may have done!)
■ The ultra-conservatives, who tend to be insecure people who vehemently oppose any ideas of change.

You are going to need the help of the first group: those who are truly committed. They should be your 'missionaries'. This is what John Neill of

Unipart did when, after his 'buyout', he started to transform his manufacturing division which everyone else urged him to close.

You will need to list those most likely to be willing to put in the effort needed to create and sustain the momentum you need to generate. They should be the ones invited to your initial 'brainstorming' sessions to talk through the need for change, and how it is to be introduced. They should be the ones who are invited to serve on any project team you form to get the process under way. They can help you build up the 'critical mass' you will need.

TEAMS

We need to make greater use of teams of people committed to a common purpose and performance goals for which they hold themselves mutually accountable. The creation of teams facilitates the development both of 'effective followers' and of leadership at every level. We will return to the need to base our organisation on teams when discussing Structures and Systems (Pillar 7).

COMMITMENT

When people are respected for their ability to solve problems, they are likely not only to come up with more creative solutions but to be far more enthusiastically committed to taking the lead in making sure that their recommendations work.

VALUES

As one guru has pointed out, the power of leaders is that they deal with values. His comment was that:

> Values turn followers on. If followers feel more fulfilled by association with someone who asks them to behave in ways and for reasons that make them feel proud of themselves, that's leadership.

BRAINSTORMING EXERCISES OR PROJECTS: 2

Collective Leadership and Missionaries

■ Do you agree that you need to create a broader acceptance of the concept of 'collective leadership'? If so, how do you do this?

■ Do you agree that you need to encourage leadership at every level, in every activity? If so, how do you do it?

■ Do you agree that to help you in your transformation, you are likely to need a number of 'dedicated missionaries'? If so, how do you identify, involve and motivate them?

■ Do you accept that you need to create 'effective' followers, and if so, how can you do this?

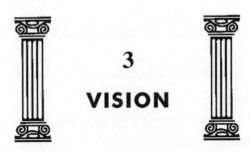

3

VISION

Whenever I use words like 'vision', 'mission', and 'meaning' at a seminar, I am invariably heckled by derisory remarks about companies with meaningless, disregarded statements framed on office walls. These are pointless. When discussing leadership, we referred to *visionary companies*: companies that are totally focused on achieving long-term success by building a **visionary organisation**. Clearly, this requires a sense of vision. So let's get down to basics with another powerful statement from Jack Welch of General Electric:

> *Workers who share their employer's goals don't need much supervision.*

If workers need less supervision we, as senior executives, can be leaders, not bogged down in management. We can have far fewer levels of executives to act as coaches and facilitators and thus do away with the need for many levels of coordinators and controllers. Some organisations have moved from 14 levels of management to four. So, how do we inspire our colleagues to share our goals?

WHAT IS A VISION?

Warren Bennis[8] says that:

> A vision should state what the future of the organisation will be like. It should engage our hearts and our spirits; it is an assertion about what we and our companies want to create. It is something worth going for; it provides meaning to the people in the organisation, in the work they are doing.

Ralph Stayer was a good paternalistic 'boss' but his survey showed that his workers saw little to commit to.

LEADER'S FIRST RESPONSIBILITY

Sir Peter Thompson explains[9] that when NFC was first privatised, he and his senior colleagues had long discussions with the Chief Executives of Britain's most successful companies. Sir Peter and his colleagues concluded that the reason for the success of these executives was that they:

> Had a clearer view of where they wanted their companies to go. They were also more determined to get there. Some of them would not embrace the word, but they all had a very clear vision for their business and most had clearly articulated business values.

A conclusion reinforced by a DTI Study.[10] Sir Peter went on to comment that:

> A company's long-term vision can only come from the leader. If the vision is totally shared, the leader has done his job. He has succeeded in getting everyone to whistle to the same tune. But it is most important to recognise the need for a vision and to be seen to be in the forefront of formulating and promoting it. Strategy emerges from the vision – strategy is merely the way in which the vision is realised. Keeping the vision bright and shining is [the leader's] most important job.

AMERICAN SURVEY

For their book, *Leaders*,[8] Warren Bennis and Burt Nanus studied 90 of America's most successful businessmen and women. They concluded that the first quality they shared was that they had created a focus of attention by a clearly articulated and communicated vision. They explain that:

> The visions these various leaders conveyed, seemed to bring about a confidence on the part of the employees, a confidence that instilled in them a belief that they were capable [of achieving the vision].

They add that the hallmark of successful executives is that:

■ they develop a compelling vision of the firm's future;
■ they translate the vision into reality by concentrating on the keys to success;
■ they remain deeply involved at the heart of things, spurring the actions needed to achieve the vision;

■ they constantly articulate the vision so that it permeates every level of the organisation, and its functions, taking the organisation where it has never been before.

As Bennis and Nanus put it[8]:

> If there is a spark of genius in the leadership function at all, it must lie in this transcending ability, a kind of magic, to assemble – out of all the variety of images, signals, forecasts and alternatives – a clearly articulated vision of the future that is simple, easily understood, clearly desirable and energising.

Professor Jonathan Brown has had a wide experience of senior management. In his view many of the CEOs who can articulate a vision, cannot identify the 'keys to success'. As I implied earlier, conventional management accounts are too focused on 'the bottom line'. What we need is to identify the 'top line drivers' that are the key to achieving our vision.

SHARED AMBITION

When Sumantra Ghoshal spoke at one of my seminars, he used the phrase 'Shared Ambition', which sums up brilliantly what we are about. How do we get as many people in our organisation as possible to share our ambition? We are not talking about a piece of paper on a wall, we are talking about an active management process.

As Sumantra said, how do we create:

■ **a sense of possibility**, that goes beyond 'business as usual';
■ **a sense of urgency**, which will challenge under-performance;
■ **a sense of unity**, with a common goal as a glue;
■ **a sense of personal responsibility**, where self-discipline stems from personal commitment;
■ **a sense of identity**, which provides meaning to everyone's efforts?

Sumantra's final challenge to the executives at our Seminar was to stress that:

> *The most basic task of leaders is to unleash the human spirit which makes initiative, creativity and entrepreneurship possible.*

We certainly cannot do this if we are bogged down trying to drive our businesses by being heavily involved in managing. We can only do this if we can step back and start to act as leaders.

A PROCESS

Let me stress what we are talking about is not a sterile statement, which remains unchanged, but an active management process. Indeed, you could argue that if your communications are truly effective then everyone should be aware of what you are trying to achieve, and you do not need a piece of paper.

In reality, this does not work. I once ran a 'workshop' for all the directors of a large group. When we came to clarifying vision, great arguments arose. We had to adjourn the meeting to allow tempers to cool. Yet these were the members of a Board who had been working together for many years and would have argued that they understood each other's point of view. (As we will discuss, the level of communication in many companies is not up to the task of imparting vision).

When NFC was first privatised, Sir Peter Thompson ensured extensive communication throughout the organisation on this issue. He held Sunday meetings to talk to everyone. They were well attended. Jack Welch ensures that at least one session is devoted to GE's mission on every single management course run within the organisation. Some 5000 people were involved in one year. As Jack Welch explained:

We want 300,000 people with different career objectives, different family aspirations, different financial goals, to share directly in our company's vision.

He adds that:

Good business leaders create a vision, articulate the vision, passionately own the vision, and relentlessly drive it to completion.

QUESTIONS TO ASK

Warren Bennis[8] says that the questions you should ask before drafting your vision statement are:

- What is unique about our company?
- What values are true priorities for the next decade?
- What would make me personally commit my mind and heart to this vision?
- What does our market need that our organisation can and should provide? and finally, and most importantly,
- What do I want my organisation to accomplish so that I will be committed, alive, and proud of my association with it?

In short, what every business needs is total dispassionate analysis of how we can gain a competitive edge (particularly at a time of stagnant or falling sales!). A continuous updated and objective view of what is needed for success is absolutely pivotal to the success of any business.

As we will discuss shortly, we need both superior strategies and superior philosophies. We will only establish this superiority if these strategies and philosophies are 'owned' by and committed to by every member of our team.

LIVE MANAGEMENT TOOL

Johnson & Johnson is one of the world's foremost companies. They too went through the phase of having a disregarded vision statement on the walls. They called it their Credo. When Jim Burt was Chairman, he called a meeting of key executives and challenged them. He said, 'Here is the Credo, if we are not going to live by it, let's tear it off the wall. If you want to change it, tell us how. We either ought to commit to it, or get rid of it.' Whatever you evolve should be a living tool. It should be a basis of the discussion at the interview to see if applicants are on the same wavelength. It should be very much part of the induction process. It should be used when considering colleagues for promotion to see if they accept that it will be their responsibility to promote this sense of vision. Let's look at the Johnson & Johnson Credo.

JOHNSON & JOHNSON CREDO

We believe our first responsibility is to the doctors, nurses and patients, to mothers and fathers and all others who use our products and services. In meeting their needs everything we do must be of high quality. We must constantly strive to reduce our costs in order to maintain reasonable prices. Customers' orders must be serviced promptly and accurately. Our suppliers and distributors must have an opportunity to make a fair profit.

We are responsible to our employees, the men and women who work with us throughout the world. Everyone must be considered as an individual. We must respect their dignity and recognise their merit. They must have a sense of security in their jobs. Compensation must be fair and adequate, and working conditions clean, orderly and safe. We must be mindful of ways to help our employees fulfil their family responsibilities. Employees must feel free to make suggestions and complaints. There must be equal opportunity for employment, development and advancement for those qualified. We must provide competent management, and their actions must be just and ethical.

We are responsible to the communities in which we live and work and to the world community as well. We must be good citizens – support good works and charities and bear our fair share of taxes. We must encourage civic improvements and better health and education. We must maintain in good order the property we are privileged to use, protecting the environment and natural resources.

Our final responsibility is to our stockholders. Business must make a sound profit. We must experiment with new ideas. Research must be carried on, innovative programs developed and mistakes paid for. New equipment must be purchased, new facilities provided and new products launched. Reserves must be created to provide for adverse times. When we operate according to these principles, the stockholders should realise a fair return.

World Wide Credo Survey

In fact, Johnson & Johnson carry out a regular world-wide study into the effectiveness of their Credo. They explain that the questionnaire that they circulate, should be a 'reflection of your thoughts and ideas regarding your company and your work'. I am grateful to Johnson & Johnson for permission to reproduce the opening questions of their questionnaire.

They also have a 'credo challenge meeting kit' to be used in running 'credo challenge meetings', which last one day, to allow enough time for groups of individuals to discuss their Credo in some depth, and prepare responses to the issues raised. The day starts with the showing of a video, and then the relevant Company President, Managing Director, or division Head, gives a presentation on the issues raised on the Credo. The meeting is then broken into syndicates to discuss it, and prepare feedback reports to the moderator of the meeting, who is described as 'the challenger'. In short, the Credo is regarded very much a working tool and, again, I am grateful to Johnson & Johnson for permission to reproduce the opening paragraphs of their discussion group questions.

Opening questions of Johnson & Johnson Credo Survey

1. **Overall**, how would you rate your COMPANY on meeting its RESPONSIBILITIES as described in this part of the CREDO?

1 Very Good 2 Good 3 Average 4 Poor 5 Very Poor 6 I have no opinion

	Very Good	Good	Average	Poor	Very Poor	Not applicable/ no opinion
How do you rate your COMPANY on						
2. Producing high quality products and services	1	2	3	4	5	6
3. Constantly striving to reduce costs	1	2	3	4	5	6
4. Maintaining reasonable prices	1	2	3	4	5	6
5. Servicing customers' orders promptly	1	2	3	4	5	6
6. Giving suppliers and distributors an opportunity to make a fair contact.	1	2	3	4	5	6

Johnson & Johnson Credo Challenge Meeting

The following questions may be useful in your discussions; however, feel free to discuss any other Credo concerns you may have.

I.   Is the Credo, in its present form, a viable philosopical guide in the day-to-day operation of our business? Should it be changed or modified?

II. What is the intent of 'Our Credo?'
   A. What does it mean in terms of our day-to-day operations?
      1. How is it implemented in our companies?
      2. How is the effectiveness of its implementation evaluated?

   B. Do the various levels of the organisation understand and accept its intent?

   C. How can we best communicate its intent to our employees?

   D. How can we determine the actual level of understanding and acceptance?

   E. Is the order of priority accepted?

BRITISH AIRWAYS

vision
2000

British Airways' vision for the future is to build profitably the world's premier global alliance with a presence in all major world markets. The alliance will have as its hallmark superior levels of service, customer loyalty, and excellent operational and financial performance, drawing on the complemaentary strengths and shared values of all employees within the alliance.

Every employee has a part to play in bringing about the wide range of changes that will be necessary if this vision is to be realised. The vision reflects and encompasses the airline's Mission and Goals. Realisation of the vision would require that. . . . . . .

◆ Our attentions are focused on our customers, both external and internal, so that customer satisfaction and retention are our prime service considerations.

◆ There is a clear understanding of our business strategy at all levels of the company and we all understand how we are involved in that strategy.

◆ Teamwork develops across all functions.

◆ There is a greater flow of information, encouraging all employees to contribute their views.

◆ Partnership prevails as a mechanism for building commitment, with all employees participating in the running of the business.

◆ Individual potential is maximised as we grasp the new opportunities that become available.

◆ High personal standards and business integrity maintain international respect for us.

◆ We work towards developing the quality framework throughout the airline ensuring that continuous improvement becomes our way of life.

Figure 3.1   British Airways Vision 2000 Statement

EXAMPLES

We have discussed the Johnson & Johnson Credo and I have shown the British Airways Vision 2000. You need to study all the examples you run across yourself.

I spoke once at a Conference of the NBS Bank of South Africa. They told me:

> *Our vision is to empower creative leaders and staff who, in turn, produce excellent results through outstanding client service.*

You might debate whether it meets the criteria set out by Warren Bennis but all the delegates to whom I spoke were highly enthusiastic, committed and very complimentary about the leadership of their Bank. Outstanding client service follows from really committed people.

Major condition for success

Let me end this discussion with one final comment from Warren Bennis[8]:

> When an organisation has a clear sense of its purpose, direction, and desired future state, and *when the image is widely shared*, individuals are able to find their own roles, both in the organisation and in the larger society of which they are a part.
>
> This empowers individuals and confers status upon them because they can see themselves as part of a worthwhile enterprise. They gain a sense of importance, as they are transferred from robots blindly following instructions to human beings engaged in a purposeful venture.
>
> When individuals feel that they can make a difference and that they can improve the society in which they are living through their participation in their organisation, then it is much more likely that they will bring vigour and enthusiasm to their tasks and that the results of their work will be mutually reinforcing.
>
> Under these conditions, the human energies of the organisation are aligned towards a common end, and a major pre-condition for success has been satisfied.

So, let's turn to that closely related pillar – Superior Philosophies.

BRAINSTORMING EXERCISES OR PROJECTS: 3

Vision, Mission and Meaning

■ Do you agree that to inspire extraordinary performance, your organisation needs to provide a strong sense of meaning and value to the work which your colleagues do by providing 'vision' of a worthwhile future, a 'mission' to achieve medium-term goals, which provide 'meaning' to the contribution people make? If so, are you satisfied that you are already doing so? If not, how do you intend to do so? How will you involve as many people as possible in arguing through vision, mission and meaning statements?

■ If you are a Chief Executive, how do you, your colleagues, and your 'missionaries' create not merely a vision statement, but a visionary organisation?

■ Should you establish, like Johnson & Johnson, regular Credo Surveys and Credo Challenge Meetings?

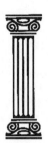
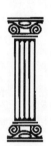

4

SUPERIOR PHILOSOPHIES

A major five year study into the world's automotive industry[11] concluded that the leading companies owed their success as much to their superior philosophies as to their superior strategies.

Mentioning this fact at one talk I gave, one very frustrated senior executive exclaimed, 'What has all this got to do with the bottom line?' The short answer is, everything.

Researchers studied 20 major American companies over a ten year period. They found that those with strong values and strong leadership at every level of their organisations, significantly outperformed companies which lacked values and leadership. The results are shown in Figure 4.1.

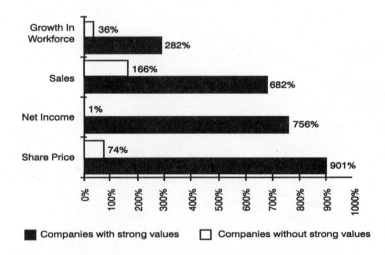

Figure 4.1 Impact of 'Values' on Performance

Source: Corporate Culture and Performance, John Kotter and James Heskett, Free Press.

ALL 'STAKEHOLDERS'

The theme of the study was that focusing just on one 'stakeholder' to the detriment of the others, destroys long-term viability. It is only organisations which integrate their approach to *all* stakeholders that truly succeed in the long term. We need to focus on what Dan Jones calls 'the extended business' or the 'value stream' of the business. Thus we need to focus on:

1. Suppliers
2. Dealers/distributors
3. Customers
4. Financiers and Shareholders
5. The Community
6. Competitors and
7. Colleagues.

Let's look, briefly, at each in turn.

1. Suppliers

For years, vehicle manufacturers sought to drive down their costs by creating intense price-based competition among numerous suppliers. During the design phase, potential suppliers were denied information which might have helped them to produce more effective components. Once the model run started, contracts would be cut or transferred.

Dan Jones and his colleagues on the MIT Study[11] highlighted the way in which the Japanese created a rational framework for determining cost, prices and profits based on a contractual framework which built a long-term, mutually viable relationship with a limited number of 'first tier' suppliers. This was based on the interchange of information which helped every supplier to optimise quality, productivity and profitability.

The first approach created a vicious circle of mutual distrust; the second a virtuous circle of cooperation. Because it works, the second approach has now been adopted by vehicle manufacturers world-wide.

Rover's recovery owes a great deal to adopting this approach. One of Rover's executives, Ed Smith, explained that 80 per cent of the final cost of components for a new car is determined in the design phase. If you don't involve the real experts – the suppliers – you lose the ability to influence cost.

By treating its selected suppliers as 'partners' to the point of sharing very sensitive strategic information years before the release of a new model, Rover achieved what Ed Smith calls technical and financial breakthroughs which would otherwise have been impossible. Note the phrase, *'If you don't involve the real experts – the suppliers'* – an attitude which echoes our earlier point of our colleagues being the people who are, or should be, the experts in the particular field of activity.

Similarly, the Somerfield supermarket chain has begun to cede responsibility for reordering stock to its suppliers as part of a 'co-managed' inventory system. Miles Clark of Somerfield describes it as a *'significant step towards the management of the supply chain as a seamless end to end process'*.

2. Dealers and distributors

Companies supplying products often use a third party to help them reach the end user, be it an agent, wholesaler, distributor, dealer, or retailer. Again, some companies create a vicious circle of mutual distrust by selfishly, unethically, putting their own interests first. Some devise short-term tactical measures to move their own stock which impact on their dealer's margins and credibility and may bypass their channel of distribution if they see the chance of supplying a major order direct.

Equally, other companies, like the Saturn franchise in America, create a virtuous circle of cooperation by leaning over backwards to build a long-term partnership with their channels of distribution. Companies which can share confidential strategic information with their channels of distribution are equally likely to gain financial and marketing breakthroughs which would otherwise be impossible. After all, those in direct contact with the end users are gleaning important marketing information.

3. Customers

Customers are the life blood of every business but we can all tell horror stories of how badly we have been treated by front-line people; those who deal face-to-face with the customer.

Tarmac has an annual award for the unit which has shown the greatest initiative. This year's winner was the company's South West of England construction division, which increased turnover by almost 50 per cent and has been winning one in three contracts, instead of one in ten as previously. How did they do this? After asking customers what improvements they required. The division held a day-long meeting for all 200 staff at a Bristol cinema to discuss how to meet customer needs. Result: a dramatic improvement in contracts secured.

4. Financiers and shareholders

Any proposal for a loan for a company with an excellent reputation for superior philosophies, backed by strong values and beliefs, is more likely to gain the support it needs. Equally, banks willing to reciprocate by sharing information and advice and behaving in an honourable way towards their customers, are more likely to build their business base.

Publicly-quoted companies are also beginning to find that their investors are interested in ethical issues. A book, *The Ethical Investor*[12], refers to the Joseph Rowntree Trust as a 'Good example of a Charity with a well structured, ethical investment policy.' So, even blue chip companies are beginning to recognise the need to project their philosophies more effectively.

5. The community

If the business develops a good reputation for the way in which it conducts all its dealings and participates in local communities it can have commercial and practical benefits, such as building up customer loyalty and even improving relationships with all the local regulatory authorities, including planning authorities.

Many large organisations are well known for their community affairs programmes, but even smaller companies can, within their local community, establish a name and reputation by local sponsorships and other activities which can build a highly favourable image in the community. One client, David Hold, Managing Director of Dave Barron Caravans, paid for the erection of numerous litter bins, each carrying his name. In fact, one client got so involved with local sponsorships and became so well known that he was able to reduce his need for advertising.

National Power makes part of their employees' performance related pay dependent on meeting environmental targets.

6. Competitors

There is no doubt that British Airways' well-deserved reputation for the way in which it turned itself round, primarily by pioneering many of the concepts we are discussing, was dented badly when it appeared that some of its executives had played 'dirty tricks' on their rivals at Virgin.

In fact, there is normally a great deal of integrity among members of the same trade and industry. The feeling is that the greater the level of professionalism, the easier it is to compete fairly and honourably. Moreover, an increasing number of industries are now becoming what are called 'open clusters': shifting networks of companies with interrelated collaborative arrangements depending on great integrity between all parties.

7. Colleagues

Let's come back to the core issue. How do we really inspire all our colleagues to give of their best: to share our ambitions? Let's take the extreme view to make a point. How do senior executives expect their workers to react when they see their organisations?

- Screwing its suppliers with almost vicious levels of mistrust and expediency?
- Talking about being 'in partnership' with dealers but acting as if they were an expendable nuisance?
- Treating customers as 'punters' and trying to provide as little as possible for as much as possible?
- Treating shareholders as idiots by milking the company of massive salary increases and share option schemes?
- Blatantly seeking to cut corners and ignoring the adverse impact of its activities on the community?
- Playing dirty with competitors?

The extent to which any organisation behaves in such ways can only debase and demotivate its people. Even a reputable blue chip company that requires its Purchase Ledger staff to duck, dive, lie and weave to avoid paying suppliers on the due date, is requiring its people to behave unethically. It's hardly likely to increase their job satisfaction, their respect for their organisation, and their motivation.

Conversely, a company which works hard to establish superior philosophies and requires its people to behave honourably and ethically towards every stakeholder, is far more likely to:

- attract and retain the most skilful suppliers, keen to use their expertise in supplying the best products;
- attract and retain the cream of the 'dealers' better able to gain and retain market share;
- attract, satisfy and retain an increasing number of customers, not least by creating a positive awareness among the community at large;
- attract and retain the required degree of cost-efficient financial support;
- gain the respect and probably the cooperation of its competitors.

But, most importantly:

■ **Will attract and retain high quality, highly ethical people with strongly held values and beliefs who, by optimising all their relationships with every stakeholder, will truly help their company to achieve its vision.**

Thus, people are highly motivated by working for a company that is highly responsible, has superior philosophies, and strongly held values and beliefs. Professor Mahoney of the LSE advocates the use of ethical codes of conduct which gives workers a sense of identity and promotes teamwork by making clear that the same high standards are expected from everyone. In his view:

> *Corporate responsibility creates a sense of satisfaction, of achievement, of working together, not just to make a living or a profit, but to make a difference to society's quality of life.*

INTELLECTUAL ASSETS

The transactional view of workers being paid to work is fast becoming obsolete.

As a leading British guru, Charles Handy, has pointed out:

> It is now widely accepted that in ten year's time, 70 per cent or more of the work we do will require brain skills, not manual skills. When that happens, the cliché that our people are our greatest asset will acquire a hard financial reality.

> When Microsoft once topped the share charts, the New York Times commented that all there was to put your money on was the 'imagination of the workers'. No one can truly own that imagination except the workers themselves, and they can walk out of the door at any time.

> Shareholders can no longer be owners in any real sense of other people's brains, but only investors or, more accurately, backers.

So, the transformational approach of seeking to optimise the intellectual talents of people is the only realistic strategy.

SELF-EMPLOYABILITY

No sports team would tolerate a team member who did not pull his or her weight: did not really 'sweat blood' to help the team to win. Similarly, no organisation can tolerate a situation where, according to some research, 50 per cent of the workforce merely do just enough to keep their jobs. Again, Jack Welch has some highly personal comments:.

> Loyalty is an affinity among people who want to grapple with the outside world and win. Their personal values, dreams, and ambitions cause them to gravitate towards each other and towards a company like GE that gives them the resources and the opportunities to flourish. *The new psychological contract, is that jobs at GE are the best in the world for people who are willing to compete.*

PROJECTING THESE VALUES

So, how do you project your organisation's philosophies, values and beliefs to everyone in your organisation? First, we have to live them in everything we say and do. Second, we have to make the time to communicate endlessly on these and related issues (yet another reason for getting ourselves off the treadmill of management). Thirdly we have to brainstorm and discuss them at every conceivable opportunity. Fourthly, despite the difficulty, we need 'in-company' training sessions, or through special project teams, to seek to establish a statement in writing. Finally, ethics must begin at the top of an organisation — it is a leadership issue. We, as chief executives, must set the example.

Example

I am grateful to John Neill for permission to reproduce the Unipart Statement of Values and Beliefs (Figure 4.2). Again, you may wish to involve a Project Team in collecting examples and evolving your own statement.

CONCLUSION

Your objective should be a very lean team of highly committed people, not requiring very much supervision, for two reasons:

1. They share your organisation's philosophies, values, and beliefs; and
2. They share your organisation's goals.

So, let's discuss the next Pillar, that of strategy.

THE UNIPART GROUP

The Unipart Group is a combination of People, Ideas and Assets which exist for the benefit of its stakeholders.

The Group will strive to be the best in everything it sets out to do and will only set out to do those things at which it could be the best.

The relationships and inter-dependencies between the stakeholders are key to achieving this position and can be described by a set of codes (values) towards

☐ *The Employee as an individual* ☐ *The Individual as an employee*
☐ *The customer* ☐ *The Supplier* ☐ *The Owner*

Among the Company's values nothing is more fundamental than its respect for the individual.

The Group will create and maintain an environment in which individual employees may contribute to and share in the fortunes of the business in a fair and consistent manner.

Our employees are our greatest asset and as such they deserve:

☐ *To be informed of what their role and tasks are* ☐ *To be appropriately trained and developed for the role and task required of them* ☐ *To be allowed the opportunity to perform* ☐ *To be regularly counselled on how they are doing and what their career potential is* ☐ *To be recognised and rewarded according to their individual achievements* ☐ *To be managed professionally* ☐ *To be given the willing assistance and support of their colleagues* ☐ *To be given the opportunities to develop their career potential to the extent of their ability* ☐ *To be informed of what their company is doing, and what its objectives are* ☐ *To know that we actively encourage promotion from within the company* ☐ *To have their ideas and opinions properly considered* ☐ *To not be burdened by those not willing to contribute.*

As Unipart respects its employees so we should expect our people to:

☐ *Support the Company, its policies, products and objectives in the world market* ☐ *Constructively appraise errors or faults in policies or practices* ☐ *Maintain within the Company all confidential information, plans and strategies about the Company and its performance* ☐ *To take a positive attitude towards their jobs and the resolution of problems and keep their managers informed at all times in order that they may manage effectively and avoid problems.*

All of our futures are determined by our ability to satisfy our customers' needs, who, whether individual, retail, wholesale or corporate deserve:

☐ *To have their needs understood and fulfilled* ☐ *An outstanding quality of product and service which exceeds the express and implied promise made when business is placed with Unipart* ☐ *To be clearly told the details of the offer before business is accepted* ☐ *Frankness and integrity from Unipart* ☐ *A positive attitude and approach to the resolution of difficulties of all kinds* ☐ *To be listened to carefully at all times* ☐ *Our demonstrable commitment to the continual developments of mutually beneficial business relationships.*

As we respect our customers, we should earn the right to be respected by our suppliers, who deserve a Company which offers:

Synergy: *through the opportunity of a long term business relationship built on mutual aspirations.*

Confidence: *by clearly defining our requirements and maintaining a good trading record.*

Trust: *by treating our suppliers with integrity and professionalism.*
Ethics: *through not using our position to the detriment of our suppliers.*

Challenge: *by setting demanding performance requirements but assisting our suppliers in meeting them.*

We have a duty to build and maintain a Company which:

☐ *Provides an acceptable rate of return with a good track record which gives an expectation of a continual growth in earnings* ☐ *Provides a readily realisable investment brought about by consistent performance in meeting commitment and forecast* ☐ *Provides a product or service which the market place sees as a continuing need* ☐ *Does not involve itself in unethical pursuits* ☐ *Gives pride in ownership.*

Figure 4.2 Unipart Statement of Beliefs and Values

BRAINSTORMING EXERCISES OR PROJECTS: 4

Superior Philosophies

■ Can you accept that strong values and beliefs, superior philosophies, can have a tremendous impact on your bottom line? If so, do you feel that you have devoted sufficient priority to defining and projecting your own values and beliefs?

■ Do you agree that to gain the benefit of great synergy, your values and beliefs, your superior philosophies, have to be applied in all your relationships with your suppliers, dealers and distributors, customers, shareholders, the community, even your competitors and – most importantly – that it is the quality of your relationship with others that determines the quality of the relationship with your colleagues?

■ How successful do you feel you and your team have been in projecting and communicating your philosophies?

■ In the light of your answers to the preceding questions, what do you and your team need to do to:

    a) Define and gain consensus on your values and beliefs?

    b) Project them effectively?

    c) Gain the commitment of all your colleagues to these values and beliefs, particularly in regard to their interface with all your stakeholders?

    d) Ensure they become the touchstone of all your actions and activities on a long-term, consistent basis?

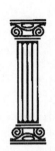

5

SUPERIOR STRATEGIES

WINNING

We will only win at business by setting and achieving the right goals. Agreed? The only way we can achieve our goals is by fully mobilising the talents and commitment of our people. As Sumantra Ghoshal pointed out:

Employees don't just want to work for a company. They want to belong to an organisation.

INVOLVEMENT AND UNDERSTANDING

In the 1970s, strategy was the latest fad: the responsibility of boffins in ivory towers. In the 1980s, strategy became more of a senior management function. To survive the 1990s strategy has to be a front-line activity.

In very large organisations, the senior executives can lose touch with the 'sharp end' of the business. Andy Grove, the Chief Executive of Intel, admits that his Board were striving to be a major player in both memory chips and microprocessors but the people on the front-line recognised – far sooner than the Board – that they had to retreat from memory chips to focus purely on microprocessors.

One of the points made by Will Carling and Robert Heller in their book, *The Way to Win*[13], is that the younger, newer entrants to a team often have a clearer perception of what is needed to win than the long-established players.

Some of our people in their early 20s have provided us, at our monthly company meetings, with penetrating insights which would have cost many thousands of pounds to obtain from a top flight management consultant! Indeed, it is doubtful if even the best of consultants would have been able to get 'under the skin' of our business to provide such insights. How many millions have been wasted by companies going to consultants for help on strategy, when their own people are the best qualified; even if a consultant helps as a facilitator? It has been said that consultants are often brought in to prove to senior management what middle management already knows!

CHALLENGE

Strategic planning is about posing questions, trying the difficult feat of looking at the organisation as from the outside to really understand where it sits in its marketplace, and thus determine the best strategic options open. Our colleagues, helped perhaps with the members of our 'value stream', like the 'stakeholders' we have just been discussing, are the best qualified people to do this.

UNDERSTANDING ENVIRONMENT

The key is to truly involve them in understanding the environment in which you operate. I once ran a workshop for all 40 members of a local business. I asked them to list all the changes that had affected their business in the past ten years or so, under the headings of the 'Five Agents of Change':

1. Legislative and political
2. Demographic
3. Economic
4. Technological
5. Cultural

Teams comprising cleaners, operatives, clerks, sales and accounting functions, came up with comprehensive lists of all the changes that had already affected their business. I then asked them to project forward the changes they saw affecting their business in future. Some of the answers were quite staggeringly perceptive.

The third part of the exercise is then to ask them how they think the business should react to these pending changes. It's a marvellous way to focus everyone's attention to the need to respond to the inevitable changes likely to affect them. Let me stress that these were ordinary front-line people.

An excellent suggestion is to create a game based on your business. For this purpose, the 'players' can be regarded as:

- **customers**; preferably broken down into relevant segments;
- **competitors**;
- **potential new entrants**; these may be existing 'players' who provide existing products or services in a totally new way, or totally new entrants who come out with a highly innovative new product or technology likely to overtake existing products or services;
- **suppliers**;
- **substitutors**; alternative players from whom customers may purchase substitute products;
- **complementors**; players from whom customers buy complementary products.

The 'game' is to create various scenarios of how each team sees each set of players interacting. Successful business strategy is about actively shaping the game you play, not just playing the game you find. Your own people are the best people to play 'your game' though from time to time; appropriate experts might be invited in to act as facilitators. You have got to find a way of involving every member of your organisation in these types of discussions and games. Arnold O'Byrne of Opel Ireland has a company-wide meeting every six weeks. In larger organisations, discussions of this type should form a major element of in-company training and communication activity.

REDEFINING CONTEXT

Theodore Levitt, in his classic report, *Marketing Myopia*[14], made the observation that too many of us become preoccupied with what *we* think we are *selling*, when the only thing that matters is what *our customers* think they are *buying*. One of the great advantages of arguing through a mission statement is that it should help to focus our attention on what our customers are buying which, after all, is the basis of all strategic planning.

Edward Vaughan was a company involved in the 'metal bashing' industries of the Midlands that suffered badly during the recession. Their then Marketing Director wrote a case study for an earlier book of mine. He explained that arguing through their mission statement was primarily responsible for ensuring that they, unlike many in their industry, did not suffer the effects of the recession. He explained:

It changed our thinking about what we did – blending lubricants – into thinking about why we did it.

Rather than considering that we sell oils or chemicals, we now recognise that we sell the means of improving manufacturing processes. This deliberate recognition of the end benefit to our customers rather than the technical processes with which we were involved, enabled our company to make significant changes: in our products profile, the markets we serve, and the way in which we position our company and its products in these markets.

Arguing through issues of this type should be an essential part of in-company discussions and brainstorms.

Your people should be going out to talk to customers, or panels of customers can be invited in for cheese and wine type discussions, with teams of your people. Everyone, from every department, should be encouraged to look at everything they do from the customer's perspective.

Ian Gibson, at Nissan, has encouraged the concept of 'the internal customer'. He encourages everyone to realise that unless they supply first-class products and services to the next step in the process, the end customer will not be satisfied.

WHAT ARE YOUR OBJECTIVES?

Every member of your team should understand clearly the goals and objectives of your organisation and should appreciate the goals or objectives they have to achieve to ensure the overall success of your business. Years ago, Peter Drucker recommended that objectives should be set for:

■ Marketing
■ Innovation
■ Suppliers
■ Human Resources
■ Physical Resources
■ Financial Resources
■ Information Resources, and
■ Social Responsibilities.

Specific, quantified goals need to be set in all these areas, not as a bureaucratic exercise, but to establish the key yardsticks needed for key, *top line drivers* crucial to the success of your business. (We will come back to 'top line drivers' later).

TACTICS, OBJECTIVES AND STRATEGY

Table 5.1 makes the distinction between tactics, objectives and strategy, which is another topic for ongoing briefing and brainstorming throughout your organisation.

Table 5.1 The distinction between tactics, objectives and strategy

TACTICS	OBJECTIVES	STRATEGY
1. Immediate activities	1. Business destination	1. Method of achievement
2. Short term only	2. Long/medium term	2. Long term only
3. Can change often	3. May change	3. Should rarely change
4. Temporary	4. Invisible	4. Highly visible, strong, consistent customer perceptions by correct positioning

Tactics are short-term reactions to immediate circumstances and should be topic of regular briefings. Every team at Nissan starts the day with a 15 or 20 minute briefing. Your objective should be understood clearly by every member of your team. Let's stop at this point.

LONG-TERM POSITIONING

There needs to be a total preoccupation by your organisation on all the processes involved in identifying, attracting, satisfying and retaining customers. In other words, all your 'marketing-related' activities. Does everyone in your organisation appreciate the need to be totally customer-driven? Are you aiming at specific customer segments?

I once ran a weekend workshop for a company, broke them into syndicates, and asked them to break down their customers into different segments. They eventually came up with 16 customer segments. They then realised that their management information system did not give them anything like enough information on the customers in these segments. When we reconvened a few weekends later, various teams had searched for the missing information and came up with the fact that 85 per cent of their sales went to just four customer segments. They also recognised that they needed much more clear-cut information on their customer segmentation; information missing from their conventional management accounting approach.

Does everyone in *your* organisation know how you need to position yourself to create the right perceptions in the minds of customers in the chosen market segments? Do they understand the need to reinforce these perceptions, and not to weaken your customers' perceptions of your products or services.

Jan Carlzon, former Chief Executive of SAS, tells the story[15] of how he preached the need to look after customers. So everyone became ultra-helpful, even to the point of delaying departures to find missing or late customers. He then had to point out that his strategy was aimed at attracting and retaining business executives who valued punctuality. Once this was explained, everyone became committed to ensuring that planes left on time.

Jan Carlzon also explained that at one point the accountants had ruled that planes should be towed from their hangars to the nearest departure gate to save costs. This meant that the customers had to chase half way round the airport to catch connecting flights. Once this was pointed out, everyone recognised the need to place connecting flights in adjacent gates.

It is back to ensuring that everyone has the information they need to understand how to satisfy their customers. More of your 'marketing' efforts needs to be devoted to marketing yourself to your own organisation. One guru claims that 40 per cent of the marketing effort should be directed internally, to the people in the organisation.

INNOVATION

Richard Pascale[16] refers to the options of:

■ optimising historic skills or
■ metamising new opportunities.

One example he gives is that Western Union strove to become better and better at sending telegrams when it ought to have seized the opportunity of pioneering fax communications.

'Change before you have to', warns Jack Welch. At Nissan every member of every team is totally committed to the Kaizen programme of continuous improvements to the way in the product is designed and produced. This is a fantastic achievement. Clearly it is a key element in producing a better product at a lower price, which we must all aim for.

But remember the Edward Vaughan story. In their case it would have been a mistake to focus purely on improving the ways in which they produced and blended their lubricants. What they had to do was to get out and about and seek to improve the way in which they could help their customers improve *their* manufacturing processes.

CLARIFYING STRATEGY

There are three other techniques which we can use to clarify the ways in which you are going to achieve your objectives.

■ *Benchmarking* is a way of establishing the performance levels of your industry. You are not interested in average levels of performance. You are interested in what the best people in your industry are achieving so that you can seek to achieve or exceed the best.

■ *Best practice* is a way of learning from other organisations on how they do things better. Jack Welch of GE gives high priority to this activity and in one of his reports explains how GE has benefited enormously from a production technique first seen in a company in New Zealand.

■ *SWOT* is a way of looking at the Strengths, Weaknesses, Opportunities and Threats facing you and your direct and indirect competitors.

These three activities make ideal in-company development projects. In passing, if you don't think you are big enough, then the students, undergraduates, and even graduates of your local Technical College, University or Business School, are often desperate for projects. When one client approached his local college he got all 56 students placed at his disposal.

OWNING – THE STRATEGY

In too many organisations, strategy is seen as the preserve of senior management. People are seen as their greatest restraint. Indeed, it is the people, not the executives, who are blamed when the organisation fails to implement its strategies effectively. Such organisations then waste vast sums investing in 'change programmes' to help their people to cope with change. It is a total waste of money.

It is more effective to involve as many people as possible in brainstorming the issues we have been discussing and the exercises I have suggested which will bring to the surface the strategies to be adopted.

The late William Giles developed what he called the 'Marlow Method'. The Board set out the broad parameters of what they thought the strategy should be. Each member of the Board then acted as mentor to a project team composed of people from every sector of the business. Where relevant, people from these first-level teams then act as mentors to a series of second-level teams, helping to cascade the process throughout the organisation in a way which expands the activity without detracting from the parameters already agreed.

COMPETING SUCCESSFULLY

One study[17] highlighted that the ability of a business to compete successfully relies on:

1. getting widespread awareness of the environmental issues and competitive forces facing the business; and
2. developing the competencies needed by the organisation and the leadership needed to achieve clearly defined goals.

OPTIMISING YOUR VALUE STREAM

In fact, it clearly makes sense to really optimise the value of the 'your extended business; or 'value stream'. When talking about suppliers, I mentioned the way in which progressive organisations share quite sensitive strategic information. Your professional advisers, bankers and lawyers, and your investors, may be ideally placed to give you invaluable information. Involving people from your community, and from your industry, can better help you to appreciate your environment. Once, Ford invited a leading automotive journalist to sit on one of their committees.

Certainly you should seek out your most forward thinking, progressive, innovative customers, since as they seek to respond to their environment, they can help you to respond to their future needs. One senior executive calls them his 'lighthouse customers' pointing the way to the future of his business! It's a good point.

YOUR PEOPLE ARE THE EXPERTS

Let me close with two stories which illustrate how perceptive your people can be on issues of strategy.

A friend asked me to evaluate the viability of a £1 million new development which he had spent a year planning. He had incurred high professional fees and 'taken his eye off the ball' as far as the running of his business was concerned. He had asked me because he had developed doubts, which were justified. The project was not viable. My client then became very concerned about the impact of the cancellation on his workers. Though they had not been told directly, they had obviously become aware of what was in the wind.

When he told them, they cheered. They had long since recognised that the idea was not viable and were worried that he might go ahead. Had he involved them from the start he would have saved himself a lot of time and money.

A different approach. Ralph Stayer's[1] factory was given the chance of a major contract. If it went well it would transform his business. But if, by overstretching his resources, it caused problems, it could be disastrous. The conventional approach would have been to agonise over the problem in endless Board meetings. Ralph called a meeting of all his 400 plus colleagues and put the problem to them. They asked for more time to think and for more information. Eventually, all but a handful voted in favour of accepting the contract. Because they were involved, they made sure it worked.

Isn't this a prime example of gaining involvement and commitment?

COMMANDING A PREMIUM

I think it was David Ogilvy who once said, 'A company with a price advantage can be undercut. A company with a performance advantage can be outflanked. But a company with an emotional difference can potentially demand a premium for ever.'

By ensuring that your people know what you stand for in terms of your values and beliefs, and by enabling them to be involved with, and identify themselves with, your strategies, you really can run a company with minimum supervision. That surely must be the way to win.

BEYOND STRATEGY TO PURPOSE

Earlier, I referred to the marvellous series of HBR articles by Chris Bartlett and Sumantra Ghoshal[6], in which they argue for the need to move beyond strategy to purpose. They reinforce the views of David Ogilvy. They say:

> Clinically framed and contractually based relationships do not inspire the extraordinary effort and sustained commitment required to deliver consistently superior performance. For that, companies need [people] who care, who have a strong emotional link with the organisation.

When he spoke at one of my seminars, Sumantra gave the example of AT&T which reinforces everything we have been discussing.

You cannot move from strategy to purpose, to creating a shared sense of ambition, if you are bogged down in 'management'. We can only do it once we have rid ourselves of the day-to-day pressures of management to focus on leadership.

EMBEDDING AMBITION AT AT&T

- **Capturing peoples' attention and interest**
  ...'Dedicated to becoming the world's best at bringing people together, giving them easy access to each other and to the information and services they want and need – anytime, anywhere.'

- **Engaging the Organisation**
  Strategy forum as a process of involving people in defining and interpreting the ambition and making it operational.

- **Building and sustaining momentum**
  Tangible commitments and measurements of progress.

FROM STRATEGIC INTENT TO CORPORATE PURPOSE

In their HBR articles, Chris and Sumantra have a case study based on Komatsu which, for many years, had the strategy of catching up with and surpassing Caterpiller. By 1989, world-wide demand for construction equipment was down, competition was up, and Komatsu's profits were in steady decline. Their President decided that they could no longer operate within the confines of a defined objective.

After extensive internal discussions, people agreed that, rather than thinking of Komatsu as a construction equipment company trying to catch CAT, they were a 'total technology enterprise', with an opportunity to leverage its existing resources and expertise in electronics, robotics and plastics. A committee was appointed to examine how Komatsu could enrich its corporate philosophy, broaden its social contributions, and revitalise its human resources.

The objective was to create an organisation to attract and stimulate the best people. In the following years, sales, which had been declining, surged, driven almost entirely by a 40 per cent growth in Komatsu's non-construction equipment business.

HARD RESULTS

These, and many more case studies which could be quoted, demonstrate that moving from strategy to purpose does ensure **Hard Results**; because it taps into the collective knowledge of people, our next ingredient.

I am grateful to British Airways for permission to reproduce the truly effective way in which they circulate their business goals (Figure 5.1).

corporate goals		targets for 1992/93
Safe and Secure	To be a safe and secure airline	◆ Undertook safety audits across all operational areas ◆ Targeted continual improvement of established safety trends ◆ Continued to improve the security awareness of staff throughout the company
Financially Strong	To deliver a strong and consistent financial performance	◆ Continued to reduce departmental unit costs with gap closure ◆ Optimised traffic mix, yields and third party revenues ◆ Improved the performance of the airline's capital assets
Global Leader	To secure a leading share of air travel business worldwide with a significant presence in all major markets	◆ Arrangements made for access to North American and Asia/Pacific markets ◆ Further presence negotiated in Europe ◆ Loyalty schemes developed in major markets
Service and Value	To provide overall superior service and good value for money in every market segment in which we compete	◆ Heathrow and Gatwick improved as transfer points ◆ Executive Club expanded to identify core customers and track their travel ◆ Sustained improvement in punctuality of the operation
Customer Driven	To excel in anticipating and quickly responding to customer needs and competitor activity	◆ Managers involved in the *In Touch* programme ◆ Executive Club members recognised by Service Delivery ◆ Mechanisms to encourage the innovation of staff and respond to customers
Good Employer	To sustain a working environment that attracts, retains and develops committed employees who share in the success of the company	◆ Half the airline's staff attended Winning for Customers ◆ Assessed training requirements and developed quality programme ◆ Developed improved performance and career management methods
Good Neighbour	To be a good neighbour, concerned for the community and the environment	◆ Key targets set from internal environmental audit programme ◆ Increased communication/dialogue with local communities ◆ Increased involvement in educational, community and conservation initiatives

targets for 1993/94	long term targets
◆ Achieve progressively higher standards of safety ◆ Lead the industry in responding rapidly to safety and security issues ◆ Provide a safe working environment for all employees ◆ Comply with all security requirements at minimum inconvenience to customers ◆ Improve security awareness of all staff	To seek constant improvement in the safety and security of the airline
◆ Focus financial management through business segmentation ◆ Enhance the strategic and business planning activities ◆ Improve asset performance including aircraft utilisation ◆ Achieve expenditure performance improvements ◆ Maintain the net debt to total capital ratio below 70%	To generate operating cash flow at 21% of traffic revenue
◆ Begin building the first effective global airline alliance ◆ Implement Executive Club frequent flyer programmes fully and consistently world-wide ◆ Agree and commit to financial targets for US Air co-ordination ◆ Set up arrangements for successful Qantas co-ordination ◆ Evaluate and determine the appropriate BA image world-wide	To establish the alliance partnership as a substantial player in all 6 of the major world markets
◆ Offer innovative services, consistency and value for money ◆ Instil a quality culture and drive continuous improvement ◆ Establish challenging service quality standards which lead the industry ◆ Improve BA's punctuality to exceed competitors on 60% of sectors ◆ Improve significantly the baggage shortlanded rate for passengers who have transferred at Heathrow and Gatwick	To plan and manage the airline so that key service delivery and schedule objectives are met cost effectively
◆ Managers listen to customers and develop front-line skills ◆ Continue the rollout of premium products and prepare the shorthaul relaunch ◆ Trial and evaluate an individualised service centre ◆ Respond rapidly and positively to complaints ◆ Track and understand customer defection to reduce its incidence	To create such customer satisfaction that 9 out of 10 passengers would recommend BA to a friend or colleague
◆ Address the key issues raised by the Input Survey ◆ Encourage a climate of openness, trust and two-way communication ◆ Develop integrated training and skill improvement plans ◆ Encourage employees to demonstrate initiative and participate creatively in generating practical ideas to the airline's benefit ◆ Redesign the performance management system to provide direction and wider involvement in achieving our business objectives	To raise employee satisfaction on attraction, retention, pay, communications and development
◆ Develop and communicate an agreed BA community relations strategic framework ◆ Increase level of investment in community relations ◆ Increase employee and public awareness of BA's environmental performance ◆ Improve waste management particularly at Heathrow and Gatwick ◆ Improve aircraft fuel efficiency and energy consumption on the ground	To ensure that BA's community and environmental achievement is maintained at a high level

Figure 5.1 British Airways' corporate goals

BRAINSTORMING EXERCISES OR PROJECTS: 5

Superior Strategies

Looking at our conclusions:

■ Do you feel that every member of your team understands the environment in which you are operating and is willing to initiate the actions needed to respond to change? If not, how do you ensure they do gain this understanding and are willing to respond to change?

■ Is every member of your team willing to take a proactive, positive role in optimising all your relationships? If not, what do you need to do to ensure that they recognise the need to do so?

■ Does every member of your team appreciate the goals they have to achieve if they are to be a member of your winning team? If not, how do you ensure they do so?

■ Is every member of your team aware of your strategies, willing to help with both input and feedback, and, above all, willing to reinforce the perceptions you are seeking to create in positioning your company? If not, how do you ensure that they are? If you do not do so already, how can you involve as many people as possible in creating and monitoring strategy?

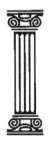

6

COLLECTIVE KNOWLEDGE

YOUR MOST INVALUABLE ASSETS

Your most invaluable asset, and mine, is the collective knowledge of every single member of our team. They are and should be treated as the real experts on the detail of the work they do.

It is not just them. Their husbands and wives, other members of their families, and their network of friends, can be an equally invaluable resource. One member of our team, Jayne McWatt, knew the Professor of Statistics at Plymouth University, Graham Crocker. As a result of her introduction to him, we were able to improve significantly the quality of our own statistical and forecasting activities.

Remember our opening quotation from Percy Barnevik of ABB which concluded: *'We have to be able to recognise and employ that untapped ability that each individual brings to work every day.'*

BACK TO PHILOSOPHY

We are back to our philosophy: the way we think about things.

It is now recognised that the West has been influenced unduly by the notions of 'Scientific Management' set out by Frederic Taylor earlier this century. He felt that workers could share in the prosperity of their organisations if they were told what to do, and how to do it, as a result of stopwatch studies carried out by their superiors. This prompted one leading Japanese industrialist, the late Konosuke Matsushita to comment:

We are going to win and the industrial West is going to lose: there's not much you can do about it because the reasons for your failure are within yourselves. Your firms are built on the Taylor model. For you, the essence of management is getting the ideas out of the heads of bosses and into the hands of labour.

We are beyond your mindset. Business, we know, is now so complex and difficult, the survival of firms so hazardous in an environment increasingly unpredictable, competitive, and fraught with danger, that their continued existence depends on the day-to-day mobilisation of **EVERY OUNCE OF INTELLIGENCE, FROM EVERY MEMBER OF THE ORGANISATION**.

Numerous British companies have reacted to this challenge successfully. They have changed their attitudes, their mindsets. As at Nissan, it is the front-line workers who are coming up with a continuous programme of improvement. British workers have proved that they can be world-class, *when led with the right philosophies.*

EIGHT ISSUES

There are eight issues which we will need to confront. They are:

1. Performance
2. Courage
3. Confidence of leaders and followers
4. Assertiveness
5. Contention
6. Openness
7. Learning organisation
8. Techniques.

1. Performance

The first very real danger is that performance may suffer in the short term. The experience which you and I have gained is based on learning from mistakes we have made. If we start to delegate to our colleagues, they will have to learn from their mistakes.

We now make each of our teams responsible for their own recruitment. The first time our Design Team did so, they made a mistake. They chose a very pleasant girl but one who came nowhere near their high levels of competence. So, at the end of the trial period, they had the responsibility of parting company with her. They made sure that their next choice was right.

It came back to me. If I wanted people to recruit their own colleagues, then I should have ensured that they received enough training. But it was the team who suffered from the disruption, they gained experience, and now that they are responsible for building their own team, they are far more committed.

What is the alternative? It is *upward delegation*. No one takes any real decisions because they feel the need to let the 'boss' cast his eye over it. He becomes the bottleneck. People do not try hard enough because they know that whatever they do will be amended. As William McKnight, the apparently uncharismatic former Chief Executive of the highly innovative company 3M, once observed:

> The men and women to whom we delegate authority and responsibility, if they are good people, are going to want to do their jobs in their own ways.... Mistakes will be made, but if a person is essentially right, the mistakes he or she makes are not as serious in the long run as the mistakes management will make if it is dictatorial and undertakes to tell those under its authority exactly how they must do their jobs.

3M is a fascinating company. One of the main reasons behind its success in innovation was that they developed an appeals process internally. Previously, if you had an idea which you thought was commercially exploitable, you put it to your boss who had the power to decide whether it should be taken any further. Because most bosses actually want a quiet life, in practice most ideas got turned down, particularly if they might be successful because this meant that the good people who were working for the boss might be moved away.

3M's appeals process worked thus: if the boss turned down the idea, the idea could be put to the boss's boss. If, under these circumstances, the boss was seen to be turning down good ideas, he was somewhat at risk himself, so the balance of advantage politically inside the business changed to those who put ideas forward from those who tried to restrict the flow of new ideas. Apparently this extremely simple change had a dramatic effect on the financial performance of the company over the years. It also changed the culture completely; an issue we discuss later.

2. Courage

If you are the owner of your business, with your money at risk, it can take considerable courage to accept this philosophy. Even if you are an employed executive, possibly on a bonus scheme, it takes courage to let more junior colleagues makes mistakes for which you bear responsibility and which may affect your bonus adversely.

The bigger problem is that your organisation is likely to be under-performing because you are trying to do far too much yourself. If you can move your people up to the fourth and fifth levels of involvement and commitment, then your productivity gains will far exceed the cost of mistakes.

Paul Layzel, former MD of BMW (GB), ran the company in an outstandingly successful way. He accepts that:

> My biggest mistake at BMW (GB) was in not realising sooner the need for change so that our people lower down the organisation could contribute more since that is where the greatest untapped talent lay.

If we are honest, most of us as executives will accept that it has been 'our biggest mistake' also.

3. Confidence of leaders and followers

We have been used to holding individual executives responsible for the results of their divisional department. We have trained them in traditional concepts of management, planning, controlling, directing and disciplining. We have paid them bonuses on their results. In all too many organisations, they have been trained to act more as upwardly reporting 'personal assistants' than independent entrepreneurs.

Your biggest challenge will be persuading them to drop their traditional, transactional approach, which often meant that they would 'shoot down in flames' any subordinate who spoke out of turn. You will need to give them the confidence to adopt the transformational approach of positively seeking and encouraging the views of the members of their team: to create *'effective followers'*.

Equally, you face the challenge of encouraging *their* followers to have the confidence to put forward their views. Many, who have been 'shot down' in the past, may be reluctant to risk another rebuff.

4. Assertiveness

Under the transactional approach, workers were expected to leave their brains at the factory gates. People were conditioned to believe that 'it was not their place' to comment. We have to change this mindset to one where it is the *responsibility of people to comment: to stop the line: to come up with their ideas.*

One of the first things I did when I started my new company in Devon was to run a series of training courses on assertiveness. The BBC have an excellent video on the topic which we used. Everyone has to accept the responsibility of speaking their minds. Every single member of our organisation of equals must accept that they have a *responsibility to be assertive.*

As Jonathan Brown points out, it is important that a company actually identifies processes that absorb the contentiousness and assertiveness that is innate in virtually everybody and puts it to constructive use rather than leaving it festering.

5. Contention

In many organisations, the culture is that you 'do not rock the boat'. Anyone who does so is treated as something of an outcast and runs the risk of being 'cut off at their knees'!

One of my most valued colleagues earlier in my career was Mike Binney, a typical blunt, cynical Yorkshireman. By speaking his mind and challenging me to think through my thoughts, he was being far more loyal than those who appeared to concur at the meeting but chuntered among themselves as they went down the stairs. Indeed, Abraham Zaleznick, a Harvard professor, once wrote[18]:

> I am constantly surprised at the frequency with which Chief Executives feel threatened by open challenges to their ideas, as though the source of their authority, rather than their specific idea, was at issue. The ability to confront is also the ability to tolerate aggressive interchange. And that skill not only has the net effect of stripping away the veils of ambiguity – characteristic of managerial cultures – but it also encourages the emotional relationship leaders need if they are to survive.

When Alfred Sloane was Chairman of General Motors, he would postpone a decision if all the directors were in agreement! He felt that at that level the issues were so complex, the options so open, that it was only after vigorous contention on the opportunities, or dangers, that he could be sure that they had explored all the issues, and were making the best judgement in the circumstances.

It's the ability to shed outmoded knowledge, techniques and beliefs, as well as to learn and deploy new ones, that enable firms to carry out strategies. The ability to do so faster and more effectively than your competitors becomes a priceless competitive advantage. This won't happen without a strong culture of contention. In fact, Richard Pascale[16] believes that our prime role as leaders is that of *maintaining a constructive level of debate.* To do this we need dispassionate analysis of *all* the options.

6. Openness

If you are determined to transform your business, you will need to take positive steps to create what is called an 'open organisation'. This is one in which there is open, informed debate involving every individual member of your team on every issue concerned with future threats and opportunities, and with the consequences of current strategies. In *Moments of Truth*[15], Jan Carlzon, the former President of SAS, starts with four key quotations:

■ 'Everyone needs to know and feel that he/she is needed.'
■ 'Everyone wants to be treated as an individual.'
■ 'Giving someone the freedom to take responsibility releases resources that would otherwise remain concealed.'
■ 'An individual without information cannot take responsibility; an individual who is given information cannot help but take responsibility.'

By giving people the freedom to take responsibility, you are releasing an invaluable resource, but they cannot take this responsibility without relevant information.

He explains that in his drive for customer service, he wanted customers to be able to pick up their luggage virtually as soon as they walked off their plane. He started publishing a league table of how long it took at every airport served by SAS. The New York team of handlers were once shown to be bottom. They were indignant. They set out to be first, gained authority to knock down a wall, and rearranged the layout. They quickly shot up the league table.

There is a tremendous competitive urge in most people. Isn't this why sport is so popular? When the local team wins, morale in the area goes up. Morale in South Africa rocketed once their rugby team won the World Cup. What a tremendous example of motivational leadership it was when their President, Mandela, emerged wearing a No 9 Captain's shirt. Everyone in South Africa and in the stadium reacted with great emotion. So, the nub is to:

■ give people the freedom to take responsibility;
■ give them the information they need to take responsibility;
■ ensure total openness so that they can go beyond the figures to see the context of the contribution they are being expected to achieve.

This may require a dramatic change of mindset particularly among middle managers since, as Robert Heller writes in his latest book,[19] *'Information is now power, but most top managers are reluctant to release it to the workers.'* What a stupid, negative, recipe for poor productivity and commitment.

We must have total openness if we want to achieve **Hard Results.**

7. Learning organisation

One important way of optimising on the collective knowledge of your people is to consciously create what has been called a 'Learning Organisation'. This is one in which everyone accepts responsibility for their own 'self mastery' and, also, accepts the responsibility for helping to develop their colleagues.

The first point comes back to the philosophy of making people responsible for sustaining their own 'self-employability'. Creating an awareness that *they* have the responsibility to keep abreast and ahead of developments so that they are better able to do an effective job on your behalf.

The second point is important: creating a culture within which every member of the team accepts responsibility for sharing information with and helping their colleagues to improve their performance. In our small company, everyone who goes on a course is required to give a presentation at our monthly company meeting: to explain what they have learned; and to highlight any ideas which could be adopted to improve our performance.

Every individual, or team, is required to give, in turn, a regular presentation of what they are doing and why, how what they are doing helps their colleagues; or how their colleagues could help them to be more effective; or maybe to give their colleagues a thorough briefing on a particular topic be it marketing, selling, data processing, librarianship, or any of our other activities.

Some of our larger clients hold regular lunchtime or periodic early evening meetings. There is tremendous value in, for example, your marketing team preparing a presentation on how they seek to position your company, and its products, the market segments at which they are aiming and the characteristics of customers in each segment, and the perceptions they are striving to create.

Other departments and specialists can prepare presentations also. In larger organisations, like Peugeot, internal videos are produced along similar lines.

Creating a culture within which everyone accepts personal responsibility for developing themselves, and their colleagues, is a tremendously powerful weapon.

8. Techniques

We have agreed, I hope, that the collective knowledge of every single person within our organisation is our single most invaluable asset and that we can achieve the **Hard Results** of improved sales, improved productivity, and react far more readily to change, if we ensure that we tap into this asset.

So, how many organisations have really thought through how to optimise upon this invaluable asset?

I spoke recently at a conference of a very switched-on organisation. Their Board of Directors had to accept that they had never once got down to discussing how to optimise upon their most important asset, the collective knowledge of their people. Such activities as did take place had grown 'like Topsy' rather than being the result of a carefully thought out strategy.

Let's look, briefly, at a few techniques.

Treat people as experts

As we said earlier, the persons or the people doing the job, are the experts. They should be the first people to be asked for their opinions on any issues relating to the work they do and they are the people who should be involved in your Kaizan programme of seeking for continuous improvements.

Stretch people

We have to stretch people by pushing as much responsibility on them as possible, and by giving them demanding targets which ensure that they have to use all their skills. Having done so, we must stop downward meddling and upward delegation. If necessary, we must let people learn from their mistakes or, hopefully, create the team spirit which ensures they go to the relevant colleague for help and advice.

Hidden talents

One way or another, perhaps at the next appraisal interview, you need to dig deep to discover the hidden assets of your people, particularly by questioning them on their spare time hobbies and interests. One client had a partsman who was a brilliant coach of a local sports team, for example. An important question at every appraisal interview, which we will discuss later, is what talents does the person feel he/she has that are not being used to the full; with the supplementary question of how the team member concerned feels that these talents could be utilised more effectively.

Discussion meetings/brainstorming

We shut down our small company for half a day a month. One client, with a team of 120, holds two evening meetings of 60 people each, on a quarterly basis. When Sir Peter Thompson was at NFC[9] he used to hold Sunday meetings on a regional basis for everyone in the area. They were always very well attended. One way or another we need to create a mechanism for regular brainstorming sessions and open discussion meetings.

Hot Group

A Hot Group is just what the name implies. A lively, high achieving, dedicated group, usually small, whose members are turned on by an exciting and challenging task. More specifically, it is accepted that they should challenge existing organisational 'correctness' to help their companies to achieve success in today's highly competitive environment.

Project teams

What we are discussing is the total delegation of day-to-day management issues, if necessary by creating a project team to solve a particular problem, in a way which draws on the talents of everyone who gets involved. Remember how Peter Nathan delegated his packing problem to Sue Stevens and her packers (page 20).

Valentines

Cross functional teams need to be established to resolve interdepartmental issues. At one point, Ford in America got each department, in turn, to set out in writing the frustrations they experienced with other departments. They were called 'Valentines'. A meeting was then organised at which the content of these 'Valentines' were discussed, openly and constructively, with the other department or departments concerned.

'Stakeholder' panels

Involving some of your stakeholders, your suppliers, dealers, people from your community, and in particular your customers (many of whom have their own areas of expertise), is an important element of optimising the value of what Dan Jones calls your 'Value Stream'.

Employee involvement

A great success at Ford, when Don Petersen was at the helm, was transforming its performance through the 'Employee Involvement Programme' which Richard Pascale explains in great depth in his book, *Managing on the Edge*[16]. There was a tremendous upswelling of initiatives from everyone at every level and impressive gains in quality and productivity were achieved. I don't like the term 'employee involvement' but by whatever name it's called, mobilising everyone's involvement must be the way to achieve **Hard Results.**

Workouts

This is the most dynamic of techniques which Jack Welch pioneered at GE. A group of people from all levels and activities from within the organisation

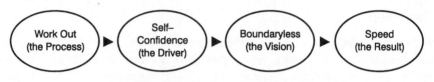

Figure 6.1 GE Workout concept

hold an extensive discussion, which can last for half a day, or up to three days. A senior executive sets the problem to be discussed. At the end of the period the senior executive returns, and the syndicate chairman puts forward the recommendations. In the process, team members gain confidence, boundaries are broken down, and there is a speedy solution to the problems being faced by the unit concerned.

Process mapping

A process map is a chart showing every step, no matter how small, that goes into making or doing something. For example, every step can be mapped from the time an order is received to the time it is delivered. It can be surprisingly difficult. To do it effectively, suppliers, team members, dealers, and even customers, must work on the map together to make sure that what they think happens, really does.

GE found that when such a process map is finished, they have the ability – often for the first time – to manage the process in a coherent way from start to finish. The result of one process map was a 50 per cent saving of time, plus a $4 million drop in inventory, resulting in an increase in stockturn to seven times a year. As importantly, by involving the people concerned, it taps into their collective knowledge. It's a valuable technique that can be used in the smallest of companies. It can now be done on computer using ATI software.

Today's most valued work is done through a complex web of interactions among highly skilled workers. The San Francisco office of Young and Rubicon deployed a Lotus Notes version of Action Work Flow to redesign their approach to creating advertising campaigns. Within months the firm reported dramatic decreases in overtime, rush charges and rework, as well as shorter cycle times and enhanced customer satisfaction. No other approach to process mapping is as powerful.

Suggestion schemes

Last, but not least, let us not forget Suggestion Schemes. QED: Quid Each Day, Quality Each Day is a proprietary scheme. At Walon, the logistics company, it resulted in 570 suggestions from 450 staff, over 350 of which were implemented successfully.

WHY SHOULD PEOPLE BOTHER?

Wouldn't it be great if you could tap into the collective knowledge of everyone involved in, or with, your organisation? It would be fantastic. It would make a tremendous difference. But why should the people concerned bother to make the effort?

Management insincerity or reciprocity

Ian Gibson, Chief Executive of Nissan Motor Manufacturing (UK) once said:

> The poor level of team spirit found among European workers is due less to cultural factors than management insincerity in cutting back on hierarchy and the perks flow from it.

Ian added:

> Inadequate training of workers and managers to take on greater roles also leads to lack of involvement. At Nissan we give shop floor workers continual training over several years so that they are able to take on projects to improve productivity, rather than passing the task on to an engineer sitting in an office.

In his recent book,[19] Robert Heller concludes that too little has changed in many company Board Rooms. We need total reciprocity, by working hard on all the twelve ingredients we have been, and will be discussing, to create a culture in which people will be 'willing to bother': keen to commit totally to your organisation. Obviously it is more difficult when external pressures may cause inevitable redundancies but involving your people is far more likely to make you responsive and competitive enough to respond positively to these external pressures.

The 'Golden Triad'

In his marvellous case-study of Honda,[16] Richard Pascale describes what he calls the 'Golden Triad' of (1) Enduring Values, (2) Trust, and (3) Empowerment, which he believes have to be in place before an organisation can tap into the commitment of its people. In a powerful piece of writing he explains:

> Values and trust establish the pre-conditions that encourage individuals to think, experiment, and improve. Once employees know what an organisation stands for, and believes it is sufficiently trustworthy to warrant their commitment and effort, they begin to truly extend themselves. If (leaders) provide

(their colleagues) with the tools, understanding and latitude to make a difference, great things are possible.

Coming back to the essential ingredient of leadership, Warren Bennis and Burt Nanus[8] write that what we should do, as leaders, is to:

Unite the people in the organisation into a **'responsible community'**, *a group of inter-dependent individuals who take responsibility for the success of the organisation and its long-term survival.*

BRAINSTORMING EXERCISES OR PROJECTS: 6

Collective Knowledge

■ Do you accept that your most valuable asset is the collective knowledge of everyone involved in or with your organisation? If so, are you tapping into this asset as fully as possible? If not, how do you set about ensuring that you optimise this invaluable asset?

■ Do you have the courage to accept that if you let people make their own decisions, they will undoubtedly do things differently, and may need to 'learn from their mistakes'? Are you willing to let them go through this learning process? More importantly, how do you ensure that all your executives are prepared to 'let go of the reins'?

■ Do you accept that to release the knowledge of people, you have to encourage a more assertive and contentious environment? If so, how do you set about doing this?

■ Do you agree that to ensure Extraordinary performance you have to create an open 'learning organisation'? If so, how do you set about doing this?

■ Looking at the suggestions given under the heading of 'Techniques', which do you feel would be most appropriate to your own organisation in terms of truly optimising the collective knowledge of every member of your team, and how would you implement them? Could you and your team come up with other appropriate techniques?

■ To what extent do you feel you have created what Richard Pascale calls the 'Golden Triad' of (1) Enduring Values (2) Trust and (3) Empowerment? What actions can you use to build or reinforce the 'Golden Triad' in your organisation?

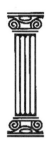

7

WINNING STRUCTURES
& SYSTEMS

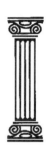

EVOLUTION NOT REVOLUTION

Reorganisations are disruptive and are not always successful. I prefer evolution rather than revolution. Going back to the Ralph Stayer case study[1], as he progressively created the culture in which his front-line people demanded more responsibility, the role of his supervisors changed. Instead of being checkers and controllers, they became coaches and facilitators.

Nonetheless, in these brutally competitive days, with margins under pressure, you have to accept that the structures and systems of your organisation have a crucial impact on your success and, if you have the wrong organisation and wrong systems, can represent a real problem. So, let's look, fairly briefly, at a number of very important issues which you and your team may wish to discuss.

WINNING: OBJECTIVES COME FIRST

Everyone agrees. Peter Drucker[20], years ago, said first decide on your objectives, and then design the organisation needed for their achievement. Another guru, Alfred Chandler[21], said 'Structure follows Strategy'. We have to optimise our existing organisation and its people; our most valuable asset. But we will not survive unless we evolve strategies that help us to achieve realistic, stretching objectives.

THE GLOBAL THREAT

When Stephane Garelli, a Professor who is also Director of the World Competitive Report, spoke at one of our Workshops, he said bluntly:

Every day low cost
Every day low price
Every day low margin.

He stressed that the name of the game is the cost efficiency of structures and systems. He quoted West German labour costs at $27.30, average EC costs at $19.70, and the US at $17.00, whereas in the underdeveloped countries of Asia and South America, labour costs ranged from $5.00 downwards, with costs in the rapidly developing markets of China and India probably lower than $1.00 an hour.

In these circumstances, there is bound to be a transfer of manufacturing to these low-cost areas with Western organisations becoming merely assemblers. Rapid developments in Information Technology (IT) mean that it is more cost-effective for some European companies to have all their centralised accounting processes carried out in India, while some American companies have their data processed in the high unemployment areas of Western Ireland.

As John Neill of Unipart once said, 'Work can now be done almost anywhere by almost anyone, heralding new waves of competitive intensity, unparalleled in the experience of many of today's leading companies.'

Earlier, I recommended that you and your team should carry out a **SWOT** analysis of your organisation. Depending on the business you are in, you may well need to look at these global issues.

IMPORTANCE OF ORGANISATION

In their book, based on their world-wide study,[11] Dan Jones and his MIT colleagues give many dramatic examples of different levels of performance from organisations in exactly the same business. The differences were startling (see Table 7.1).

They also analysed the reason for such a significant productivity gap between two factories. They concluded that 52 per cent of the difference could be traced back to differences in sourcing, processing and manufacturability but that the biggest reason for the productivity gap, at 48 per cent, was superior organisation (though better sourcing, processing, design and manufacturability are themselves the result of better organisation).

Table 7.1 Differing performance levels

	Company A	Company B
Hours to assemble car	31	16
Defects per 100 cars	130	45
Assembly space per car	8.1	4.8
Average stocks	2 weeks	2 hours

So let's accept that in these highly competitive times, we have to look hard at our structures and systems.

DON'T SHOW CUSTOMERS YOUR ARSE!

Your core objective must be to identify, attract, satisfy and retain an increasing number of customers in a way which optimises the resources available to you.

Sadly, too many companies have been vertically driven, financially oriented, and authority based, with the Chief Executive looking down from his exalted position on apparent order, symmetry and uniformity, with an ever-widening pyramid of divisions and departments. Those at the bottom of the pyramid, the front-line executives, look up at a phalanx of controllers whose demands soak up most of their energies and time. The result, as Jack Welch puts it, 'Is an organisation with its face towards the CEO and its arse towards the customer!'

This is very true. How many times have you, as a customer, been treated as if the organisation's structure and systems were more important than meeting your needs? Could this be happening in your organisation?

Your structure and your systems should be designed to exceed the expectations of your customers. One of the great benefits of starting to draw organisation charts as an upturned triangle, with the front-line, customer-facing people at the top, is that it makes the important psychological point that it is the people at the sharp end, at the customer interface, who are important and that it is a function of middle and senior executives to support them.

As Jan Carlzon puts it in his marvellous book[15], it is literally their millions of 15 second contacts with the members of his team which built the reputation of SAS in the minds of their customers. Years ago, you may remember, there was a training film called *Who Lost the Sale?*. In it the switchboard operator, the receptionist, the van driver, the clerk, all played their part. We have to create organisations in which everyone accepts responsibility for 'adding value' to every contact they have.

FRONT-LINE ENTREPRENEURS

We have to drop our assumption that those at the top are the only entrepreneurs in the business.

As Sumantra Ghoshal points out[6]:

> Few front-line initiatives survive bureaucracy's smothering assumption that top managers are the best visionaries for their organisations and are alone responsible for leading their companies into new areas. Any bottom-up ideas that survive the top-down directives are likely to be crushed in the documentation, review, and approval processes that supply senior managers with the information and feedback they need to operate as a company's strategic gurus.

Upturning your organisation will only work effectively when you recognise that the role of the front line is transformed from implementors to initiators, and when you recognise that our role as senior executives is to provide the culture, the context, in which our front-line colleagues will feel free to use their initiative and, hopefully, even be entrepreneurs on our behalf.

When Jim Maxmin was at Thorn EMI, he once worked out that if his service people had had the freedom to negotiate with customers over warranty claims, the total cost to the company would have been far less than the bureaucracy which had been created in referring these claims back to Head Office for verification and reluctant approval. But, as he pointed out to me, it was not merely the cost, it was the customer dissatisfaction caused which was the more important issue.

ENCOURAGE INNOVATION

One of the world's most innovative corporations is 3M where a former Chief Executive, William McKnight, believed that his company was best served when senior executives trusted those with direct knowledge of the market, the operations, or the technology involved.

His philosophy has rewarded 3M with thousands of breakthrough entrepreneurial initiatives, so it is little wonder that belief in the individual is one of 3M's core values, as it should be in every organisation.

As Andy Grove, the Chief Executive of Intel admits, their most important strategic decision was made not in response to some clear-sighted corporate vision but by the decisions of front-line managers who knew what was going on. We, as leaders, have to hold in high regard every member of our organisation if we want the hard results that will follow from their commitment to striving to excel on our behalf.

LEAN BUT NOT MEAN

As Julia's illustrations portray, many organisations resemble a carriage pulled by six blindfolded horses, kept on course by outriders, and whipped fiercely by the coachman because they are uncertain of the road ahead (Figure 7.1).

It was Dan Jones and his MIT colleagues who first introduced the concept of *'lean manufacturing'* which Dan updated in his more recent *Harvard Business Review* article,[22] with his colleague James Womack. They write:

> by eliminating unnecessary steps, aligning all steps in an activity in a continuous flow, recombining labour into cross-functional teams dedicated to that activity, and continually striving for improvement, lean companies can develop, produce, and distribute products with *half or less the human effort, space, tools, time and overall expense. They can also become vastly more flexible and responsive to customer desires.*

No organisation can afford to miss out on these benefits. Lean does not necessarily imply mean – in fact the reverse. People are more often demotivated by slack, wasteful organisations. If the right culture is created, people get far more of a 'buzz' from being given responsibility.

Your organisation should resemble Julia's second illustration, a carriage pulled by fewer, better motivated horses, needing only minimal guidance because they can see the road ahead, and enjoy the exhilaration of their performance. It comes back to our central theme that colleagues who share your goals and your values won't need much supervision.

Let me give you one example. I had three executives on one of my workshops. Each had broadly the same level of turnover, and were in the same type of business. One had 38 staff, one 32, and the third only 18. Can you imagine the difference in profitability?

TRANSACTIONAL APPROACH

Many organisations resemble a carriage pulled by six blindfolded horses kept
on course by outriders and whipped fiercely by the coachman because they
are uncertain of the road ahead.

TRANSFORMATIONAL APPROACH

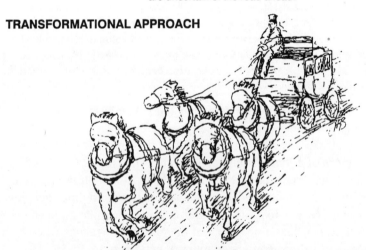

Organisations should resemble a carriage pulled by fewer, better motivated horses,
only needing minimal guidance because they can see the road ahead,
and enoy the exhilaration of their performance.

Illustrations By Julia Howarth

Figure 7.1 The organisation culture

WHAT'S YOUR CORE BUSINESS?

In the past, those of us, myself included, who have built up their own businesses, have tended to measure our progress by the size of the organisation. Rather than talking about turnover or profitability, it has been easier to say 'I employ 70 people', or whatever. In today's highly competitive environment, this is no longer a valid approach.

Stephane Garelli sees an organisation with three elements (see Figures 7.2 and 7.3):

1. A **compact core** representing as small a team as possible of dedicated, completely committed people, focusing on truly 'adding value' to the unique expertise by which their organisation satisfies its customers.
2. An **inner periphery** of people on short-term contracts. BP advertised at one point for an economist on a non-pensionable, three year contract. In fact, this is a very sensible route for a small, rapidly growing organisation to take. Too many small companies have crippled themselves by taking on, as full time employees, people whose skills were only relevant to that stage of the company's growth. Once the company expanded beyond their competence, they became a hindrance. So, short-term contracts for a particular short-term need, make sense.
3. An **outer periphery** of work which is 'outsourced'. This is an increasing trend among companies large and small. The Inland Revenue is reputed to pay a billion pounds a year to EDS to manage its data processing functions. BP Exploration has outsourced all its Information Technology operations in an effort to cut costs, gain more flexible and higher quality IT resources, and refocus the IT department on activities that directly improve the overall business.

The *American Management Association*[23] magazine once quoted a case study on Tomima Edmar, an ex-IBM employee, who chafed at the amount of time she 'wasted' on office politics, personnel issues, and countless meetings. When she started out on her own, she determined to spend time on doing business rather than managing. She grew her Topsytail hair care gadget to sales of $80 million, with only two employees.

The AMA article gives five reasons why people outsource:

■ Outsiders are more efficient – 70%
■ Focus on your own products – 45%
■ Save costs of benefits – 42%
■ Less investment needed – 41%
■ Lower regulatory burdens – 21%

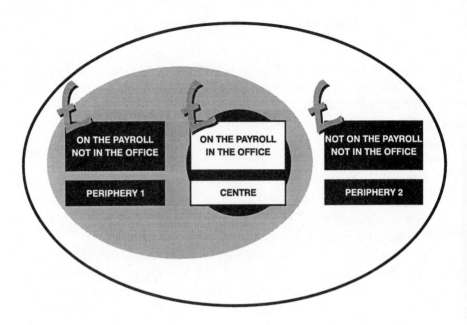

Figure 7.2 The core contracts, the periphery expands

1st PERIPHERY			CENTRE			2nd PERIPHERY	
Job Status	–middle mgnt –project driven		Job Status	–senior –full time		Job Status	–project oriented
Structure	–permanent –part–time –job sharing		Structure	–permanent		Structure	–temporary
Revenues	–salaries –fees –variable		Revenues	–salaries/ options etc		Revenues	–business contracts
Office	–virtual –at home		Office	–in house		Office	–external –linked
Social Benefits	–partial –and private		Social Benefits	–full		Social Benefits	–external
Sense of Belonging	–medium		Sense of Belonging	–strong		Sense of Belonging	–low

Figure 7.3 The redefinition of jobs

It's all too easy to slip into the trap of adding on activities. For example, because my company produces a lot of information, we invested heavily in desktop publishing. At one point it seemed logical to develop an internal print operation. It then seemed a logical step to try to recoup some of the capital outlay by selling print outside the business. This then became a distraction. We sold it, and now subcontract all our printing.

At Walon, the Logistics and Distribution organisation, John Merry has been very stringent in requiring every department or activity to assess critically the extent to which the services they provide, or receive, are truly adding value. We all need to do the same. We need to have a lean organisation focusing on our particular strengths, make greater use of people on short-term contracts, and wherever possible, outsource activities which are not part of our core business.

Although problems can arise from its social aspect, more companies are making use of short-term or temporary staff. It has enabled one company to significantly increase its responsiveness while lowering its costs, but it can also be counterproductive if taken too far; a loyal core of committed people is vital. Problems can also arise when an activity is transferred into a new company with the people transferred facing a real culture shock.

Increasingly companies will need to look outside for specialist advice; sometimes in areas in which they do not have the expertise to judge the competence of their advisors. It is one area in which mistakes can be hideously expensive. Take care on this issue.

WORKING AWAY FROM ORGANISATION

Regarding the changing nature of work, Garelli suggested that in future far more work will be done at home. Given the high costs of property it makes sense.

Space in submarines is at such a premium that bunks are shared. Stephane was talking of a company in Holland which uses a similar concept. Everyone has the equivalent of a large left-luggage locker. They put all their personal papers in this locker. If they come into the office, they take the equivalent of a supermarket trolley, collect their papers from their locker, and then go to find whichever desk happens to be empty.

Many of our clients at the Stephane Garelli meeting became very worried by the new ideas he was explaining of 'The Virtual Organisation', where work is done outside the traditional office structures. Charles Handy had an interesting article on this point in the *Harvard Business Review*[24]. He explains that executives need to move beyond the fear of losing efficiency

'Does your firm realise that its most sensitive work is being handled by a 14 year old working on a vague promise of extra pocket money?'

Figure 7.4   Working from home

and the desire to impose checks and controls. Handy proposes seven rules of trust:

1. **Trust is not blind**. It needs fairly small groupings so people can know each other well.
2. **Trust needs boundaries**. Define a goal, then leave the worker to get on with it.
3. **Trust demands learning and openness to change**.
4. **Trust is tough**: when it turns out to be a mistake, people have to go.
5. **Trust needs bonding**: the goals of a small unit must gel with a larger group.
6. **Trust needs touch**: workers must sometimes meet in person.
7. **Trust requires leaders**.

All very valid points which apply to colleagues working inside and away from our businesses. Obviously, it depends very much on the type of business you are in. Many organisations already have significant numbers of people out in the field. Certainly, most would feel that 'being a member of a team' is a very important motivational factor but the overheads of running an office are significant, so the concept of 'hot desking' is one to be borne in mind.

BOUNDARYLESSNESS

Jack Welch, has written and spoken a great deal on the need for a 'boundaryless' organisation, in which everyone is responsible. He said in one of his Annual Reports:

> Our dream for the 1990s is a boundaryless company ... where we knock down the walls that separate us from each other on the inside and from our key constituencies on the outside.

In Jack Welch's vision, such a company would remove barriers among traditional functions, *'recognise no distinction, but ignore or erase group levels such as "management", "salaried", or "hourly", which get in the way of people working together.'*

Two other gurus[25] developed the concept put forward by Jack Welch. They write:

> One of the premier challenges of 'leaders' is to design more flexible organisations. Companies are replacing vertical hierarchies with horizontal networks: linking together traditional functions through inter-functional teams; and forming strategic alliances with suppliers, customers, and even competitors. (Leaders) are insisting that every (colleague) understands and adheres to the company's strategic mission without distinction of title, function, or task.

They add that:

> The traditional organisation map describes a world that no longer exists ... In the new organisation, subordinates must challenge in order to follow – while superiors must listen in order to lead.

The last sentence is important. It comes back to the issue of leaders and effective followers which are our first two ingredients. Let us look at some of the issues that arise from this.

HORIZONTAL NOT VERTICAL

For years, businesses have been built on the basis of largely autonomous functions, often referred to as 'chimneys' (see Figure 7.5). Individuals saw their careers as moving progressively up their functional ladder; switching from company to company, to move further up their particular 'chimney'.

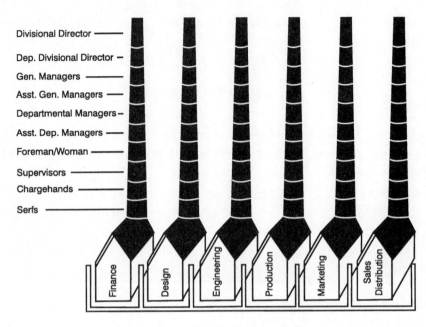

Figure 7.5 The dissipation of effort

You must be well aware of all the conflicts that have resulted from this type of organisation. In one notorious case, the people in Design would not meet or even speak to the people in Engineering on the telephone. Their only contact was through memos! It's a nonsensical way to run an organisation. The internal focus means that nobody is really focusing on 'adding value' to the customer, their failure to share information adds to cost and lowers productivity, while the people within the activities and their suppliers are 'switched off'.

As a result, they lose out against their more flexible competitors.

Figure 7.6 Internally focused interdepartmental conflicts and rivalries

We are back to the difficult issue of 'mindset', of deeply ingrained thinking. Our success will be based on creating very flat, horizontal organisations. Four immediate issues arise from the new approach.

Span of control

It became perceived wisdom at one point that an executive's span of control should be limited to five subordinates. One of Jack Welch's initial actions was to extend the span of control of most of his executives to 15 or more. He argued that if an executive only has five people reporting to him, then he has time to manage, to interfere. If he has 15 or more, he has no time to manage, he is forced to lead.

The book *Re-Engineering the Corporation*[5] refers to spans of control of up to 30. When Larry de Monaco of GE spoke at one of our seminars, he referred to one executive who is directly responsible for over 250 people. Larry added that by Tuesday morning, the executive concerned is searching for things to do!

Levels

Years ago it was not uncommon for organisations to have up to 16 levels of management. Truly professional organisations, including Unipart and the AA, recognise that even quite large organisations can be run on three, four or, at the most, five levels.

Titles

It follows that there is much less scope for grand titles. *Management Today* once referred to an American company which had abolished all titles. Everyone, from the highest to the lowest, was termed an 'Associate', and was expected to work diligently with colleagues, with only one objective – how they could 'add value' for the customer and thus help their organisation to succeed.

Progress independent of promotion

This raises a very important social and motivational issue. If there are fewer levels and the organisation is more horizontally organised, then there are only two ways of switching people on. They must feel a valued member of a worthwhile organisation. They can see that their personal development is enhanced by a broader, more rounded appreciation of, and involvement in the total process, rather than limited specific tasks. Let us develop this point.

PROCESSES NOT TASKS

For 200 years, businesses have concentrated on breaking down work into simple tasks on a 'production line' basis. This happens even in offices. The approach incurs high supervision and coordination costs. Workers quickly become bored and quality and productivity suffer.

Years ago, Peter Drucker[20] was writing of a Direct Mail Fulfilment house where one clerk slit open the letter, the next smoothed it flat, and so on. It took some 20 steps to fulfil an order! The result? A high level of employee and customer dissatisfaction. Peter Drucker advised the firm to make each colleague totally responsible for their own group of customers. Motivation and customer satisfaction rocketed. More recently, Michael Hammer and James Champy took up this theme in their book, *Re-Engineering the Corporation.* They write of the need for companies to virtually reinvent themselves:

> What matters in re-engineering is how we organise work today, given the demand of today's markets and the power of today's technologies.

They argue that it's not a question of asking ourselves:

- How do we do what we do faster? or
- How do we do what we do better? or
- How do we do what we do at lower cost?

But asking:

- *Why do we do what we do at all?*

In their extensive research, they found that:

> Many tasks had nothing to do with meeting customer needs ... Many tasks were done simply to satisfy the internal demands of the company's own organisation.

They add that:

> Programming people to conform to established procedures remains the essence of bureaucracy even now.

They argue that achieving a competitive advantage *'isn't an issue of getting people to work harder but of learning to work differently'*.

If you have not already read it, the book is well worth reading. Even better, form one of the Hot Groups mentioned earlier, buy each member of the group a copy, and get them to report back to you on how its principles could be applied in your organisation.

The two authors raise numerous points.

■ Combine several tasks into one process. The central issue.
■ Abolish supervision. Let workers make decisions.
■ Organise work concurrently, not sequentially.
■ Create different levels of response: computerise the straightforward, train confident people to deal with the 15 per cent plus of minor variations and only involve the higher level of expertise needed in balance of the more difficult.
■ Let work be performed more effectively elsewhere, delegating some tasks to suppliers or even customers.
■ Reduce checks and controls by training and trusting front-line people.
■ Reduce reconciliations, particularly by integrating the whole process.
■ Provide customers with a single point of contact.
■ Use new technology to get the benefits of centralisation and decentralisation.
■ Create multi-dimensional work by creating teams of people with different complementary skills.
■ Move from controlling to empowering.
■ Move from training to education (a point to which we will return).
■ Measure results rather than activities.
■ Change people from being protective to productive.
■ Get managers to change into coaches and from score keepers into leaders.

All these are very valid points and your Hot Groups should be able to come up with interesting answers.

The two authors define 're-engineering' as the

> Fundamental re-thinking and radical re-design of business processes to achieve dramatic improvements in critical measures of performance. Fundamental questions are, why do we do what we do, and why do we do it the way we do?

They define *processes* as a collection of activities that create an output of value to the customer. One very basic example is order fulfilment which begins when a customer places an order, ends when the goods are delivered, and includes everything between. Typically the process involves a dozen or so steps performed by different people in different departments. No one in the company oversees the whole process and no one is responsible. Errors are inevitable with so many people having to handle, and act separately on, the same order. Hence the importance of having one customer contact point.

The book is full of fascinating examples. A Finance House discovered that work which actually took only 90 minutes, often took more than seven days because it was spread over five people. It slashed its seven-day turn-around to four hours, without an increase in headcount, and the number of deals handled has increased one hundred fold.

It is now accepted that most of the 'Re-engineering' projects completed have only achieved modest improvements. As I said at the outset, no technique, however excellent, will work unless all 12 ingredients are in place. I come back to my point of evolution not revolution. Your best first step would be the exercise on 'Process Mapping' I suggested earlier. If you and your team understand all the processes involved, and challenge yourselves with whether every step is truly adding value to the end user/customer, then this could be the way of easing into the re-engineering of your business.

What we are talking about is moving from the situation where different individuals or departments handle a sequence of tasks, to one where a team of people accept mutual responsibility for adding value to your customers by handling the complete process from start to finish. This may require a team to be composed of different specialists and thus require a different lay-out, so that all the members of each team can work as close to each other as possible. Unipart operates in this way, having an open plan office subdivided into teams of development, marketing, technical, administrative and other specialists working together on specific products or projects.

TEAMS NOT INDIVIDUALS

We in Britain tend to pride ourselves upon being a nation of individuals (perhaps it is one of our problems when we strive to take part in team sports at an international level?). Certainly, in business, the focus is on the individual. Job descriptions, pay schemes, career paths, performance evaluations, focus on individuals. We feel uncomfortable if our career prospects depend upon others.

Wisdom of Teams[26] by Jon Katzenbach and Douglas Smith should be essential reading if you are concerned to create a high-performance organisation.

The Team Performance Curve

One of the crucial illustrations of this stimulating book refers to:

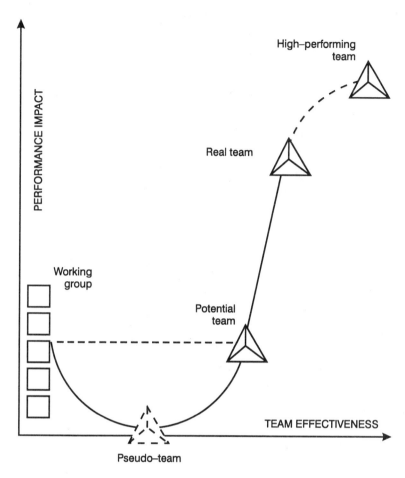

Figure 7.7   The Team Performance Curve

- working group
- pseudo-team
- potential team
- real team
- high-performing team.

Let's look at each in turn, but first, what is a 'team'?

A team defined

Katzenbach and Smith's definition is that:

A team is a small number of people, with complementary skills, who are committed to a common purpose, performance goals, and an approach for which they hold themselves mutually accountable.

Small, because a smaller number of people are better able to work through their differences to achieve their purpose.

Complementary skills are needed if a team is to be effective. So, you might end up with a team from Design, Supply, Marketing, Sales, Delivery and Administrative departments.

Purpose and *performance* go hand in hand. The specific **performance** goal helps a team track progress and hold itself accountable; the sense of **purpose** supplies both meaning and emotional energy.

Committed to a common approach requires team members to agree on who will do what, what skills need to be developed, how continuing membership is to be earned, and how the group will make and modify its decisions.

Mutual accountability, in which the teams hold themselves collectively responsible for their team's performance.

The two authors criticise many organisations for imprecise thinking about teams, confusing it with teamwork, for example, and for the lack of discipline in applying every aspect of their careful definition. They conclude:

> We believe that the truly committed team is the most productive performance unit (leaders) have at their disposal – provided there are specific results for which the team is collectively responsible and provided the performance ethics of the company demands those results.

Against this thought-provoking definition let's go back to Figure 7.7.

Working groups

A working group relies primarily on the individual contributions of its members for group performance. It is typically the committee formed by the heads of each department whose bonuses may well be geared to the performance of their own department. Thus, while they may liaise together to resolve areas of friction and even brainstorm good ideas, they are essentially concerned to protect their own activity. As the two authors point out, rugged individuals – and there are many, especially at the top – cannot contribute to real team performance without taking responsibility for their peers, and letting their peers assume responsibility for them.

Pseudo team

The authors warn that there is a real danger that in trying to adopt a 'team' approach, people get diverted from their individual goals but are not willing to commit to working as a real team. Hence their collective performance drops.

Potential team

This is a team which is trying to improve results. But it requires more clarity about its purpose and goals and more discipline in hammering out a common working approach. Its members have not yet accepted collective responsibility. The authors add that such teams are to be found in many organisations.

Real team

This is a small number of people, with complementary skills, who are equally committed to a common purpose, performance goals, and a working approach for which they hold themselves mutually accountable. As shown in the diagram, they can significantly improve performance.

High performance team

Even higher levels of performance can be achieved once the members of a team get deeply committed to each other. Each generally helps the others to achieve both personal and professional goals. The authors quote examples of team members who paid for the training they felt they needed to keep up. The authors describe how some team members tried to resign because they felt they were letting the side down. Their colleagues refused to let them. Instead, they provided the training, coaching and support they needed so that they became truly competent members of the team. It would be great if the same things happened in your own organisation.

THE WISDOM OF TEAMS

Summary of key lessons

A demanding performance challenge tends to create a team. No team arises without a performance challenge that is meaningful to those involved. In fact, teams often form around such challenges without any help or support from management. Conversely, potential teams without such challenges usually fail.

Leaders can foster team performance best by building a strong performance ethic rather than promoting teams for the sake of teams. Real
teams are much more likely to flourish if leaders aim their sights on performance results that balance the needs of customers, employees and
shareholders. Clarity of purpose and goals have tremendous power in our
change-driven world.

Individualism need not get in the way of team performance. Real teams
always find ways for each individual to contribute and thereby gain distinction. Indeed, when harnessed to a common team purpose and goals,
our need to distinguish ourselves as individuals becomes a powerful
engine.

Groups become teams through disciplined action. They *shape* a common
purpose, *agree* on performance goals, *define* a common working
approach, *develop* high levels of complementary skills and *hold* themselves mutually accountable for results. And, as with any effective discipline, they never stop doing any of these things.

Source: *The Wisdom of Teams* by John Katzenbach and Douglas Smith, Harvard Business Press

Elite case study

One of their wide range of case studies mentions an American Regional
newspaper, *The Democrat*, which sought to resolve its problems – primarily
dissatisfied advertisers – by a reorganisation which failed. It then solved its
problems by creating a project team.

The team had a strong mix of skills (twelve of the best people from all
parts of the paper). It used their goal of eliminating errors to create the
name of **Elite**. Advertising accuracy, never before tracked, rose sharply and
stayed above 99 per cent. Lost revenue from errors, previously as high as
$10,000 a month, dropped to near zero. Advertiser satisfaction rocketed.
But the authors write that:

> The impact of Elite went beyond numbers. It completely redesigned the
> process by which the Democrat sells, creates, produces advertisements. It
> stimulated and nurtured the customer obsession and cross-functional coopera-
> tion required to make the new processes work. In effect, this team of MOST-
> LY FRONT LINE WORKERS transformed an entire organisation with
> respect to customer service.

We are back to our central theme. The front line can do it. I urge you to set
up a small team of people, buy them each a copy of this marvellous book,

and get them to research the basis on which high performance teams could flourish in your organisation.

ENSURING YOU HAVE SKILLS TO WIN

Because most of us run a car, let's use the example of a dealership. Most are functionally organised with sales, service, bodyshop, parts and accounting departments. What is, or should be, the role of a Sales Manager? It should be to market (M) new and used cars through a good team of people (P), in a way which achieves a financial result (F) based on good technical expertise (T).

If we then ask what are the key tasks of every other departmental manager, we come up with the same three tasks of marketing, people and finance based on sound technical expertise. But since sales, service and parts managers tend to be promoted from salesmen, technicians and partsmen, they are hardly likely to have these three skills. They have gained promotion because of their 'technical' expertise.

Table 7.2 Functional or skills based?

Sales	Service	Bodyshop	Parts	Accounts	Skills based
M	M	M	M	M	Marketing coach
P	P	P	P	P	People coach
F	F	F	F	F	Database facilitator
T	T	T	T	T	Team leaders

Functionally Based Approach

Looking at Table 7.2, is it logical to organise a dealership on the vertical, functional basis, where all the managers lack the depth of expertise needed in three crucial areas, or would you organise it on a horizontal basis, where you still rely on the technical expertise of the departmental people by turning them into skilled coaches but ensure that they have the support they need from a marketing coach, a people coach, and a database/information facilitator?

Often this problem arises out of a misplaced sense of loyalty to the people who have helped us to start our business. We want to promote them as a reward. You may be lucky, you may have somebody with the capacity to grow with you. Three of the people who first joined me in Devon at a junior level have grown into valued senior colleagues. Equally, it is easy to promote somebody who is truly unable to cope, with the result that you block out the possibility of recruiting somebody with the skills you need. It needs very careful thought.

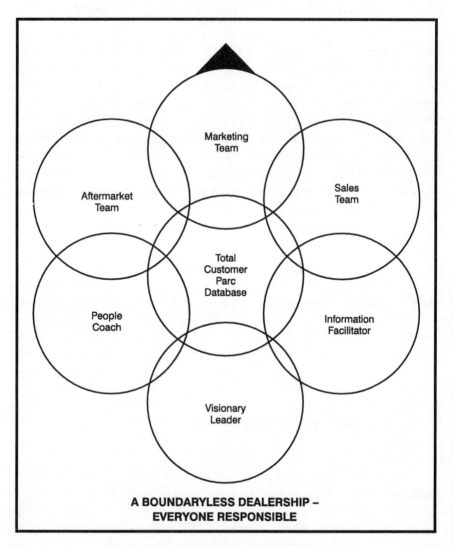

**A BOUNDARYLESS DEALERSHIP –
EVERYONE RESPONSIBLE**

Figure 7.8   The customer focused business

Spearhead of your business

Looking at Figure 7.8, the spearhead of your business, of every business, should be your marketing team. The core of your business should be a totally integrated customer database, giving comprehensive profiles of every customer, both individually and collectively in terms of the segments into which they can be identified. The openings created by the marketing team need to be followed up by the sales team and reinforced by the aftersales team. The customer database and other essential information, including financial information, should be coordinated by the 'information facilitator' (I would abolish the term 'accountant'). Every member of the team should be helped by a good coach, while the whole enterprise should be inspired by and driven forward by a visionary leader.

To be successful, you have got to create a customer-focused, skills-based, horizontal organisation – not, as so often happens, a technically based, functionally-organised, vertical organisation.

The growth of our organisation will be related directly to the competencies we can develop. Responsibility for developing these competencies should be pushed down to our front-line colleagues. They should have the challenge of creating the competencies they need, as a team, to achieve their objectives.

Our role as senior executives is, first, to create the context within which people can develop these competencies and then to ensure that they are shared throughout the organisation by cross-flows of resources, knowledge, and people.

VALUE ADDING SYSTEMS

When we were discussing re-engineering, did you notice the comment that the research carried out by the authors found that *'many tasks had nothing to do with customer needs'*? If data processing is geared towards providing our front-line people with the information they need, fine. Too often our data processing functions are geared to providing 'wouldn't it be nice to know' style information for bureaucratically-minded controllers.

Going back to 'process mapping', we have got to ensure that we provide the front line with the information they need to add value to their customer-facing activities, and that we, as senior executives, focus on measuring the right results.

Nonsense of bottom line

Recently I sat in at the Board Meeting of a group of companies worried about their lack of profitability. They spent several hours discussing their 'management accounts' which were not providing them with the answers they needed.

It is a nonsense to talk, as some do, about being 'bottom line driven'. The bottom line is an 'end result'. Fixed overheads are fixed. Variable overheads vary with the level of sales. What matters is the **'top line'**. A friend became a millionaire using a very simple formula. He had to make ten phonecalls to gain an interview. From five interviews he would gain one sale. So his formula was simple. Fifty phone calls, five interviews, one sale. Obviously, he was selling a 'large ticket' item, but the principle is simple and applies to every business.

What are the 'Top Line Drivers' of your business? How many phone calls, or visits, do your sales team have to get to achieve a sale? How often do you get invited to tender or quote for business and how frequently are you successful? If your advertising is designed to get your potential customers to phone you, how many of these incoming phone calls result in a sale? Or, if you entice people into your showroom, how many are converted? How many of your customers do you retain?

In short, how much do you know about all your customer-related activities?

Customer-related measurements

Jan Carlzon[15] has a very interesting cameo on the point I am trying to make. For maximum efficiency and profitability, commercial airlines try to fill the 'empty bellies' of passenger planes with air cargo. So, SAS measured its performance by the amount of freight carried and, typically, had a 'yardstick' on the percentage of space utilised, be it 60 per cent, 70 per cent, or whatever. The kind of figures we have all seen.

But customers are not interested in space utilisation. They want *prompt deliveries to specified locations.* Jan Carlzon ran a test. He arranged for 100 packages to be sent to various addresses throughout Europe. He admits that 'the results were devastating'. All the parcels were due to arrive next day; on average, it took four days.

He admits that SAS had caught itself in one of the most basic mistakes a service-oriented business can make: promising one thing; measuring another. They were promising prompt, precise delivery, yet they were merely measuring their own cost-efficiencies. In fact, they had no system for tracking late deliveries.

He delegated the problem to the people at the front line. They devised a **QUALI CARGO** system to measure the precision of their service. How quickly did they answer the telephone? Did they meet the promised deadlines? Did the cargo actually arrive on the plane they had booked it on? How long did it take from the time the plane landed until the cargo was ready to be picked up by the customer?

I can only leave you with the question, *Are your systems truly geared to measuring effectively all the activities you undertake in relation to identifying, attracting, satisfying and retaining customers?* Or, are your systems geared to providing your accountant with the information he needs for the ritualised 'post mortem' on your monthly results (often bedevilled by arguments on the basis on which 'fixed' costs have been allocated)?

Self measurement by front line

Let's see the importance of your 'Top Line Drivers'.

Charles Schwab became a millionaire running steel mills in America. He once visited one of his furnaces and asked them how many 'heats' they had achieved that shift. When they said six, he drew a large 'six' in chalk on the floor. When the next shift arrived, they asked what it meant, and – to prove they were better – they achieved seven, rubbed out their colleagues' 'six' and proudly drew a large 'seven'. Eventually the number of 'heats' achieved grew to twelve. Charles Schwab doubled productivity by writing a number in chalk on the floor!

How much scope do you have for devising similar, simple figures which can be displayed easily in each location?

Visible management

The thing which most impressed me about my visit to the Nissan plant in Sunderland was their system of what they call 'visible management'. Each team has its own 'boardroom' area, in which are displayed their crucial performance yardsticks.

I took a close interest in some of the figures. I can't forget my accounting training. I pointed to some figures which appeared to be low. The executive showing me around told me that I had committed a cardinal sin. The team in that area had to be trusted to have enough pride to correct any area of under-performance themselves. If management were to come round commenting on poor figures, 'creative accounting' would take place, and the figures would become meaningless. Leaders had to have enough trust and respect for their people to accept that they were aware of the problem and would be putting it right as soon as possible.

Nissan is achieving world-class performance in terms of productivity and quality.

Progressive companies are adopting a technique called **ABC**: Activity, Based, Costing, which has been described as the technique which *'helps companies become the one everyone else is copying'*. The underlying principle is as simple as Charles Schwab drawing a large chalk 'six' on the floor of his steel mill.

Personalised information

This is the crucial issue. How can you provide your front-line people with their own highly personalised information? Or, how can you personalise existing information? One quick example. What is your debt collection period? It's probably in your management reporting system as 60 days, 70 days, whatever – yet another anonymous figure considered by 'Head Office'. But if Betty is the person in charge of collecting your debts, isn't it better to have a whiteboard note or chart on her office wall headed, 'Betty's Success in Collecting our Money'. It comes back to how you can introduce concepts of individualised, visible self management for the front-line people in your organisation: those responsible for the 'Top Line Drivers' which will achieve your Hard Results.

The third in the series of articles by Chris Bartlett and Sumantra Ghoshal[6] points out that planning and control systems were once the tools that enabled companies to grow. But the systems that allowed managers to control their employees also inhibited creativity and initiative. Today, they claim the challenge is for leaders to engage the knowledge and skills of everyone in what they call an **'Individualised Corporation'**.

They have conducted research into 20 high performing corporations. They have concluded that systems, no matter how sophisticated, can never replace the richness of close personal communication and contact between leaders, coaches and front-line colleagues. In the successful corporations, the leaders create an environment in which individuals monitor themselves. It has been proved that, given the same information, incentives, and authority to act, front-line colleagues and coaches will reach the same decisions that top level managers would have reached.

THE ORGANISATIONAL DILEMMA

Some years ago, a book appeared, *Small is Beautiful*[27], which had a dramatic impact. Its effects are still being seen today as industrial giants like ICI and others start to hive off their activities. *Small is Beautiful* because it motivates your front-line people and, as importantly, enables them to focus on serving the special needs of a particular customer segment.

3M has achieved dramatic growth, not least by the ways in which it focuses on innovation but by the way in which it then enables the people who create the new product to turn it into a business unit for which they are responsible.

ASEA Brown Boveri has split itself into 1300 separate operating companies on what is called a *matrix structure*. Thus the managers of each front-line unit have to report both to a Regional Manager and to a world-wide business head.

Percy Barnevik, Chief Executive, takes a dim view of complex, formal business structures.

> They tend to be slow, inflexible and bureaucratic. Worse still, such organisations create barriers between themselves and their customers, take initiative away from those who need to exercise it, and attract and promote the type of people who operate well in that kind of environment. We wanted to build an organisation with the opposite characteristics. To be simultaneously global and local, big and small, centralised and de-centralised.

To do this, Barnevik and his top management team have had to redefine key organisational relationships and behaviours which has taken them several years to accomplish.

Richard Pascale[16] refers to the need for:

1. Fit
2. Split
3. Contend
4. Transcend.

Fit: This relates to the attempt we all make to ensure coherence and to achieve synergy from a totally integrated organisation. This is not always easy to achieve, as Richard Pascale points out. It can be achieved only by ensuring that all twelve ingredients are blended correctly.

Split: To provide totally customised services to specific segments of our customers can require teams of people dedicated to meeting specific needs. You may have to find ways of splitting your organisation; though creating separate subsidiaries can add to cost, not least in audit fees! You have to develop new techniques for achieving synergy despite diversity. It may be rather like managing one team playing rugby, while another is playing football, another hockey, and yet another cricket, while every team is a member of the same 'club' dedicated to winning.

Contention: is inevitable. Indeed, Richard Pascale feels it's healthy in challenging your organisation to respond to its external competitive pressures.

Transcend: Is the ability which you, as the leader of your organisation, will need to orchestrate these conflicting concepts of fit, split and contention. It may require a totally different approach such as 'Activity Based Costing'. It will certainly require a totally different social architecture and mindset.

Federalism

Charles Handy is a highly respected guru whose books are always well worth reading and I am grateful to the *Financial Times* for permission to include a major quotation from one of his articles.

He writes:

> Organisations could ultimately become a collection of project teams, harnessing the intellectual assets around a task or an assignment.

> To the individual, the organisation will offer, not the promise of a planned career, but a series of opportunities which one's skill profile may or may not fit. All the world will then, in a sense, be a stage: a sequence of teams with a changing cast of performers, backed by a small continuing production team.

> That will not be an easy or comfortable world, or even a very desirable one, but the tide of technology and competition cannot be halted, even if you don't like the stuff it brings in with it. We must ride the tide, not fight it. The challenge for businesses will be to find ways to bind themselves to players on whom they can depend for the future.

> Good conditions of work and employment will not be enough, for there will often be comparable ones around the corner. To be a *'preferred employer'* it would be necessary to make the vital staff into quasi-partners, with more share ownership and bonus schemes, so that they share the future of the organisation, good and bad, and to invest at the same time in the constant regeneration of their intellectual assets, despite the possibility that the regenerated assets will leave.

> It would not be unreasonable, for instance, to expect to invest the traditional 10 per cent depreciation (or regeneration) allowance of both time and salary in the education and development of each individual. Keeping staff is one thing, working them efficiently is another. Project leadership will become the key to corporate performance.

> To build a cohesive team out of the requisite mix of different roles and talents is never easy, as any theatre director will confirm. Hierarchy cuts little ice with stars, for as their leader you have only as much power and influence as they allow you. Leadership in the world of people assets draws its power from the people over whom it is exercised. It is a world where loyalty has to be earned from the individual, not demanded. Do all this, and there is more. A collection of project teams, no matter how well led and how well starred, is not in itself an organisation. These teams have to be welded together to give them the clout they need in the market.

The 'intellectual organisation' needs to be both small and big, local and global, tight and loose. It needs, in short, to be federal. Federalism is built on shared power, compromise and negotiation. Unfamiliar, unpopular and hard to make work, it is nevertheless the way all organisations are heading, because centrally directed systems are too expensive, too often wrong, too restrictive and too imprisoning for the human soul. When that human soul is your key asset, you have to give it heed. To do that, and remain efficient, is the leading challenge facing our organisations.

CREATING A WINNING CULTURE: THE RIGHT SOCIAL ARCHITECTURE

Warren Bennis and Burt Nanus[8] write:

> The design and management of social architecture is one of the pivotal responsibilities of the leader. Leaders who fail to take their social architecture into account and yet try to change their organisations resemble ... King Canute.
>
> *Leaders*, Bennis, W and Nanus, B, Harper Row

You have to ask yourself what type of people you need to help you to achieve your objectives: buffaloes or geese? You then have to ask yourself what type of culture you need to create to get the best out of your people. In their book, Bennis and Nanus give three types of social architecture, summarised in Table 7.3.

Table 7.3   Three types of social architecture

Values/ Behaviour	Formalistic	Collegial	Personalistic
Basis for decision	Direction from authority	Discussion, agreement	Directions from within
Forms of control	Rules, laws, rewards, punishments	Interpersonal group commitments	Actions aligned with self-concept
Source of power	Superior	What 'we' think and feel	What I think and feel
Desired end	Compliance	Consensus	Self-actualisation
To be avoided	Deviation from authoritative direction, taking risks	Failure to reach consensus	Not being 'true to oneself'
Position relative to others	Hierarchical	Peer	Individual
Human relationships	Structured	Group oriented	Individually oriented
Basis for growth	Following the established order	Peer group membership	Acting on awareness of self

Source: *Leaders*, Warren Bennis and Burt Nanus, Harper Row

What type of social architecture do you feel you have at present? Which of the three do you think will best help you to achieve your objectives?

The personalistic approach may suit a young boffin-type organisation, but most should settle for the collegial style. In this, power, influence and status are based on peer recognition which, in turn, is based on how competent people are thought to be, and on their interpersonal skills. We are back to our earlier discussion on assertiveness and contention. Warren Bennis and Burt Nanus write:

> People are expected to fight hard for what they believe in, but to fight in an above board, open, clear and clean fashion.

The important point is that decision making is participative and based on encouraging the flow of ideas across, up and down the organisation so that all people who implement, or are affected by, a decision have a say. The operating principle of such companies is to 'strive for excellence'. It requires a high level of interdependence among teams and individuals.

Mindset/paradigm

We are back to the critically important issue of the attitudes, the mindset, the paradigm of your organisation. The two senior executives of the Kepner-Tregoe management consultancy, which specialises in the human dimensions of organisational change, summarise the fundamental difference in mindset shown in Table 7.4.

Table 7.4   Differing attitudes

	Mechanistic organisation	People-wise organisation
Defining principle	A set of structures and systems	A community of people
Main thrust	Efficiency	Creating and deployment of knowledge
Approach to change	Re-engineer, and the people will follow	Prepare people for change
Time frame	Do it now	Do it forever
Competitive advantage	Business systems, processes and structures	People – their knowledge and skills
Impact	Under-utilises human potential	Diffuses responsibility
Key job requirements	Technical skills	Critical thinking, intuition, experience – and technical skills
Result	Dependability	Commitment

First we have to change our own mindset, second change the mindset of our missionaries, and third change the mindset of our executives. In most organisations, front-line people are only too willing to respond once they test the sincerity of their leader's values and beliefs.

WINNING MEANS CHANGE

Very few people like change. Sir Brian Wolfson once said, 'The only people who like change are wet babies'. But our customers are changing, our competitors are changing, the environment is changing, the whole world is changing.

To create and sustain your competitive advantage, you have got to find ways of focusing people on change. Ideally, you must get them to initiate the responses they feel necessary. It is your ultimate responsibility to intervene directly to shake up operating units that may have grown staid or comfortable. The theme of Richard Pascale's book[16] is that *'nothing fails like success'*. GM and IBM were once companies with a dominant market share. They grew staid and comfortable. They are now having to fight hard to recover lost ground. They have years of accumulated reserves to help them survive the process. Smaller companies do not. You cannot afford to lose ground in this way. You have to make sure you have a deliberate policy of creating the social architecture, the mindset needed to ensure that you take Jack Welch's advice of 'change before you have to'.

IT'S BACK TO LEADERSHIP

A friend of mine runs a group with over 100 subsidiaries. If he has one doing exceptionally well, and one doing very badly, it's a reflection of the manager concerned. If he were to switch the two managers, the high performing company would go downhill, while the results of the poorly performing company would rocket upwards.

Robert Heller and Ian Carling make the same point in their book[13]. If you take an interest in sport, how often have you seen a team languishing at the bottom of the relevant table, shoot to the top when a new, more effective leader is appointed?

In 1989, ABB acquired part of Westinghouse's troubled power transmission and distribution business. It was a mature activity with an ageing product line that generated only modest products and expected only limited growth. Yet, within three years of being integrated within ABB, the unit was behaving like a young growth company. Operating profits had doubled, and with the help of its sister companies, the unit had developed a significant new capability in microprocessor based relay technology. The General Manager was the same man who had been running the business for Westinghouse. But he has been transformed by ABB's culture.

The result you get from your people, and your executives, rests entirely upon the structures, the systems, and the cultures which you generate.

TIME, THE ESSENTIAL INGREDIENT

I had lunch recently with a dynamic young tycoon who is thoroughly enjoying the frenetic pace at which he is chasing his tail, acquiring companies and developing his group. He is on a real 'high' but I warned him that he was on a slippery slope to potential disaster.

As he was honest enough to admit, he did not have enough time to communicate his vision to the senior executives of the companies he has acquired. While they were doing a sound competent job on their own, they were not developing the dynamic growth which should result from the synergy which should be being established.

I told him that to really grow his business he had to devote at least 40 to 50 per cent of his time on communicating his vision, talking to and developing his senior executives.

Percy Barnevik's fundamental objective in developing ABB's decentralised organisation was to modify the behaviour and transform the underlying values of all their people world-wide. To achieve that objective, he and his top management team spent most of their time, for more than five years, improving organisational processes designed to encourage entrepreneurship from those closest to customers: to integrate and leverage the resources and capabilities developed in the front-line units into a company-wide asset; and, most of all, to ensure ABB's commitment to a continuous renewal process.

ROLE OF HEAD OFFICE

If you now accept the importance of leadership, the role of your 'Head Office' has a tremendous impact. It helps to set the culture, the social architecture, of your organisation.

The General Motors Headquarters in Detroit was notorious for its bureaucracy, for stifling dissension and blocking any attempt to adapt to increasingly severe competition. One of the first things the new Chairman, Jack Smith, did was to move his office to the GM Technical Centre ten miles away to symbolise his desire to be close to the action. GM's results are improving.

CONCLUSION

Table 7.5 may help to encapsulate the points we have been discussing.

Table 7.5   Creating a winning culture

FROM	TO
Top-down organisation	Upturned organisation
Many levels	Few levels
Narrow spans of control	Wide spans of control
Tightly defined departments	Boundarylessness
Teams of specialists and teams of skills	Mix of specialists and skills in process focused teams
Tightly controlled individuals concentrating on tasks	Self-led, autonomous teams focused on contribution
Line managers	Coaches
Staff-specialists	Facilitators
Directors	Leaders
Excessive concern with titles and rank	Concern to gain respect for contribution to team
Achievement of budgets of department	Achievement of customer satisfaction, goals and vision of organisation
Large corporate power-broking Head Office allocating physical and financial resources of plans, controls and information	Lean Head Office ensuring horizontal integration of cross-organisation coaching, technology and skills transfers to aid process of continuous organisational learning

LEAN THINKING

In their book *Lean Thinking*,[28] Dan Jones and James Womack stress the need to optimise the 'value stream' of every process needed to satisfy customers. Thus one example they give is that it can take between 300 and 400 days to make a tin can, though the actual processes only take three hours. Every organisation involved has large warehouses full of the materials they need and the products they produce. If every organisation involved could operate their 'lean thinking' approach of looking at the efficiency of the entire 'value stream', tremendous savings could be achieved by every participant, particularly in warehousing costs.

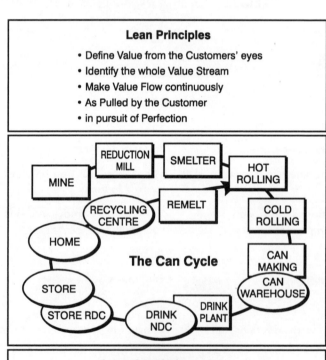

Figure 7.9 Lean Thinking

BRAINSTORMING EXERCISES OR PROJECTS: 7

Designing a Superior Organisation

■ Is there any possibility that you have a traditional, bureaucratic bottom-line driven organisation, with emphasis upon titles and departmentalisation? The equivalent of our drawing of six blindfolded horses? If so, do you and your team accept the need for change to the equivalent to four clear-sighted, self-motivated horses? If so, how do you set about starting the process of change?

■ What style of 'social architecture' do you feel that you have in your organisation at present? Is it appropriate? If you feel another style would be more appropriate, how would you introduce the change?

■ In your particular circumstances, do you need to concentrate on improving the effectiveness of your 'working groups', or are you prepared to accept the challenge of seeking to build 'high performance teams'? Do you need a special project team to look at how you achieve this change (basing their work on *The Wisdom of Teams*)?

■ Do you need the same, or a different project team, to study the book on *Re-engineering the Corporation*, and to recommend to you how to apply its principles in your own organisation?

■ Do you need to break away from traditional departments, by creating cross-functional teams focusing on value added processes or specific customer segments? If not, how could you do so in future?

■ Do you motivate all your colleagues by projecting your organisation in such a way that they can see the importance and value of their own specific contributions? If not, how could you do so in future?

■ How relevant are Richard Pascale's ideas on 'fit', 'split', 'contend' and 'transcend' in terms of creating a totally new mindset of the way you and your team approach organisational issues? (Do you or a project team need to study his book, *Managing on the Edge*, in greater depth?)

■ Have you created a 'lean' Head Office which seeks horizontal integration to ensure continuous organisation learning? If not, how do you and your team intend to do so?

■ Do you think 'lean'? Should you establish a project team to study how to apply the recommendation of 'lean thinking'?

8

BUILDING A WINNING ORGANISATION

A STRATEGIC ACTIVITY

If we accept that to gain a strategic advantage we have to focus on people, then every activity related to building your organisation *is of strategic importance.* But under the day-to-day pressure of striving to 'manage' business, these strategically important activities are often perceived to be irritating interruptions amid all the other pressures.

There are nine activities to be considered:

1. Attitudes
2. Capacities
3. Recruitment
4. Induction
5. Reviews
6. Promotion
7. Demotion
8. Progression
9. Pruning.

In addition, there is the vital tenth activity of **TEAM BUILDING**.

These activities have to be carried out so thoroughly that not only do you achieve hard results but, just as importantly, you have time for the real role of the visionary leader.

ATTITUDES: FOUNDATION FOR SUCCESS

When Toyota started recruiting for their new plant at Burnaston, they were overwhelmed with a flood of applications. For their initial screening they totally ignored technical qualifications, looking only at the attitudes of the applicants. Those they deemed to have the wrong attitudes were not considered. Those that had the right attitudes were then considered on the basis of their technical qualifications and competencies.

Dentsu's ten rules of the demon

Dentsu is one of the largest advertising agencies in the world and controls a significant share of all advertising in Japan. Its guiding precepts were set out by its Chairman, Hideo Yoshida. They focus on a successful *Dentsu person*. Should you not evolve similar 'rules' for your own organisation?

1. Initiate projects on your own instead of waiting for work to be assigned.
2. Take an active role in all your endeavours, not passive.
3. Search for large and complex challenges.
4. Welcome difficult assignments. Progress lies in accomplishing difficult work.
5. Once you begin a task, complete it. Never give up.
6. Lead and set an example for your fellow workers.
7. Set goals for yourself to ensure a constant sense of purpose. This will give you perseverance, resourcefulness and hope.
8. Move with confidence. It gives your work focus and substance.
9. At all times, challenge yourself to think creatively and find new solutions.
10. When confrontation is necessary, don't shy away from it. Confrontation is the mother of progress and the fertiliser of an aggressive enterprise. If you fear conflict, it will make you timid and irresolute.

In *Re-engineering the Corporation*[5], Michael Hammer and James Champy make the point that in a reorganised organisation, colleagues should hold beliefs such as:

■ Customers pay all our salaries: I must do what it takes to please them.
■ Every job in this company is essential and important: I *do* make a difference.
■ Showing up is no accomplishment: I get paid for the value I create.
■ The buck stops here: I must accept ownership of problems and get them solved.
■ I belong to a team; we fail or we succeed together.
■ Nobody knows what tomorrow holds: constant learning is part of my job.

This implies, of course, that we need to make far greater use of psychological and similar tests to ensure we recruit those with the attitudes we require.

The Test Agency, near High Wycombe, once helped a major client by testing all the organisation's most successful sales people. Interestingly, the one feature which all their top sales people shared was 'conscientiousness'. Building a profile in this way of the attitudes and competencies of your more successful colleagues, can help to determine the profile of those you need to recruit or promote.

Again, it is the ideal topic to be discussed extensively within your own organisation, at in-company briefing sessions or in-company training courses. Everyone should be well aware of the attitudes expected from every member of the team.

Surveying attitudes

In 1992, Rank Xerox won the European Quality Award – the first year the award was granted.

In their very impressive submission to the EFQM, Rank Xerox described their ten year journey to become a quality company. They described how, in 1982, they had measured the performance of their business against four measures. These were:

1. Growth – measured by market share.
2. Profitability – measured by earnings per share.
3. Customer satisfaction – measured by appropriate indices.
4. Employee satisfaction – measured by appropriate indices.

By the time they reached 1992, they reported that they learned that if they concentrated totally on points 3, customer satisfaction and 4, employee satisfaction, then points 1 and 2 seemed to take care of themselves.

As my friend Martin Wibberley points out, it illustrates the importance that one world-class company gives to carefully measuring and acting on customer satisfaction and employee satisfaction. In fact, the two are linked. It has been suggested that in future, 40 per cent of the money spent on marketing will be on 'internal marketing' to employees, on whom the success of the company depends.

Martin points out that one of the most skilled retailers in the UK spends almost nothing on advertising, but it spends hugely on ensuring employee commitment. So, tracking corporate culture (an issue we have yet to discuss) and employee attitudes and *acting on results* is an important strategic issue.

When Martin was with Allied Dunbar (from 1993–1995) they instigated an annual measuring process (dubbed VIVA) to become part of an integrated programme of measuring the movement they wanted to make towards becoming 'market led'. I am grateful to Martin and to Allied Dunbar for permission to reproduce a section of the questionnaire (Table 8.1).

Table 8.1 Extract from Allied Dunbar Employee Survey

My view and values	Strongly agree	Agree	Disagree	Strongly disagree	Don't know	Don't care
1. I enjoy the company of people I work with	1	2	3	4	5	6
2. Allied Dunbar is one of the leading UK Financial Services companies	1	2	3	4	5	6
3. My job makes good use of my abilities	1	2	3	4	5	6
4. I am learning through my present job	1	2	3	4	5	6
5. I am put in the picture about Allied Dunbar's Corporate plans and performance	1	2	3	4	5	6
6. I have confidence in the management ability of my immediate boss	1	2	3	4	5	6
7. Allied Dunbar is committed to satisfying needs and wants of consumers and clients	1	2	3	4	5	6
8. There is good cooperation among the people I work with	1	2	3	4	5	6
9. I'm proud to tell people I'm part of Allied Dunbar	1	2	3	4	5	6
10. People in Allied Dunbar can be trusted	1	2	3	4	5	6
11. I'm building the career I want inside Allied Dunbar	1	2	3	4	5	6
12. I get a fair reward for my effort	1	2	3	4	5	6
13. I am put in the picture about issues that directly affect my work	1	2	3	4	5	6
14. I have confidence in the fairness of my immediate manager	1	2	3	4	5	6
15. My physical working conditions are OK	1	2	3	4	5	6
16. People in Allied Dunbar generally know what they are doing	1	2	3	4	5	6
17. Allied Dunbar has a clear set of corporate values or beliefs	1	2	3	4	5	6
18. Please list what you think Allied Dunbar's corporate values are:						
19. Our team is well organised to achieve results	1	2	3	4	5	6
20. Allied Dunbar provides value for money products and service	1	2	3	4	5	6
21. I am encouraged to contribute my ideas towards improving things	1	2	3	4	5	6
22. People in Allied Dunbar are generally energetic and enthusiastic	1	2	3	4	5	6
23. Open and honest two-way communication is encouraged around here	1	2	3	4	5	6
24. My manager has communicated clearly the results that are expected of me	1	2	3	4	5	6
25. I feel that high achievers get appropriate recognition and reward in Allied Dunbar	1	2	3	4	5	6
26. Allied Dunbar's top management is capable of building a successful long-term future	1	2	3	4	5	6
27. Allied Dunbar's corporate values are relevant to future business success	1	2	3	4	5	6
28. I get the support I need from other parts of the organisation to do a good job	1	2	3	4	5	6
29. Allied Dunbar has a good range of products	1	2	3	4	5	6
30. I get regular and accurate feedback on how I'm performing	1	2	3	4	5	6
31. I'm committed to Allied Dunbar's corporate values	1	2	3	4	5	6
32. It's OK to confront issues in Allied Dunbar	1	2	3	4	5	6
33. I like Allied Dunbar's approach to Conventions for top sales achievers	1	2	3	4	5	6
34. People inside Allied Dunbar behave in a way which is consistent with our corporate values	1	2	3	4	5	6
35. People inside Allied Dunbar are committed to helping the Company achieve its objectives	1	2	3	4	5	6

COMPETENCIES AND CAPACITIES

If their attitudes are right, people can be developed. But, clearly, it is important to ensure that they have the right level of competence in relation to the team of people they will be joining. Given the discussion we have just had on the need to rethink your structure, you may need to rethink the competencies you will need as you work towards establishing your lean, horizontal, boundaryless, customer-focused organisation.

The authors of *Re-Engineering*[5] raised the issue of moving from training to education. As they point out, *'training increases skills and competencies and teaches employees the "how" of a job. Education increases their insights and understanding and teaches the "why".'*

Earlier, we agreed that what we needed to do was to create 'effective followers'. You have to ask yourself whether each recruit has the capacity to be developed into an effective follower.

'Change agents'

Like most organisations, you are bound to have some long-established 'characters' with, perhaps, some deeply ingrained, irritating attitudes or habits you may be unwilling or unable to move. This is not to say that, if necessary, you should not reorganise and restructure, even if it does cause disruption. But, quite definitely, every recruitment or promotion window must be used by you to change your organisation.

The ultimate responsibility

Before we move on to other issues of building a superior organisation, there is one salutary point to consider:

If the person was wrong to start with, we are to blame.
If the person was right to start with, but then failed to perform, we are to blame.

So when we, or one of our subordinates, criticises the performance of one of *their* subordinates, we all have to remember that they are criticising themselves.

Our success depends on having the right people. If we have, then we have no problems other than the pleasant task of coaching even better performance. If we have a problem, the nagging concern of a poor performer, it is because we have failed to spend enough time on all the issues we are discussing.

BOSS:	"How on earth did you manage to fall down so badly..."
SUBORDINATE:	"Trouble is Sir, I have seven idiots working for me in my department!"
BOSS:	"Aren't you lucky, I have got eight working for me!"

If you now accept that you will need to move your organisation from *individuals performing tasks* to *teams performing processes*, then you may have to have a fundamental rethink about the type of people you wish to recruit or promote, and will need to place far more emphasis on recruiting good team players.

RECRUITING THE BEST

There are many excellent guides to recruitment so I do not want to take up time unnecessarily.

First, let us re-emphasise the importance of devoting enough effort. I once worked out that if a sales team leader were to achieve 'top quartile' results, he and his team could achieve a gross profit of nearly £1 million. If he and his team only achieved 'bottom quartile' results, they would only earn a gross profit of £0.25m: a difference of £0.75m. Assuming he was in his post for an average of three years, this would make a difference of £2.25m!

If a company were to spend this sum on any other activity, days, if not months, would be spent. Yet the same amount of effort is not devoted when recruiting an executive who could either make or lose the organisation £2.25m.

When Toyota first opened its plant in Derby, some papers criticised the fact that it spent an average of 14 hours interviewing each person. I did not see why. It demonstrated great professionalism and a high level of ethics. It is vital to your organisation to recruit the right person. Nothing is worse than recruiting somebody who is not good enough to keep, nor bad enough to sack. It is equally important for the person selected to ensure that they are making the right decision for themselves and for their families. They should not be put through the disruption of changing to a job for which they are not truly suited.

Compatibility

In earlier sections, we have discussed the need for our colleagues to share our vision, our values, and our goals. It follows that when we recruit a new member of our team, these ingredients need to be discussed fully.

- Which of the applicants is most excited by your sense of vision: which of them shares your values and beliefs? You need to spend time on this issue alone.
- Which of them appreciates the strategies you are trying to adopt to achieve your objectives? Can they appreciate them; more than this, can they make comments about how they can see themselves adding value to their achievements?
- Do they appreciate that they will be expected to be assertive and contentious, would they be willing to speak their minds, and play their part as an effective member of the team?
- Would they be willing to share their knowledge with, and learn from, their colleagues in your open organisation?
- In short, how compatible are they to the ideals you are striving to achieve?

We send all our shortlisted applicants a copy of our 'Company Charter' with a covering letter explaining that we are willing to provide them with 110 per cent support, provided they can promise us 110 per cent commitment. In fact, we stress that they should not take their application any further unless they are prepared to do so.

Competencies

When I was more actively involved in running seminars, I used to talk about the eight hour interview. The executives on the course would express surprise and ask why it should take so long. I then used to set them the exercise of defining the questions they needed to ask to determine whether an applicant was likely to achieve all the goals he or she would be set. Invariably, they ran out of time in seeking to define these questions.

In the case of a Sales Manager, does he understand all the issues arising from every aspect of identifying, attracting, satisfying and retaining customers, including gaining referrals from satisfied customers? How good is he at team building issues? Does he understand all the financial implications?

Collective approach

Recruitment should involve as many people as possible. Ideally, the team needing the recruit should do the recruitment themselves. It should be a team effort. The chauffeur who meets them at the station, the receptionist who receives them, the secretary who gives them the initial tour of the building, the people to whom they are introduced on the tour, everyone should have an input. I am always amazed how otherwise sensible people 'let their hair down' with my Secretary or other front-line colleagues as if they 'do not count'.

Testing

In my view, it is absolutely essential that you get the best possible advice from a professional organisation on the best type of psychological or other tests to use to avoid the element of 'double bluff' which can otherwise creep in.

Demonstrating an edge

How far can you get people to demonstrate whether or not they have the edge over their rivals? Can you, in your advertisement, set an exercise along the following lines:

> Given your experience of the type of position for which you are applying, can you set out the two, three, or four things which, in your experience, are crucial to achieving success?

Can you send selected respondents some form of test? If we are seeking an editor, we ask for copies of articles of which they are proud. If we are seeking an abstractor, we send them a selection of articles and ask them to abstract. What can *you* do to get people to demonstrate an edge?

Trial period

Everyone should join for an initial trial period. It should be a real trial period. It should be made plain that their performance will be reassessed at the end of three or four months. Applicants should be warned that if they are not up to par by the end of the trial period, then, while consideration might be given to extending the trial, they will probably be asked to leave. You cannot afford to carry people unable to achieve the competencies required by their peers.

'Working initially as'

The final point is that the contract of employment of any new colleague should be phrased to say that they will 'work initially as ...', implying that in a rapidly changing environment their roles will also change.

Supervision at Nissan

Peter Wickens was Director of Personnel at the time that Nissan was being established in Sunderland. He wrote about his experiences in *The Road to Nissan*[29]. The section of the book I found of particular interest was where he described how they set about recruiting supervisors. They decided to do everything possible to minimise the chances of making mistakes. They therefore developed their own assessment centre, a technique whereby a number of candidates undertake a variety of tasks so that their performance can be judged by various people from different angles. Peter writes that:

> There is no doubt that the assessment centre process is both time-consuming and expensive. However, at the end of the process, when we have spent something over one hundred manager days selecting twenty-two supervisors, the effect on the participating managers was like a conversion on the road to Damascus. To them, now, there is no other effective method.

There is a cautionary note on Nissan recruitment advertisement: *'Very few people will reach our standards'*, which has significant implications for society as a whole.

MOTIVATION BY SUPERIOR INDUCTION

If insufficient time is taken on recruitment, even less is taken with induction. Often the new recruit feels totally demotivated by lunchtime on the first day. Having taken a great deal of care to recruit people who share our philosophies, and are committed to our strategies, it is vital that we turn them into enthusiastic 'missionaries' when they join. We need to 'fire them up' during a carefully structured induction programme.

It is the mark of a truly professional organisation that they are equally concerned to provide in-depth induction to temporary workers. Thus the Disney organisation has a high labour turnover but every new person is inducted as thoroughly as if they were likely to remain with the company for 25 years. MacDonalds do the same.

When Martin Wibberley started the Robert Bosch green field site in Wales, he arranged a two-week induction programme. A cleaner, speaking of his induction course, said: *'It was the best fortnight I ever had – no one has treated me like this before – I am involved and part of the organisation.'* What a wonderful quote. Wouldn't it be great if every new recruit is given a 'mentor' to help them through their first few weeks.

At Lawrence of Kemnay, Elaine Creighton has developed a different one-month induction programme for every department (Table 8.2). This includes an effective set of exercises to make sure that new colleagues can find their way around the business, transfer phone calls, in fact everything they need to know to settle in successfully.

Table 8.2   Induction at Lawrence of Kemnay

Service Department On Job Training – Week One

Name:_____

Be able to:	Trainee's initials	Trainer's initials
1. Transfer a phone call from one department to another		
2 Find out where the *Yellow Pages*/phone books are kept in your department		
3. Answer the telephone in your department in a polite and courteous manner		
4. Name the two telephonists		
5. Know what number to dial to get through switchboard		
6. Find out where to get a brochure on a new car		

COACHING PERFORMANCE REGULARLY

I do not believe in the traditional, bureaucratic job description. The 'psychological contract' between the colleague and the company can be explained in a Company Charter. Everything relating to the standard terms and conditions of employment can be spelt out in a standard manner.

What every single member of our team needs is a straightforward, quantified explanation of the one, two or three 'key tasks' they and their fellow team members are expected to achieve.

Sustaining performance

We have to create mechanisms by which we can sustain performance by regular coaching. Hopefully, we can create a climate in which every team member can receive on-going coaching from their peers, their team leader, and from the organisation's coaches and facilitators. Nonetheless, I fervently believe that every one of our colleagues deserves the opportunity of a regular 'heart-to-heart' with their immediate team leader.

Creating the performance ethic

The objective is simple: to help each colleague to perform better so that they can derive greater satisfaction from feeling a valued member of the team. To thank and praise them for what they have done well. To ask them what help they need from us to perform better. Are there some frustrations we can remove? What are they doing to help themselves to sustain their own 'self-employability': is there anything we can do to help? Have they any talents which are not yet being fully utilised, and if so, what do we or they have to do to stretch these talents to the full?

I do not see criticism as an element of any review meeting. Every executive has to accept total responsibility for the performance of his subordinates. If they are underperforming, he has to reflect on what he has done, or failed to do, to achieve the right levels of commitment and motivation. If necessary, it is up to the appraiser to apologise for letting down his subordinate. The objective is to build both confidence and competence: the underlying philosophy we should adopt towards every colleague.

This is not to say that there should not be straight talking. Issues of underperformance need to be tackled head on. But if the right people have been recruited, or promoted, then they should respond to positive counselling.

Frequency

If we go back to the point with which we started, moving our colleague commitment index from 50 per cent to near 100 per cent justifies a performance review meeting every four months. Yes, I know it takes a lot of time but it is the way to get hard results. It's part of creating the open, learning, contentious organisation.

Ranking

One of the things we developed during our monthly company meetings was our Company Charter, which spelt out our Performance Review procedures. We agreed that our colleagues should be ranked out of five in terms of competence, and out of ten in terms of attitude. The rankings were then considered at the Board Meeting following the series of reviews. I felt them to be of tremendous importance.

Many executives hate the process of 'playing God'. Undoubtedly, it reflects on them. If they give low marks, then they are clearly not developing their people. High marks are only acceptable if their activity is exceeding its performance objectives. I was interested to see that Jack Welch of GE and Sir Peter Bonfield, the former Chief Executive of ICL, both had to take a very strong line on this issue with their own executives. Jack Welch writes:

> We had a long discussion about this in GE. How can you put a number on how open people are, how directly they face reality? Well, they are going to have to give the best numbers they can come up with, and then argue about them. We have to know if our people are open and self-confident: if they believe in honest communication and quick action. If the people we hired years ago have changed. The only way to test our progress is through regular evaluation.

Self assessment

There is certainly a great deal to be said for moving away from the hierarchical, military style, appraisals. I am advocating a much more collegial approach, a two-way process. This leads on to the concept of self assessment which Ralph Stayer has done with his team, as you will see from the short cameo case study below[1]. Note the final paragraph of:

> *'Workers invented it, administer it, revise it, and the person in charge is an hourly paid worker.'*

JOHNSONVILLE SAUSAGE COMPANY

Ralph Stayer's 300 wage earners evaluate their own performance every six months, assessing themselves on a scale of 1 to 9 in 17 specific areas. Each member's coach (immediate superior) fills out an identical form, and later both people sit down together and discuss all 17 areas. In cases of disagreement, the rule is only that their overall point totals must agree within 9 points, whereupon the two totals are averaged to reach a final score. If the gap is bigger, an arbitration group is available, but, so far, has not been needed. The marks are then grouped into five categories of performance, superior, better than average, average, below average, and poor (those likely to lose their jobs).

The total pool of profit available is then shared between the workers, average performers getting 100 per cent of the average share but superior performers getting 125 per cent of the average share, while below average performers may only get 95 per cent or 75 per cent of the average share.

Ralph Stayer admits that some people do complain but they then try to help the individual concerned to improve his or her performance. Overall satisfaction is high primarily because **fellow workers invented it, administer it, and constantly revise it in an effort to make it more equitable.** The person currently in charge of the Johnsonville profit-sharing team is an hourly paid worker from the shipping department.

Upward assessment

Perhaps another more challenging technique is 'upward assessment' where people assess their immediate supervisor. Clearly this has to start from the top and work downwards.

When I met George Simpson, then Chief Executive of Lucas, he had just had his 'upward assessment' carried out by his immediate colleagues as the first step in cascading the concept throughout his organisation. It takes courage but it can be an extremely worthwhile exercise.

PROMOTING THE RIGHT PEOPLE

Peter Principle

We are back to the Peter Principle, the mistake we all make in terms of not devoting enough time to the act of promotion; with the result that we end up promoting someone to their level of incompetence. The common mistake is to assume that we know the person concerned. He or she may have worked with us for some time. So, we assume that he or she will be able to take over a much more demanding, or even a totally different job. You may have seen that the word assume can be broken down into making an ASS of 'U' and ME.

Critically important task

If the success of your business depends on the attitudes and competencies of the team members you recruit, its success depends even more on the attitudes and the competencies of the team leaders, coaches and facilitators you appoint. This is what happened at Ford in the late 1980s. Don Petersen used the granting of promotion or the withholding of promotion as a potent tool to build a team of executives willing to help him to transform Ford.

Leading change

We have agreed, I hope, that we need to abandon the transactional concept of a 'manager' who plans, directs and controls. We need transformational leaders willing to create effective followers. So, we have to think through the attributes of those we wish to promote, as David Oldroyd of Ixion Motor Group has done.

Table 8.3 Promotion: Defining attributes of a successful General Manager

Criteria	Definitions
1. Low cynical views	Open to new approaches
	Not rely on the tried and tested
	Not play the role of the negative critic
2. Low change uncertainty	Low needs and reliance on structure
	Flexibility in responding to change
	Reduced need to minimise unpredictability
	Lower levels of caution, reticence to shift plans, etc
3. High self-confidence and self-esteem	Good personal morale
	Genuine self-confidence
	Balanced stability and objectivity

Trial period

I have known people go home on a Friday to tell their wife 'I have been promoted'. When the wife asked what that meant, they have not been able to tell her. They themselves have not been told. We cannot afford the situation where, because everybody is under pressure 'managing', people are thrown in the deep end.

Leaders must ensure pre-promotion, induction, and post-promotion support. Everything possible must be done to ensure that it works, but it must be for an initial trial period. It can be presented as part of the colleague's management development programme. If it works well, then he will be confirmed in the appointment. But if it does not look like working effectively, then he must revert to his previous position until such time as he can be given another opportunity.

One thing is certain, we cannot afford to leave people in any position in which they cannot achieve the level of contribution needed if your organisation is to achieve its objectives.

DEMOTION

If we do make a mistake, the person concerned has to be demoted. We cover this in our Charter.

> You can be sure that the leaders of our company will be keen to provide every effective form of help, coaching and counselling to ensure that you can handle your promotion effectively and successfully. But it would be unfair to you, your team, and to our company to allow you to retain your position, if, in the event, you found that you lacked the confidence or the competence to handle the work effectively.
>
> In this event, you would be expected to relinquish your appointment voluntarily until such time as you have gained the experience and training needed to be considered for a future vacancy of the same, or a different nature.

CMG case study

The computer management group CMG is owned and controlled by its workers. All decisions are made in a very open manner. People are promoted and demoted at meetings of an appropriate committee. CMG is open and frank about non-performance. In the words of one former executive, *'The process reduced the loss of face by encouraging honesty.'*

An executive who is now a Managing Director suffered a demotion when he was a more junior executive. He recalls:

> It was tremendously disappointing at the time – but I had a big shareholding. So, I wanted the company to do well. Not just me. I just didn't know what I was doing. Demotion was better than the sack.

CMG is a particularly progressive company. The executive's reaction was affected by being a shareholder. Nonetheless, every company must take a similar tough line. The pressure on us is such that we cannot carry passengers. We cannot afford underperformance. Above all, it is a betrayal to all who are 'working their socks off' if they see that we are prepared to tolerate underperformance by others.

PROGRESS INDEPENDENT OF PROMOTION

We have agreed already that we need a very lean organisation with very few levels of management. One finance house cut its levels from fourteen to four! We have to find a way of finding progression independent of promotion and self-esteem independent of titles.

Empowerment

For your people to feel that they are 'in charge' of their own destinies, and they can make a difference to how your company performs, is highly motivational.

Leadership at every level

Hopefully, you have agreed that the way forward is to work towards the creation of teams at every level of your organisation. This offers the opportunity of progression to a 'team leader' role. However, the authors of *The Wisdom of Teams*[26] comment that as a team develops, leadership becomes shared across the entire team. We are back to our 'flock of geese', taking turns to take the lead as and when necessary. So, teams become an invaluable way of ensuring leadership at every level.

Self development

Secondly, teams become a powerful agent for self development. At

Motorola, a member of one team, who could not read, asked to be replaced so she would not slow down the rest of the team. The team insisted on teaching her to read and went on to achieve its goals.

Just as importantly, team members often develop interchangeable skills. One team started with seven men focusing on the seven activities of marketing, operations, sales, strategy, finance and planning. It was not long before they were developing interchangeable skills which reinforced their mutual confidence and capability and gave them greater flexibility than they would otherwise have had.

Recognition

Teams exploit the power of positive feedback, recognition and reward. The benefits of this extend to people at every level. Some teams showed great sensitivity towards developing the shy members of their team. Successful leaders would deliberately single out each team member for praise; tying the compliment to a specific contribution the member had made to the team's objectives.

Rewarding knowledge

Tom Peters makes a valid point when he talks about the need to reward knowledge. If we accept that our success depends on the capabilities of our team members, then, as Tom says – we ought to reward those who enhance their capabilities by becoming multiskilled.

Summary

In your lean organisation you will have to provide progression without promotion by encouraging self development, the opportunity to gain new capabilities, and with it, greater self-confidence, and by giving respect, recognition and reward far more positively than has been the case in the old transactional style of management.

THE INTEGRITY TO PRUNE YOUR ORGANISATION

Before dealing with this issue, let me quote Jack Welch of GE.

No one at GE loses a job because of a missed quarter .... a missed year .... or a mistake. That's nonsense, and everyone knows it. A company would be paralysed in an atmosphere like that. People get a second chance. Many get a third, or a fourth, along with training, help, even a different job. There is only one performance failure where there is no second chance. That's a clear integrity violation. If you commit one of those, you are out.

Let me also clarify why repeated failure to deliver ... is unacceptable in our culture. That failure hurts every (stakeholder) we deal with. It hurts employees ... [suppliers], ... the communities where we operate ... the shareholders who have invested in us. It hurts the customers.

No one wins (with) lower performance standards. Everyone loses.

Integrity

I agree with Jack Welch. We need a standard of ethics, and we cannot tolerate those who break them. GE has policies on ethics which are clearly articulated and enforced. Each year, people in GE have to sign a statement that they know of no wrong-doing, or have reported it. Jack Welch urges every member of his organisation to take what he calls the 'mirror test', critically examining their own actions for integrity. That test is tougher than it sounds.

Performance

A large organisation, with nearly 300,000 employees, has the scope to find somebody another job more suited to their talents. The smaller the organisation, the more difficult it can be to transfer people into an alternative job.

No organisation can afford to retain an under-performing colleague, and we certainly can't afford to carry an under-performing executive. As Jack Welch says, they need effective coaching, counselling and development. It is better to demote than to sack. But in the final analysis, someone who is either unable or unwilling to make an effective contribution cannot be sustained.

It is surprising how many companies hinder their progress by tolerating under-performance out of a misplaced sense of loyalty. If a football team had one player who was dragging down the performance of the team, the other ten players would be quick to take him to task.

Hopefully, as we develop team concepts, the members of the team will be the first to put pressure upon anyone letting them down. But if we, as leaders, fail to take action, then the message we send is that we are not serious about seeking Hard Results. The authors of *Built to Last*[7] comment that in their visionary companies:

> Only those who fit extremely well with the core ideology and demanding standards of a visionary company, will find it a great place to work. (Those who don't will be expunged.) There is no middle ground. Visionary companies are so clear about what they stand for and what they are trying to achieve that they simply don't have room for those unwilling or unable to fit their exacting standards.

BUILDING A TEAM

It's not easy

As we have seen, choosing eleven cricketers or footballers, or choosing 15 rugby players capable of beating their opponents, is not easy. It is not easy to blend an effective team of people together to achieve the Hard Results you need. It takes time – something you will only have if you transform yourself from a manager to a leader.

Martin Bartholomew, Chief Executive of Lattelkom PTT, once got every member of his team to complete the Myers-Briggs personality questionnaire. This takes about 20 minutes to complete and the results are fed back by an Occupational Psychologist. Each person, they learn, tends to operate as one of 16 types. Profiles were discussed privately with individuals and then fed back to teams as a whole.

What Martin learned was that his organisation had too few practical people for the work they predominantly did. So he kept this in mind and redressed the balance as they brought in new people. Some moved to more suitable jobs. They redesigned some jobs around the people. They learned to listen more to each other and take advantage of different perspectives, especially in project teams. Martin felt that the organisation became more tolerant and more assertive. Recruits are encouraged to complete the questionnaire and they update the whole exercise from time to time. He concluded:

> Financial performance and customer satisfaction have improved. Staff turnover, sickness and absentee rates are where we want them. People comment favourably on the atmosphere. Formerly, they most certainly did not.

BRAINSTORMING EXERCISES OR PROJECTS: 8

Building a Superior Organisation

■ If you agree that your success depends on recruiting and promoting people who share your values and beliefs, have you defined the attitudes you need for those you recruit? If not, how do you do this? Can you modify the examples given? Do you need to look for a different, stronger set of attitudes in those you promote? Are you aware of attitudes prevalent in your organisation?

■ Do you very carefully establish the competencies you require in each person to be recruited? If not, how would you do so in future? Can you define the specific competencies needed in those you promote, bearing in mind their need to be effective coaches?

■ Do you now recognise that every act of recruitment and promotion can be a way of introducing a 'change agent' into your organisation to speed its transformation? Does this alter the way in which you tackle these all-important activities? If so, how do you ensure that this is recognised by everyone involved?

■ Does every member of your team accept that when they criticise a subordinate, they are criticising their own ability to recruit/promote effectively, or their inability to coach or coax performance? If not, how do you create this awareness?

■ Are you willing to push responsibility for recruitment down to the teams concerned? If so, what training is needed, and how will you ensure that the highest level of priority is given to all recruitment activities?

■ Do you feel that you fire people up by the care you devote to induction, and the enthusiasm with which they are welcomed into your organisation? If not, how can you ensure that this level of motivation is achieved in future? Do you need a project team to evolve or improve your induction procedures?

■ Do you agree that if you want to create a performance achievement culture you need to ensure regular coaching review are held on a tri-annual or biannual basis? Do you feel that your existing procedures are making a positive contribution to your success, and that they are used to enhance performance? If not, how might they be improved? Is this a potential project; particularly focusing on the introduction of self-assessment or upward assessment?

■ Have you created an environment within which people can make progress, independent of promotion? If not, what actions do you need to take to ensure that people can progress in this way?

■ Do you maintain your values by terminating those unwilling to do so? Are you prepared to sustain your 'culture of performance', finding alternative positions, or dismissing those either unable or unwilling to live up to the standards set by peers?

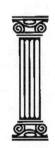

9

DEVELOPING YOUR
WINNING TEAMS

TOO LITTLE: TOO LATE: TOO FEW

Professor Peter Hall, then of Cranfield, once said that

> In spite of enormous national investment in management training, the performance of large sectors of British industry and business is not improving.'

He adds that much of the training has been what is called 'maintenance learning', entrenching past behaviours. Or it has been a waste of time, particularly when more senior executives have not permitted the training to be put into effect. His recommendations follow many of the ingredients we have been discussing, and are based on the excellent diagram shown in Figure 9.1.

An organisation can have a lot of well educated people who are not making much difference to the way in which the business is run.

Learning must be supported by the right structures and systems. But above all, learning must be driven by a 'leader' who demonstrates his total commitment.

Peter Hall believes that:

> (Leaders) must actually believe in management development and be able to recognise the difference between management training and educational activities. The behaviour of top people must present a model of the behaviour required to meet the organisation's strategy.

For some years, I headed a significant training organisation. We found that delegates were sent on courses with no effective briefing: they did not understand why they had been sent. They would then get enthused by the

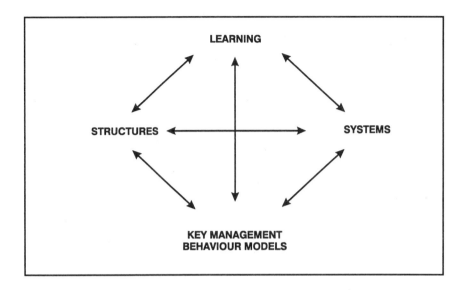

Figure 9.1   Effective training

course only to comment, sadly, that while it was great, their immediate boss would not let them apply anything they were learning. Typically they predicted that the greeting on their return would be, 'Right, now you've had your holiday, let's get back to work'.

Back to leadership

When we first started our business, we were very much involved in helping our clients by, in effect, 'training the troops'. Eventually we were able to persuade our better clients, the ones with whom we wished to continue working, that the first essential was to start with them and their senior management team.

Bill Cullen, of Renault Ireland, was right to take himself off to Arizona. It all starts from the top. But let's look at some of the issues involved.

SELF-EMPLOYABILITY: WILLINGNESS TO COMPETE

Jack Welch has written that 'The new psychological contract .... is that jobs at GE are the best in the world for people who are willing to compete.' The hard issue is that every single member of our team has the responsibility to ensure their continued employability. This must be stressed at the interview stage, in the letter offering them their appointment, and at every subsequent performance review meeting. You have the right, the duty to your organisation, to say to people, to an individual, or to a team:

■ This is the goal, or the goals, you need to achieve.
■ Do you have a clear action plan on how you and your colleagues can achieve these goals?
■ Do you think you will need any more training or development to achieve these goals?
■ If so, can you organise this for yourself, or for yourselves?
■ What help and support do you need from me, or your leaders? Tell us, and we will provide it.
■ Which of your talents do you feel we are not using effectively, and what do we need to do to make sure that we do use them to the full?
■ How do you visualise yourself progressing in our organisation; what do you need to do, and what do we need to do, to ensure that you can progress?

Contractual responsibility

In short, training should never need to be imposed. It should be demanded by those who accept that they have a contractual responsibility to ensure that they receive the on-going training they need to sustain their own self-employability.

BUILDING COMPETENCE

Coordinating training

Winning implies a total commitment to training. At Nissan MM UK, Ian Gibson explains that shop-floor workers receive continual training so that they are able to take on projects to improve productivity.

In the Ritz Carlton Hotel group, the initial training process comprises a two-day cultural orientation, a 21 day follow-up, a 60 day technical certification, while their ongoing training process includes the daily 'line-ups' or briefing sessions, workshops and process team meetings, and yearly recertification and reorientation.

Large organisations can employ skilled Training Advisers. In our small company one of our colleagues, Jayne McWatt, is responsible for acting as our Training Coordinator. For smaller organisations, the relevant Trade

Association can often provide advice, if not the training itself, geared to the relevant NVQs.

As part of their own development programme, individual colleagues can be asked to accept the additional responsibility of acting as a 'training facilitator' perhaps for a short period such as four months. For this period, they take responsibility for organising in-company activities. Ideally, every organisation should seek to have a full- or part-time 'people coach'.

On-the-job coaching

As indicated earlier, one of the prime reasons for having a regular performance review (ideally three times a year) is to be able to keep this issue of performance improvement under constant review. It's an excellent opportunity for discussing training and development needs.

Having said all this, there is no doubt that the best way to build competence is by on-the-job coaching both from sharing knowledge with other members of the team, and by having a first-class coach in the shape of the team leader or, as at Nissan, the team supervisors.

CREATING CONFIDENCE

Learning from sport

When Will Carling spoke at a conference I was chairing, he told of the way they prepared for the English rugby matches by building confidence. This included producing a set of videos for the team and sometimes for each player, showing them in their best light, pulling off their most fantastic performances. The objective was to build confidence by stressing how well they could play. The book which Will has written with Robert Heller[13] makes interesting reading on a very important topic.

Positive thinking

Thoreau once said that, 'The mass of men live lives of quiet desperation.' It is surprising how many people lack confidence because of low feelings of self esteem. As a shy, introverted accountant with a stutter, I was greatly helped by the book by Norman Vincent Peale, *The Power of Positive Thinking*[30]. More recently, Anthony Robbins has taken over his mantle with books and cassettes on the theme of unlocking the power which lies within each individual.

Nightingale Conant, at Paignton, have a wide range of self-motivational, confidence building tapes. I feel that every organisation should build up a small library of books, tapes and videos on this all-important theme of building confidence.

Executive review

One of the key skills you need from those you appoint as team leaders, coaches or facilitators, is their ability to develop the confidence of their people. It needs to be high on the list of the topics to be discussed at their regular review meetings. As we have discussed, developing assertiveness, contention, openness and learning, are all factors in building confidence.

Involvement

Involving people is the key to developing your organisation. We have already touched upon the topics on which they should be involved. Getting them to debate and improve your statements of vision, mission and meaning. Asking them to help evolve your statements of values and beliefs. Gaining ownership of strategy by involving them in discussions on all the changes which have, or might affect you: developing a game of all the participants likely to impact on your business; and carrying out a SWOT analysis.

All exercises designed to help clarify the context in which your business should operate. Involving them in discussions on your objectives and, in particular, the concept of optimising the 'value stream' of your extended business. Many of the techniques we discussed in terms of making full use of the collective knowledge of everyone involved in or with you, will also help to build confidence.

What other ideas can you think of to develop everyone's awareness of the issues which have to be confronted if your organisation is to win?

World class performance

John Neill of Unipart is dedicated to achieving 'World Class Performance'. He gives this his personal, total commitment; ensures the commitment of his senior management team; and the funding necessary. He put his former Personal Assistant, Sue Topham, in charge of a People Development programme, and she has developed five on-going programmes:

1. You make the difference
2. Putting people first
3. Mark in action
4. My Contribution Counts
5. Our Contribution Counts Circles.

All are geared to encouraging and recognising the contribution of people. The Awards are presented by John Neill as a real event. When the Queen visited them she made some of the Awards, to the delight of the recipients. It's an impressive example of what can be done in-house by a committed team member like Sue.

MBWA

Some executives display a real genius for walking into a situation where something has 'just gone wrong'. Thus they are ideally placed to 'blast' those concerned.

The objective of Managing by Walking About (MBWA), is, *find someone doing something right.* I believe that the following paragraph should appear in the job description of every coach and facilitator.

> Your success depends on your ability to get the best out of every member of your team. So, one of your most important tasks is to build their confidence in themselves, and in you as their coach and supporter. You will only do this by praise and encouragement. You will not do it by criticism even if you excuse your actions by talking about 'constructive criticism'. All criticism is essentially destructive. You need to lead by example, by building competence and by giving recognition for progress and achievement.

Let me give you two contrasting points.

Three salesmen were worried about the lack of showroom customers. They met one evening over a few pints, and decided to totally reorganise the showroom displays. Next morning, they all worked very hard, with great enthusiasm to remodel the displays in a way which they felt would entice more customers. At the end, like eager puppies with tails wagging, they waited for their efforts to be recognised. Their boss had a cursory look, muttered a few unenthusiastic words of praise, and criticised a missing price tag. The salesmen felt, *'Why did we bother!'*

Their boss was worried and preoccupied, but he could and should have been enthusiastic, praised them, and either ignored the missing price tag or found some tactful way of saying, *'I expect you missed off that price tag to catch me out".'*

In their book on leaders[8], Warren Bennis and Burt Nanus write:

> Leaders with positive self-regard rarely, if ever, have to rely on criticism or

negative sanctions, whether they lead a large multinational company, or a football team. Coach, John Robinson, of the Los Angeles Rams told us that he '*Never* criticises his players until they are convinced of his *unconditional confidence in their abilities*.' After that's achieved, he might say 'Look, what you are doing is 99 per cent terrific, but there is that 1 per cent factor that can make a difference, let's work on that.'

What an approach! Perhaps you, or some of the members of your team, should seek permission to study some of the coaching techniques used by the leading sporting clubs of your area? Above all, we have to create a climate of trust which is the foundation for self-confidence.

DEVELOPING THE CAPACITY TO GROW

It is equally important to think about 'capacity'. This is the ability to accommodate and react to change and accept increased responsibilities. It could be held to be a function of '*education*' but many people who left school at sixteen have been found to have high capacities. They may well have educated themselves, not least by applying their keen intelligence to reading and collecting knowledge.

Continuing education

Allowing for this, we need to find a way of raising the capacity of our colleagues by encouraging either formal or informal educational activities. Many American and British companies have found that they need to run educational courses for their team members to rectify deficiencies in their education; particularly as they seek to delegate more responsibility to their front-line team members.

Lucas has a Continuing Education and Training programme open to every member of its team. Small companies may be able to use the facilities of their local colleges; preferably by getting some of the lecturers to come in to run sessions for small groups of people.

The thinking organisation

Some of the companies within the Frost Group set out to create what they called a 'Thinking Organisation' by teaching thinking techniques such as Tony Buzan's *Mind Mapping*[31] and Edward de Bono's *Sixth Hat Thinking*[32]. They then meet in groups three or four times a year to generate new ideas for the business using these techniques of 'lateral thinking'. One small group came up with an idea that is saving £70,000 a year. The pressures of business are such that it is all too easy to develop tunnel vision. A technique which encourages a group of people in the organisation to have fun developing new skills must be good, and if it results in **Hard Results**, so much the better.

Corporations as universities

General Electric has a Management Development Centre which has been described as the 'Harvard' of Corporate America. Unipart has created its own university in liaison with Dan Jones. The Credit Accumulation Transfer Scheme developed by the CNAA has enabled many companies to liaise with local Education Centres to develop degree facilities. Lex has its own MBA course. Even small organisations can do the same, encouraging colleagues to use the Open University or a correspondence course to gain appropriate qualifications.

Specific skills

The priority task is to improve the skills you need to achieve your objectives. Once, most of the training at ICL was generalised. Now more than 80 per cent is specific to the needs of the company. Moreover, while they still use outside facilitators – of the calibre of Rosabeth Moss Kanter – there is a greater emphasis on using their own staff. This must be right: you, and your team, are the ones who truly understand what you are trying to achieve, and the skills you need.

In-company presentations

We can all learn a great deal when we have to prepare and give a presentation to others. So at our own company meetings we require each team and their leaders to stand up and make presentations. For some, it is the first time that they have ever had to stand on their feet to speak in public. When Karen spoke for the first time, she hung a large 'L' plate around her neck. There are many opportunities for such presentations.

Your Accountant could explain your management accounts, and give a lesson on profit planning. Your Marketing Executive can talk about your market place. Your Sales Executives can not only talk about how your customers are reacting to your products and services, but also give everyone an awareness of how to sell themselves and their company. If you have a Copywriter, he or she can give lessons on writing good letters. Virtually every member of your team possesses a field of expertise they can share with their colleagues. Alf, our 'post boy' gave a brilliant presentation.

Cascade briefings

Your company may be too large to close down for half a day a month. You may need to use the principle of 'cascade briefings'. In brief, an expert talks to a group of his colleagues. Each member of the group then gives the presentation to another group, and so on, in turn, until the briefing has cascaded throughout the organisation.

Cost-effective aids

Many organisations, such as Management Learning Resources, can provide some very cost-effective aids. BBC television often runs management-related programmes which can be recorded and used for in-company meetings. Sometimes they issue 'study packs' to go with such programmes. Often, large franchisers will provide videos and other training aids to their franchisees. For a keen internal facilitator, there is no shortage of such aids, in addition to being able to hire training videos from the many companies which specialise in this field. Gower, and other publishers, have manuals designed to help organisations run internal training courses.

PULLING TOGETHER: COHESION

Upturning your organisation allows a great deal of freedom and initiative. You have to make sure that everybody still pulls together: that there is cohesion. Let's look at some of the issues which arise.

Strategy

The precise way of ensuring cohesion is for everyone to have a clear understanding of your objectives and be involved in creating the strategies by which they will be achieved. Lord Montgomery made sure every soldier in his command knew his objectives, since he had to rely on their dedication and initiative to achieve those targets; despite the confusion of battle. We need to do the same so our colleagues can cope in the day-to-day pressures of business.

Disciplines

Rosabeth Moss Kanter, a world authority on change, points out that those to whom we are delegating responsibility, and allowing to use their own initiative, must operate within standard sets of disciplines if essential cohesion is to be maintained. There are three important areas:

1. Problem solving and decision making
2. Quality in its widest sense
3. Communications.

Selecting the eleven best players for each position to play for England does not – of itself – ensure a successful team. What *is* needed is a common set of basic disciplines which gives the team the cohesion they need to excel. When this quality is present, then the team can excel. The sum total of the efforts of the players will be greater than the sum of the individual parts. The same is true of your organisation and mine. We have to have a unifying set of disciplines.

Honda's rational thinking process

In his brilliant case study on Honda, Richard Pascale[16] highlights the emphasis which Honda puts on identifying problems. Co-founder Takeo Fujisawa believed the most important trait of a good executive was the ability to ask the right questions. In the West we worship 'answers'. In the East, there is a deep reverence for questions. So in the West, we tend to solve symptoms, in the East, they resolve the underlying problems.

In the 1950s Fujisawa learned of the *Kepner Tregoe* method. This teaches a structure for thinking systematically and getting to the root cause of problems. (Studies show that only 12 per cent of decisions made in US companies are soundly researched and decided.) The methodology was licensed and developed into the 'Honda Rational Thinking Programme'. Honda executives world-wide believe that it gets them beyond superficialities to underlying root causes. It trains them to examine alternatives which provide a stimulus for innovative, lateral thinking.

Toyota has a similar approach called the '**Five Whys?**'. Their executives are trained to keep asking 'why?'. It has been said that the biggest enemy of effective decision making are the emotions of fear (including anxiety and self doubt), anger and impatience. When we talk about fear, we come back to the need to build self-confidence in all our colleagues and to adopt Tom Peter's recommendation of praising people for making a mistake. We also come back to the vital need for dispassionate analysis.

General Electric routinely trains every new employee in decision making. It is something you might like to consider, partly because it is important for your front-line colleagues to have the skill of making sound decisions on your behalf. It will also ensure the effective cohesion which is so vital.

Quality

Once more, Richard Pascale[16] makes an extremely important point when he writes, 'Quality is not simply a desirable attitude, but an organisational discipline. Few concepts are more widely misunderstood.' He explains that when quality is defined as a systematic process or discipline, it links values with strategy. He also adds that while many find it hard to get into a full appreciation of strategy, the pursuit of quality has a great motivational appeal. As he points out, 'Everyone, at every level, can do something about it, and feel the satisfaction of having made a difference. Equally "quality" can be quantified and process tracked against goals.'

Communication

Ensuring cohesion requires a much higher level of communication both on our part and on the part of our colleagues. Once I slipped up. On two separate occasions I indicated to two colleagues what I felt we should do. They both used their initiative and did the exact opposite. With hindsight, I realised that I focused on *what* we should do and did not brief either of them fully enough on *why* I felt we should act as I suggested. Equally, both, while right to use their initiative, could have communicated their reservations to me more effectively.

It does emphasise that the whole process rests on a much higher level of communication – a point to which we must return when we consider communications as our eleventh pillar.

CREATING A LEARNING ORGANISATION

Our ability to learn

Richard Pascale[16] writes about the eight specific factors which influence an organisation's ability to learn. These are:

1. The extent to which an elite group, or single point of view, dominates decision making. Typically, Finance can exert too strong an influence

and has been known to discourage meetings by working out the cost of the time of all the people involved. Do you have one department which is too dominant?

2. The extent to which colleagues are encouraged to challenge the 'status quo'.
3. The way in which new members of the team are inducted and socialised.
4. The extent to which information on performance, quality, customer satisfaction and competitiveness is cultivated or suppressed.
5. The fairness of the reward system and the degree of emphasis on status.
6. The extent to which colleagues, at all levels, are given the freedom to take responsibility.
7. The culture of the organisation (which we will discuss later).
8. The integrity of the 'contention management' processes; particularly in facing hard truths and confronting reality.

In America, companies are beginning to develop what is known as 'Open Book' management. The companies concerned totally open their books to everyone in the organisation. This aims to make team members feel and act like owners. Clearly, workers need to be trained on what the numbers mean. But, as John Case, author of a book on Open Book management[33] says, 'it fills in a lot of gaps'.

For instance, a colleague may be considered empowered if he has the authority to stop an assembly line because of a perceived quality problem. But with Open Book management he has also been taught to understand what quality means to the bottom line, and exactly what the cost is of shutting down the assembly line for a few hours. That allows him to make an informed decision.

We have to be totally sincere on all these points. While Richard Pascale is highlighting the eight specific factors which influence an organisation's ability to learn, I feel, as you might expect, that all 12 of our pillars have to be in place before you can develop your winning team.

LEADERSHIP: AGAIN

At Unipart, John Neill has created their own university. Following the opening of Unipart 'U' in September 1993, he committed six hours per week to teach *The Philosophies and Principles of the Ten(d) To Zero Supplier Relationship Programme* to all employees. Since that time, many external stakeholders have attended the course, including the Director-General of the BBC, many of Britain's business leaders as well as the Permanent Secretary of the Treasury. Following his attendance on the course, over 60 Treasury officials have also attended these courses. In addition, many of Unipart's Directors, Managers and employees at all levels, are now responsible for teaching work related subjects in the 'U'.

When British Airways initiated a 'Putting People First' programme for every member of their organisation, Sir Colin Marshall, then Chief Executive, visited 97 per cent of the sessions held. Kenneth Macke, the former Chairman and Chief Executive of Dayton Hudson spent 40 per cent of his time on training-related activities. Jack Welch visits GE's own university on a regular monthly basis, and while he is there, he submits himself to intensive grilling by all the delegates present, on any of the issues they wish to raise.

We need time to develop a winning organisation.

Wasting or saving money?

Millions of pounds have been wasted on what I call 'mid air' training which, because it was not seen as one of our 12 pillars, was not perceived as part of the 'psychological contract' of total two-way commitment.

The way is to save money by having a much leaner, more competitive team than your competitors, and by tapping into the collective knowledge of all your people. I think it important to reiterate some of the savings mentioned in the Introduction. Alf saved us £10,000. Sue Stevens saved Peter Nathan £15,000. 'My Contribution Counts' circles at Unipart have saved £2 million. The people at Premier Exhaust saved £300,000. On one Tarmac contract, initiatives by the front-line people saved £500,000. It is truly a matter of both saving and making money if you have a lean but totally committed, highly trained organisation.

This takes money. Nissan spends 14 per cent of its salary bill on training. On average, workers will receive nearly 9 days of training a year 'off-the-job' and 12 days a year 'on-the-job'. The trainees will get an average of over 60 days a year 'off-the-job' training. Continuous development programmes exist for every member of staff.

When Sir Colin Marshall spoke at one of our client briefings several years ago, he suggested a minimum training budget of 5 per cent of sales.

As Charles Handy has pointed out, we need half the people doing three times the work (Figure 9.2).

One final point. Don't train people what to do (it's called maintenance training). Develop people to be aware of what has to be achieved, and let *them* develop the competencies they need to achieve your objectives in the best way possible.

| EMPLOY HALF AS MANY FULL TIME | PAY THEM TWICE AS MUCH | WORK THEM THREE TIMES AS HARD |

Figure 9.2 The new productivity formula
Source: Adapted from Charles Handy

For example, Peter Nathan stopped training his team on how to produce a Devon pasty. He ran sessions on all the relevant regulations which had to be observed so that his team could both appreciate the boundaries within which they had to work, and suggest ways in which they could meet these standards more effectively. He explained to them the importance of achieving the right 'yield' from the ingredients they were using. These cost Peter some £750,000 a year. If the team were over-generous and used, perhaps, 10 per cent more product than needed, this would cost a further £75,000 and make a significant dent in net profitability. If they used too little, they would lose customers and break the law. Awareness of all these and related issues made Peter's team far more aware and self-disciplined in terms of achieving the right yield.

Like Peter, you have to demonstrate leadership.

The 'bottom line'

To come down to earth we are talking about how we survive profitably in an increasingly competitive environment. Two companies were in the same highly competitive sector of the engineering industry. Their customers were demanding more for less: higher quality at lower margins. Both companies invested heavily to stay in the 'game'. One concentrated on more automation. The second clearly needed to keep pace with advancing technology but it doubled its investment in training – from £250,000 to £500,000. The first company closed: the more highly trained and committed team at the second gained new contracts and is continuing to grow, profitably.

BRAINSTORMING EXERCISES OR PROJECTS: 9

Developing your Organisation

■ Do you operate a system of self-led development? If so, do you need to think through how to improve the effectiveness of your system? If not, how do you and your colleagues feel that you can start such a system?

■ Does every individual and team have clearly defined goals, and the responsibility, authority, information, competence, capacity, and coaching they need to achieve these goals on your behalf? If not, what elements are missing and how can they be supplied?

■ Do you have a plan for developing your long-term performance based on stretching people's goals, giving them additional responsibilities, gaining greater acceptance for the need for self and team development; and having an in-company 'development facilitator'? If you have, do you now feel that it can be improved? If you have not, how would you and your team set about creating such a plan?

■ If you accept the need to upturn your organisation and give your front-line colleagues responsibility for using their initiative and taking decisions, how do you ensure cohesion? By making sure they fully understand your objectives, strategy and positioning? By ensuring the application of key disciplines throughout the organisation, vastly improved communication, and by leadership? Can you and your team improve the effectiveness of these activities?

THANK YOU FOR COMPLETING THIS QUESTIONNAIRE ....

PLEASE RETURN by email to Alex Harrison: bjaharrison@compuserve.com

Or post to: 33 Rollscourt Avenue, London SE24 0EA

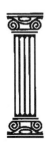

10

MOTIVATING A WINNING
PERFORMANCE

MOTIVATIONAL THEORIES

Douglas McGregor, in *The Human Side of Enterprise*[34] wrote about theory X and theory Y. Theory Y said that:

- Work is as natural as play if the conditions are favourable.
- Qualities of self-control, and self-motivation are present, and people welcome the opportunity to exercise them.
- Many people have the capacity for coming up with highly creative solutions to organisational problems.
- People can be motivated by the sense of status and self-esteem, as well as needing a sense of security and direction.
- Many people will be motivated to achieve clearly defined objectives, on their own initiative, once properly motivated to do so.

Professor Herzberg[35] said that good working conditions, by themselves, do not motivate. People are motivated by:

- the opportunity of achievement
- recognition of that achievement
- interesting and challenging work
- genuine job responsibility
- some scope for advancement.

One of the diagrams to his book, shown in Figure 10.1, illustrates the point. Achievement and recognition have a high impact on motivation, but for a relatively short period. The work itself and achievement tend to have more impact but, as you can see, it is responsibility that has the longest impact.

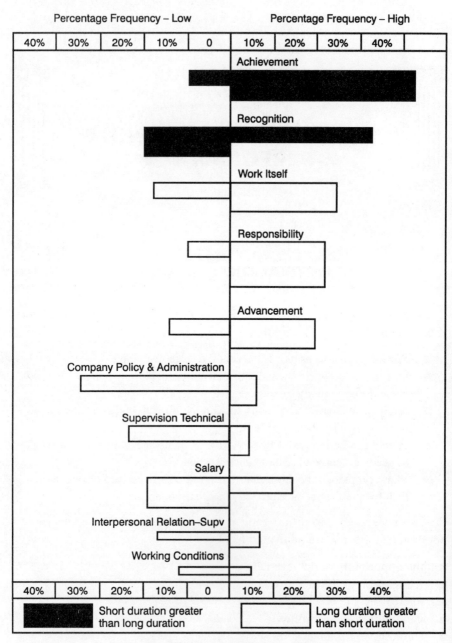

From *Work and the Nature of Man*
by Prof Frederick Herzberg (Staples Press)

Figure 10.1   The Motivation-Hygiene Theory
Comparison of Satisfiers and Dissatisfiers

The work of Frederick Herzberg was put into practice by one of his colleagues Bill Paul with the concept of **job enrichment.** One of ICI's paint products had shown no improvement in sales for some time, despite being competitive in price and quality. Bill took one group of salesmen and gave them a much higher level of responsibility, while the rest of the salesmen continued on the old basis. Those with greater responsibility increased sales by nearly 19 per cent, while sales of the rest of the sales force dropped by 5 per cent.

Carol Kennedy's book, *Guide to the Management Gurus*[36], provides an invaluable shortcut to the ideas of these leading management thinkers. Yet, despite all this research into motivation, Dr David Parsons, when at the Institute of Personnel Management, said:

> On most available measures, UK employees have lower levels of work motivation and employer commitment than in other major developed economies. New thinking is called for... a culture that facilitates and sustains more effective staff motivation is a critical success factor.

So, let us look at motivation under four headings: Motivation is Emotional; Creating the Desire to Win; Creating Winning Teams; and Rewarding Success.

MOTIVATION IS EMOTIONAL!

In a powerful piece of writing, Professor Noel Tichy – who has written a book on Jack Welch entitled *Control Your Destiny or Someone Else Will*[37] and who ran for two years GE's Executive Training Centre – wrote:

> Most organisations don't know how to deal with emotion, so they try to pretend it doesn't exist. Corporations seem emotionally barren. Feelings, one understands, are best expressed at home, where they won't gum up the machinery of scientific management. The emotional sterility of the business environment is a *cordon sanitaire* around the fear, jealousy, resentment, rage, longing, pride, ambition and God-knows-what-else that seethe in the human heart.

> Work, inevitably is an emotional experience; healthy people can't just drop their feelings off at home like a set of golf clubs. Yet management theory long neglected this realm, and we are just beginning the search for ways to harness the vast power of workers' emotional energy.

Have you thought about motivation in these terms? Harnessing the vast power of workers' emotional energy? Richard Pascale once wrote[16]:

> The Eastern perspective reminds us that the real organisation you are working

for is the organisation called *yourself*. The problems and challenges of the organisation that you are working for 'out there' and the one 'in here' are not two separate things. They grow towards excellence together.

Most people bring three kinds of needs to their organisational existence: a need to be rewarded for what they achieve, a need to be accepted as a unique person, and a need to be appreciated, not only for the function performed, but also as a human being.

These two quotations provide a different slant to the way we should approach motivation. First let us look at two problems.

Negative emotions

A 'bad atmosphere' demotivates. Negative emotions can exist. Insecure people criticise: some play 'politics'; 'stirrers' enjoy creating dissension. Careful recruitment and, even more, careful promotion should screen out such people. Building confidence removes insecurity. Creating an open, assertive, contentious, team-focused culture should drive out antisocial behaviour, or drive out the individuals concerned. They cannot be allowed to disrupt.

Personal emotions

Many people have horrendous personal problems. One man's wife is shattered by having a baby with Down's syndrome. A woman's son is in a coma following a motorbike accident. Another has a mother with Alzheimer's disease. There is no end to the range of personal traumas. For some, their period at work is a blessed relief from the tensions and tragedies of their personal lives. We have to show compassion. Insensitivity demotivates. We have to get team members to be supportive, we may need to provide or arrange counselling, but the team has to sustain its performance and achieve its objectives.

Visualising success

We cannot motivate our colleagues unless we visualise them as being successful on our behalf. Research has shown that teachers who have high expectations of the abilities of their pupils get a 25 per cent improvement in performance, compared to those who don't. Equally, it has been proved that gardeners who visualise getting good crops, get them. Golfers and other sportsmen need to visualise success. So do we. We must:

- build on the strengths of people, and not be preoccupied by their weaknesses;
- look at the opportunities in the situation, and not the difficulties;
- visualise a successful outcome to a situation, rather than a disastrous one;
- believe in our colleagues and anticipate their doing a good job on our behalf.

Motivation starts with how we *think* about our people. Thoughts are powerful. People respond to our expectations. If we expect them to be successful, they will live up to our expectations. If we expect them to fail, they will!

Pride

Robert Schaeffer[38] wrote a brilliant article in the *HBR* on the theme of demanding high performance. He quoted two Motorola workers who were involved in a project for Nippon Telephone and Telegraph, who explained:

> The customer came and told us that nothing except absolute excellence would be accepted. The team was turned on by the challenge of doing something that was considered impossible. People were challenged every day. There was a strong drive to succeed. It was the most exciting time of my life.

Robert Schaeffer was recommending that leaders should have 'clearly conveyed, 'non negotiable' expectations.' He adds that, 'if your subordinates are like most, they will respond to the higher demand. They will be able to accomplish what is expected – or most of it. And, despite a bit of testing, most of them will enjoy a more result-oriented environment. Thus you will be creating greater job satisfaction and mutual respect, better relationships among all levels and a multiplied return on the organisation's human and material resources.' It's a very important point.

Champions

Tom Peters is right when he talks about the need to treat people as champions. We need to motivate, by actively projecting the concept that everyone involved in your organisation are the members of a unique '**Winning Team**'.

Recognition

As Sir John Harvey Jones[2] has said, 'people work for recognition as much as reward'. You can see this every night on TV as the long list of credits for people such as 'Best Boy', 'Gaffer' and 'Grip' roll out. Some of the 'Employee of the Month' type schemes can become hackneyed, but they are still important to the people honoured. TMI have their 'Double Bagger' award. This is geared to recognise the person at the supermarket checkout who, if you have a lot of heavy shopping, will take the trouble to put one bag inside another to ensure the safety of your shopping.

Tarmac have their 'Golden Arrow' award scheme for the unit which has shown the greatest initiative in improving their performance or in resolving a difficult problem. John Lovering, Chief Operating Officer, has said that the benefits of the many initiatives now stemming from front-line colleagues are, 'being spread across the group. When they work well we all win prizes through group bonus schemes based on the improved profitability of all our businesses.'

Fun

But it's not only the formal schemes, it is the more spontaneous acts of recognition that count. Tom Peters is right, we need more of what he calls 'Hoopla'. One telesales company encourages those who clinch a sale to ring a bell and shout with exhilaration! In our small company, those who do something special get a Mars Bar. From time to time, when everything has gone well, everyone gets a Mars Bar. At one GE company, they offered to provide free coffee and doughnuts to workers once the plant met its monthly production quota. 'It sounds like a small thing,' said the Plant Director, 'but it proved how interested [people] are in being recognised for a job well done. We dug the business out of the hole it was in, and the doughnut guys got rich.'

A company called Successories, based at Paignton, have a range of mugs, T shirts, caps, posters and other aids to create this type of 'buzz' in your office or plant.

Meaning

Finally, an important motivator is to provide a sense of meaning. Many people choose to work in lower paid locations because it provides meaning to their lives. But if your company is providing a value-adding product or service to its customers, then this should provide you, and your team, with a sense of meaning. As Jack Welch once said,

People have the freedom to be creative, a place that brings out the best in everybody. An open, fair place where people have a sense of what they do matters. And where that sense of accomplishment is rewarded in both the pocketbook and the soul.

His last point is important, motivation has to involve the 'soul' and the pocket.

CREATING THE DESIRE TO WIN

How do we set about creating the desire to win? It is by focusing on the other 11 Pillars of our formula. Let's look at each in terms of their ability to motivate.

Leadership

The essence of leadership is motivation. Jack Welch has what one close associate calls, 'an absolute desire to win'. One of his main goals as a leader has been to stimulate positive emotional energy in his subordinates so that they come to see themselves as *winners*. His secret? Noel Tichy explains that

> [He believes] in the principle of human equality [and] treats subordinates as his intellectual and social peers, and rewards merit where he sees it. Welch's focus is on creating a team of like-minded people who believe in what they do, and work better as a result.

One of his rules is: 'Give your people every chance to identify with their business. Their enthusiasm is your most valuable asset.'

All this sounds fine, but there is a problem. The leaders studied in the survey carried out by Warren Bennis and Burt Nanus[8], put having a feeling of 'positive self-regard' high up their list of essential qualities. Many business executives fail to motivate because they have low or negative feelings of self-regard so they opt out and use financial incentives. Self mastery is vital.

Leadership at every level

Every leader, at every level, has to work hard to build up a strong feeling of positive self-regard about themselves before they can motivate others. Executives should be selected on the basis of their 'positive self-regard' so that they are able, in turn, to support and coach the members of their teams. Being a 'team leader' is a way of providing Herzberg's motivating factors of advancement, responsibility, more interesting work, recognition and achievement.

Vision

Your long-term vision, your medium-term mission, and the sense of 'meaning' should be powerful motivators *if* they are communicated effectively. Everyone wants to feel that they belong to an organisation which is worthwhile and has a future. Again, Warren Bennis has an apt quotation: 'People talk about the decline of the work ethic. But what there really is, is a "commitment gap". Leaders have failed to instil vision, meaning and trust in their followers.'

Do not be constrained by reality

Terry Keen, the Principal and Chief Executive of South Devon College, now one of the leading colleges in the country, advised his new colleagues when he joined the college: *'Do not be constrained by reality'*, when discussing with them how to draw up their strategic plans.

It is an important fact that most really successful organisations today began with visions that were out of proportion to their resources at the time. Where the vision is shared and understood, it creates a sense of belonging and purpose for colleagues and customers. Terry believes that leadership and vision are linked directly, and are a necessary concept for enterprising and innovative businesses. When a truly empowered workforce is established, people do things they never would have believed they would do, or would be able to do. Many of today's successful enterprises owe their success to linking leadership, vision and strategy.

Strategies

Commitment is reinforced when people are fully aware of the environment within which their company operates; are aware of – and ideally – are involved in the strategies to be pursued; and have a clear commitment to the objectives, the goals, to be achieved. They are even more committed when they have their own personal or team goals, a point to which we will return.

Philosophies

People are motivated when *their* organisation requires them to act with integrity in all their dealings with suppliers, dealers, customers, shareholders, competitors and the community. Equally, the right sort of people are demotivated when required to behave unethically or deviously. Of crucial importance are the philosophies the organisation has towards its workers and their emotions. An outline of the philosophies to be adopted is shown in Table 10.1, though it is for every organisation to establish their own.

Collective knowledge

Any degree of 'powerlessness' corrupts. Conversely, for people to feel regarded as experts, that their ideas are welcome, and their involvement appreciated, and that the 'collective knowledge' of them and all their colleagues is genuinely perceived as the most valuable asset of the organisation, is highly motivational.

Most of us can win over people with whom we can develop a face-to-face relationship. As we grow, it becomes increasingly difficult to have close relationships with every member of our organisation. We have to find ways of earning the allegiance of relative strangers. It has been said of Jack Welch that he solves this problem by 'acknowledging and respecting the considerable power that even the most junior employee commands – the power of independent thought.' Your success will depend on mobilising this power. If you do, you will have a highly motivated team of people.

1. Term **'EMPLOYEE'** abolished: replaced by: **COLLEAGUE**
   TEAM MEMBER
   ASSOCIATE

2. Term **'MANAGER'** abolished: replaced by: **COACH**
   FACILITATOR
   TEAM LEADER

3. Acceptance that:

   ■ Most team members come to work wanting to do a good job and to feel happy doing so: to have fun.
   ■ People do not deliberately make mistakes but do so out of lack of confidence based on lack of information.
   ■ People who are **NOT** given information cannot accept responsibility.
   ■ People who **ARE** given information cannot but fail to accept responsibility.
   ■ Self-control by individuals is indispensable if your organisation is to be successful.
   ■ The person doing the job is – or should be – your organisation's expert on how best the job should be done.

■ Members of the team have the expertise, the willingness and the creativity to solve the problems facing their organisation.

■ People are motivated by feeling a valued, respected member of a team which they feel is making a measurable contribution to worthwhile goals which will contribute to the overall success of the organisation, and thus helps to achieve a shared vision of a worthwhile future for everyone involved.

4. Under-performance is the responsibility of leaders.

■ If the individual was wrong to start with, then the leader made a mistake in recruiting or promoting him or her.

■ If the individual was right to start with, then the leader failed to induct, develop, coach or review effectively.

Superior organisation

For people to be on a 'production line', whether in the factory, or in the office, is highly demotivational. Arthur Hamper, worked for nine years on a GM assembly line. In his book *Rivethead*[39] he describes the slow mental disintegration of himself and his colleagues:

> The clock sucked you on as you awaited the next job. It ridiculed you each time you'd take a peep. The more irritated you became, the slower it moved. The slower it moved, the more you thought. Thinking was a very slow death at times.

You need to ask yourself, how far does the organisation, its structure, systems and 'social architecture' motivate or demotivate? As one example, over-tight systems of checks and controls can demotivate. Conversely, people involved in a process which they can see to be adding value for the customer, have the comradeship of working as a valued member of a team, perhaps with job rotation, but – above all – who are given genuine responsibility for organising their own work, and are given the information they need to do so, will feel highly motivated. Generating a feeling of trust motivates. Peter Nathan's 'girls' now know not only *what* they are doing but *why* they are doing it.

Building organisation

People are motivated by being involved in building your organisation. They should be able to recruit, or at least have a say in recruiting, additional members of their team. As we saw with Ralph Stayer, they can be involved in designing their own appraisal system, but above all, ongoing coaching and support, reinforced by regular review meetings with their coach, which praises them for their performance and reaches mutual agreement on future self-development and has a significant impact on motivation.

Developing organisation

The opportunity for progress, independent of promotion, and – above all – the challenge of self-development, is a very powerful motivator. We have to work hard at building up people's self-confidence and self-regard. It is probably the most important motivational technique we can use.

Communication

All the above activities both rely upon, and are reinforced by, truly effective communication. A point we have yet to consider.

Charter and culture

Finally, all these activities need to come together into a *psychological contract* between the organisation and its workers. Ideally, all these 'soft' philosophies, and 'hard' structural issues should be hammered out into your own 'Company Charter' and culture.

Summary

At the risk of being repetitive, it is vital to see how each of the 12 Pillars impacts on motivation. You cannot consider motivation as an isolated activity. It is the end result of focusing upon *all* the Pillars. Bill Paul argued that higher pay may be sought *as compensation for the lack of interest and opportunity at work*. He suggested that financially based incentives encourage employees to seek higher pay instead of seeking commitment to their work.

If you want to secure 110 per cent commitment you will have to demonstrate 110 per cent commitment to the ideas we are discussing. This leads us to a very important point.

CREATING WINNING TEAMS

'A motivational technique that works'

Professors Edwin Locke and Gary Latham have carried out extensive research, in many industries, and set out their conclusions in their book, *Goal Setting, a Motivational Technique That Works*[40]. It is one of the books which every executive should read. They state that goal setting led to an average improvement in performance – in terms of quantity and quality of output – of 16 per cent, with the better organisations achieving improvements of well over 50 per cent. In one study, 900 supervisors were broken down into one of three categories:

1. Stays on the job but does not set specific production goals.
2. Sets specific production goals but does not stay on the job.
3. Sets specific production goals, stays on the job to support and coach his team.

They found that the third group of supervisors, those who set specific targets *and* stayed on the job to support their team, brought about significant increases in productivity. Yet the two professors found that the systematic and effective use of goal setting is the exception rather than the rule in most organisations; because most managers do not know enough about the goal setting process. The two professors say that,

> Paradoxically, people do not do their best when they are trying to do their best! 'Doing your best' is a vague goal because the meaning of 'best' is not specified. The way to get individuals to truly do their best is to set challenging (specific) goals that demand the maximum use of their skills and abilities.

They found that:

- *Stretching goals* produce greater motivation than easier ones.
- *Specific goals* lead to higher performance than more general 'Do your Best' goals.
- *Feedback* is essential and may of itself have additional motivating factors. We are back to Charles Schwab's chalked figures on the furnace floor.

Faced with a specific, challenging goal, people are motivated by a sense of satisfaction from knowing what they are about. They feel a sense of direction. They gain a sense of accomplishment and pride in their ability to achieve their goals which make their effort worthwhile. Moreover, they are prepared to be persistent, and often work long hours if they are to meet commitments. The three words **direction, effort** and **persistent** are important.

Goals that cannot be reached fully will still lead to high effort levels provided that partial success can be achieved and will be recognised. The motivation to achieve long-range goals can be helped by setting a series of shorter-term goals. Some people may be 'switched off' from too challenging a goal. Either they, or their supervisor, are lacking in self-confidence. Confidence is a vital motivator.

'Behavioural Observation Scales'

Locke and Latham explain their idea of 'Behavioural Observation Scales' (BOS). In this, the activities or behaviours needed to attain a goal are broken down. Thus, a salesman may have to make 50 prospect calls and achieve ten interviews to sell one unit. So, measuring his willingness to prospect and his ability to gain appointments may be more important than achieving a unit sale; particularly if this then starts to involve other people in the negotiation. The two professors believe that the advantage of a BOS is that 'individuals are given credit for trying for difficult goals, *even if they do not fully achieve them, since their score depends upon the degree of attainment of the activities such as prospecting*'.

Group or individual goals

Rensis Likert, well-known author and psychologist, argued that *group goal setting* fosters a higher degree of cooperation and commitment than *individual goal setting*, and is thus preferable.

Gaining commitment

Ed Locke and Gary Latham explain that there are at least eight methods to secure commitment from team members.

1. *Support.* 'People whose boss behaves supportively had the confidence and trust to set or accept higher goals (and thus achieve high levels of performance) than those whose boss was non-supportive.'

   You can prove this for yourself. Role playing exercises can be used where some teams are 'thrown in at the deep end', while others are supported by an experienced coach. Invariably, the second group out-performs the first. (In passing, in-company role playing exercises are a marvellous low-cost way of developing people).

2. *Instruction.* If team members trust their leaders, and perceive the goal to be fair and reasonable, then simple instruction and explanations will ensure acceptance.

3. *Participation.* Provided trust is present, team members do not necessarily have to participate in setting goals, though it can be helpful, but they certainly need to participate in how these goals are to be achieved.

4. *Coaching.* Goals are accepted when team members are given the necessary degree of coaching to gain the competence and confidence they need.

5. *Selection.* Commitment depends on careful selection of team members, especially those with the right attitudes.

6. *Pleasure.* Individuals within the team like to gain pleasure by pleasing their leader; particularly one *willing to praise and give recognition* for exceeding, achieving, or coming close to the goal, or even for making the effort.

7. *Feedback.* Essential and often generates informal competition which introduces an element of excitement, challenge and pride.

8. *Action Plans.* Every individual, or team, given a goal, should set out the actions they need to take to achieve their goal in the form of an 'Action Plan'. This has a number of benefits. It:

   ■ aids the search for more efficient methods;
   ■ tests whether the goal can be achieved;
   ■ develops a sound basis for estimating time/cost requirements and deadlines for accomplishing sub-goals;
   ■ identifies areas of coordination;
   ■ may uncover unanticipated snags;
   ■ determines resources needed;
   ■ identifies reporting/feedback systems;
   ■ identifies support needed;
   ■ facilitates the process of true delegation.

Goal setting and stress

In my experience, it is the feeling of *powerlessness, of not being informed, of not being aware of what is expected*, which is a prevalent source of stress in most organisations. Setting goals can be a way in which stress is reduced, and motivation increased. Ed Locke and Gary Latham write:

> The challenge of overcoming obstacles can provide excitement and joy – it can be the fuel that impels (people) to great achievements. When goals, especially difficult ones, are attained, the individual not only feels satisfaction over a job well done but pride in accomplishment. If the task requires, as

most do, the productive use of the individual's mind, success heightens self-esteem. This is as true for the CEO who turns a declining company around as it is for the unskilled, unemployed worker who masters his or her first job skill. When people succeed, they feel an increased sense of efficacy; they feel, in the context of their work, that they can cope, that they can master reality. The conviction that they are competent lessens the threat posed by future assignments and makes people more willing to take on challenging tasks in the future.

Summary

The two professors endorse the theme of our discussion. They endorse the importance of the 'collective knowledge' of every member of our team; and reinforce the need to develop the right attitudes and behaviours. They point out that 'Careful attention to engaging in, and rewarding appropriate behaviours, can have a significant effect on the aspirations of individuals.'

Finally, they endorse our central theme that every member of a team has to understand thoroughly the philosophies and strategies with which we are seeking to establish our vision of a worthwhile future. **In short, motivation must be seen to be only one Pillar out of the twelve to ensure extraordinary performance.** In fact, provided pay is perceived to be fair, the motivational impact of the 12 Pillars is the most powerful, creative and cohesive way of building a team. It is worth remembering a highly apt comment by Frederick Herzberg:

If you want to motivate people to do a good job ...
...give them a good job to do.

REWARDING YOUR TEAM FOR THEIR SUCCESS

Performance Related Pay (PRP)

Research carried out by the Institute of Personnel Management indicates that it is rather doubtful that incentive and profit-related pay systems motivate. The Institute once studied Profit-Related Pay schemes covering 4.2m workers in Britain. Its conclusion was that while PRP may motivate 20 per cent of employees, it is at the expense of the other 80 per cent, while the driving force in most firms was to reduce wage bills rather than to improve staff performance.

Clive Fletcher, Professor of Occupational Psychology at Goldsmith College, and co-author of the IPM report, said, 'PRP programmes do not change attitudes positively, but they can sometimes change them negatively. Whenever I talk to managers, they all laugh when I ask if they are motivated by money. They talk instead about satisfaction and achievement.'

However, Peter Nathan has found that PRP has helped him to lower his gross wage costs while increasing his team's net take-home pay.

An abdication of management

It is now accepted that incentive schemes are an abdication of management. As Professor Michael Beer of Harvard has pointed out:

> Managers tend to use compensation as a crutch. After all, it is far easier to design an incentive system that will do management's work than it is to articulate a direction persuasively, develop agreement about goals and problems, and confront difficulties when they arise.

Financial incentive schemes do not last long before they need to be modified. They tend to focus on short-term performance. Salesmen pull forward sales to enhance their commissions, executives enhance work-in-progress and stocks to improve their end of year bonuses. Shortfalls in performance then result in the next financial period. Dissension is caused when one group, typically salesmen, can earn high commissions, while equally important and hard working colleagues in other activities, cannot.

The *Harvard Business Review* regularly debates this issue. Let me give you some key comments from earlier debates.

Against incentives

Alfie Kohn writes that, 'I believe incentive plans must in some way fail, because they are based on a patently inadequate theory of motivation.' He goes on to quote a survey among Human Resource executives which concluded that, 'At best, their incentive plans didn't do too much damage.'

Professor Michael Beer of Harvard said:

> A prevailing mythology today holds that pay can be re-designed to motivate individuals to work differently. That's simply not true. Pay is not the right tool to effect change. Telling people you are going to change the compensation system rallies them around compensation when what you want them to do is to rally around making teams work.

Professor Beer argues forcefully that organisations should change how they work before they change how they pay, and should defer changes in pay. He continues:

Workers resist formal changes such as pay redesign because they are perceived as final decisions about new roles and responsibilities that haven't been accepted yet. Instead, change should be an organic process that evolves as people learn and adapt to the new work structure.

For change

Professor Lawler of the University of Southern California is equally adamant:

Major transformations in the way organisations operate require major transformations in pay systems. The pay system is part of the very fabric of an organisation; it is either against you, or with you. When it is against you, it is like fighting with one hand behind your back. Therefore, despite the difficulties .... it is important to try to align an organisation's pay systems with its management approach.

Capabilities, not numbers

Donald Berwick, an Associate Professor at Harvard Medical School, advises strongly against numerical targets. He writes:

Payment by numbers invites expensive investment in internal gaining: managers and employees will play by the numbers instead of improving their methods. Results will be rewarded. This may feel good for a while, but the underlying organisational competence will not progress. If we focus on the capabilities that create results, we will get results that we never imagined.

His views are reinforced by Professor Lawler who recommends 'skill-based pay systems'. He writes:

Instead of reinforcing hierarchy, they reinforce skill acquisition and personal growth. Skill-based systems also have the advantage of allowing organisations to pay outstanding individuals higher amounts of money.

'Sweating the details'

Nothing is more disruptive and damaging than to spend a great deal of time planning and introducing an incentive scheme only to find that it fails. As one contributor to the HBR study commented, 'There is no area of management where "sweating the details" is more important than pay.'

Deborah Smith, Vice President of Human Resources at Xerox commented that, 'At Xerox, we have seen four critical levers can either facilitate transition or prevent progress. If anyone is neglected, the change process will not occur effectively.' Her four levers were cohesion, communication, training and reward. She agrees that:

> Pay is one of the many tools that can be effective in bringing about change. Making sure that recognition and reward are tied to the desired end results and behaviour needed to achieve those results, can increase the likelihood that goals will be met. Whatever compensation programme is designed, it must be integrated into the company culture and have the support and understanding of employees. It should balance both group and individual recognition to reinforce teamwork and encourage individual innovation and creativity.

Expanding on her first point, Deborah Smith refers to the need for 'A common set of values, a common approach to problems, and even a common language to overcome functional barriers.' All points we touched on earlier when discussing the need for cohesion. Ideally, whenever a new scheme is to be introduced, a dummy run should take place, calculating what people would be likely to earn if the scheme were to be introduced.

Involvement

You will remember that Ralph Stayer's workers designed, introduced and operated their own incentive scheme. Similarly, a team of technicians at Motorola developed their own pay programme and brought their plans to the executives in charge of compensation. Though these executives had some reservations, it was approved. Rightly, they felt that 'ownership' of the plan was important. It worked.

Colleagues as shareholders

An increasing number of organisations are now taking the issue of team member involvement to what they regard as its logical conclusion, by involving them as shareholders. Both NFC and Unipart are organisations with a significant measure of employee shareholders. CMG, a computer software company, has an impressive employee shareholder scheme. Over the years, employees have invested over £50m.

CONCLUSION

Motivation cannot be discussed in isolation. It should be the end result of getting the motivational impact of every one of our twelve Pillars right.

Once this is done, then the motivation technique that works is to set specific, stretching goals, provide the feedback – and above all – provide the support needed. Pay must be perceived to be fair, and the question then is, what role, if any, should incentive compensation play? If we are genuine about involvement, then our front-line colleagues should be involved in this discussion but I like the recommendation that 'If we focus on the capabilities that create results, we will get results that we never imagined.'

Above all we want to motivate people so they should look forward to coming to work, because it can be fun, and they have the confidence, competence and capabilities to ensure successful outcomes, to be part of a '**winning team**'.

BRAINSTORMING EXERCISES OR PROJECTS: 10

Motivating Superior Performance

■ Do you and your colleagues view motivation as a way of harnessing the vast power of your colleagues' emotional energy: by accepting their personal emotions; visualising success; generating pride; treating them as champions; providing recognition; having fun; and – above all – generating a sense of *meaning*? If not, what actions do you and your team need to take?

■ Have you created *an absolute desire to win*, giving your people every chance to identify with your business, and use their enthusiasm as your most valuable asset? If not, what actions do you and your team need to take?

■ Does your organisation demonstrate *reciprocity*? Do you generate an environment that demands a great deal of your colleagues but, equally, goes to great lengths to take them and their ideas into account? If not, what actions do you and your team need to take that ensures genuine reciprocity exists?

■ Have you created a winning team: does everyone know the goals they have to score? Do you have an eight-point plan for gaining both commitment and achievement? If not, what actions do you feel that you and your team need to take?

■ Do you need to set a project team to study, and come back to you with recommendations on how you can apply the principles set out in the book by Edwin Locke and Gary Latham?

■ Are you effective in rewarding your team for their success? Are you using potentially divisive financial incentives? Do you and your team feel that you could create a more integrated approach to both non-financial and financial rewards, which give emphasis to developing the capabilities you need for your long-term success? Is this a topic worthy of creating a special project team? How far could you delegate this task to the people themselves?

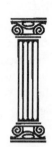

11

COMMUNICATE TO ACHIEVE EXTRAORDINARY PERFORMANCE

LEADER'S GREATEST OBLIGATION

It has been said that 'A leader's greatest obligation is to preach'. He or she has to focus primarily on four areas:

1. Communicating the vision so that it is understood clearly and people are highly motivated to play their part in its achievement.
2. Creating the culture to translate intention into reality.
3. Creating a symbolic 'picture' of the organisation.
4. Breaking through your 'Cultural Web'.

To set the scene, let's look at a case study, summarised from an HBR report.

THE PURPOSE AT THE HEART OF LEADERSHIP

When Kye Anderson was thirteen, her father died of a heart attack. The result was a single-minded career in medical technology which led to her starting her own company to develop and sell innovative systems for diagnosing heart and lung disease. At one point, she had two weeks to build a system to save the life of a baby who could not breathe on his own when he slept. But, when sales started to climb to $10m she was persuaded that she lacked the financial and managerial expertise to carry her business from 'exuberant adolescence' to 'profitable maturity' so she stepped aside.

But, while the bottom line improved, focus on logistics and management had 'put out the fire in people's guts'. The company was losing its way. So, after an 19 month 'sabbatical' Kye Anderson came back. She picked new board members who could act as her 'mentors'. She reasserted her original 'core values'. With help, she put together a statement of higher purposes, mission, eight values, and three strategies. She writes:

When mission and value statements talk about filling unmet diagnostic needs, about improving the quality of patients' lives, about maintaining competitive advantage through quality and innovation, about profit, human dignity, ethics, cost consciousness, cost effective medicine, about listening to customers, patients, and employees – and when these values are spelled out under a banner proclaiming, as a higher purpose, 'to prevent heart and lung disease, the leading causes of death and rising health care costs', the result is a guide to behaviour, to planning, and to problem solving.

In a key sentence, she concludes, *'I've been able to trace back every difficulty I've ever encountered at Medical Graphics, trivial as well as serious, to violation of one of these principles.'*

Kye Anderson realised that a leader's greatest obligation is to preach, and she began to spend much of her time communicating with her own employees about the purpose, mission, values, and strategy that could carry the company into a billion dollar primary-care market.

Abridged with the permission of the Trustees from *Harvard Business Review*, reprint 92301.

COMMUNICATING THE VISION

Leaders are only as powerful as the ideas they can communicate. They inspire their followers to high levels of achievement by showing them how their work contributes to worthwhile ends. It is an emotional appeal to some of the most fundamental of human needs – the need to be important, to make a difference, to feel useful, to be part of a successful and worthwhile enterprise.

This quotation from *Leaders*[8] by Warren Bennis and Burt Nanus, serves as a very powerful challenge to those of us responsible for leading our organisations.

Personal commitment

Kye Anderson concluded her 'First Person' article in the *HBR* by saying:

When I came back, I began for the first time telling people the story of my father's death. To my surprise, nearly everyone I worked with had a similar story. It turned out that all of us were in it for something more than money, and for 10 years I had let that sense of higher purpose go unexpressed and unfulfilled. It may be difficult, even painful, for an entrepreneur to expose the private emotions that drive him or her, but it is an indispensable piece of *good entrepreneurial leadership*.

As Kye Anderson says, it can be difficult, even painful, to expose the private emotions which drive us. I had a very disrupted childhood which left me extremely introverted, loath to communicate my private feelings. Initially this hindered my progress in my business. Once, I told a long-established colleague about my background. His response was that he felt cheated by not having known earlier. He was enthused by our 'heart-to-heart'.

Truly successful executives project their vision with almost missionary zeal. Undoubtedly you can think of many examples for yourself. Tom Farmer of Kwik Fit is constantly visiting every one of his depots to talk to staff on duty. It was once said of Jan Carlzon of SAS that whenever there was a group of people having a chat, it was highly probable that Jan was one of them. When Sir Colin Marshall was at British Airways, he took every opportunity to talk to his staff on the planes, and at the terminals. He took an interest, asked questions, and expressed appreciation. He focused on things that people are doing right.

But as we said earlier, no one person can do it all by himself. Just as there has to be leadership at every level of the organisation, so, too, must there be communication at every level, indeed, throughout the organisation.

Extensive participation and consultation

When I went to Japan with a client once, he, his assistant, and I, found ourselves facing nearly twenty Japanese executives. They involved everyone likely to be affected by our discussion so that they would know how to react. Sir John Harvey Jones, in his fascinating book, *Making it Happen*[2] writes on this theme:

> Those of us who have worked with the Japanese and who admire their business achievements, as I do, know how long it takes the Japanese to reach a decision. One is lulled into a totally false sense of security by the apparently endless debate and the thoroughness of the involvement of people at every level of the organisation in the decision, because when the action stage comes they move like greased lightning.

> Some years ago we licensed a process to build a paraxylene plant to the Japanese ....We were simultaneously building an identical one in the UK and we had each taken the decision to go ahead at the same time. After four months we were already breaking ground and priding ourselves on being well ahead of the Far Eastern opposition who were still endlessly debating items of the design and equipment. Imagine then our chagrin when not only did they complete their plant seven months before us but also it worked at first go while ours suffered the usual teething troubles and only achieved its flowsheet some three months after start.

'The Japanese get their commitment in the process of discussing the "How".'

The Machine That Changed the World[11] gives a different dimension to this point. When Japanese vehicle manufacturers start to design a new model, hundreds of people are involved to resolve all the potential problems. Nothing is allowed to move forward until somebody accepts commitment for resolving the problems. So thorough is this process that as it develops fewer people are needed. In the West, we used to do the reverse. At the beginning of the design process, fewer people were involved. Difficult issues were deferred. The people initially involved did not accept responsibility. The result was that more and more people were needed to resolve problems as the process developed.

The process of communication in Japanese factories was such that they could practise simultaneous engineering, doing many differing functions concurrently. In the West, at that time, we tended to do them in sequence. Now, as a result of the work of Dan Jones and his colleagues, the West is racing to catch up. We realise that the more we involve those who are actually going to be involved, the more likely it is that the task will be completed successfully.

In a marvellous chapter on 'Setting the Direction'[2], Sir John Harvey Jones emphasises:

> [Setting the direction]...can only be accomplished by hours of talk. We have found that this sort of discussion requires a certain amount of structure, but a great deal of flexibility, and is best carried out [outside] our normal working environment. We wear sweaters and jeans, we do not keep minutes of what individuals say, we do tremendous amounts of work on flip charts, we form a lot of our conclusions 'on the run'. The outcome of perhaps three days' work is often no more than 10 points on a flip chart, and we would consider that a good rate of striking. The discussions are always ... highly informal and we encourage each other to produce ideas, no matter how fanciful.

> We find the process simultaneously tiring, frustrating and rewarding, when at the end of tussling with some problems, we reach a shared view and a commitment to that view, which is usually of a different order to that which we can achieve by any other means.

Involvement in decisions

In his book *Sharing the Success*[9], Sir Peter Thompson writes that his objective was to make NFC employees the best informed workforce in the UK. He set an example from the top by making sure that they had an open communicative management style. The Head of Communications was required to attend all executive Board Meetings and to prepare a broadsheet of items to be communicated down the line. Subsidiary companies then added any items of interest from their own management meetings and passed the information down to the Branch Manager. Branches added their information, and this became the basis of the briefings. He also states that:

> Any policy issue was always passed down the line for discussion before a decision was taken on high. It was slow, but it then made implementation of the policies that much easier.

AWWA

Jan Carlzon[15] tells the story of how, earlier in his career, he took over a loss-making subsidiary of SAS called Linjeflyg. He summoned all the staff members from throughout the country to a meeting in the main hangar. He climbed a tall ladder and addressed the crowd from 15 feet off the ground. He said:

> This company is not doing well. It's losing money and suffering from many problems. As the new President, I don't know a thing about Linjeflyg. I can't save this company alone. The only chance for Linjeflyg to survive is if you help me – assuming responsibility yourselves, share your ideas and experience so that we have more to work with. I have some ideas of my own and we'll probably be able to use them. But you are the ones who must help *me*, not the other way around.

He explains that their reaction was fantastic. Once upon a time, the concept of MBWA, Managing By Walking Around, was popular. I feel it should become AWWA – Asking When Walking Around. The emphasis needs to be on debriefing, releasing expertise, gaining intelligence. It really does boil down to a willingness to turn round and ask a question such as:

> *'What do you think?'*
> *'How do you suggest we tackle this?'*
> *'How well are you achieving, or making progress towards your goals?'*
> *'How can I help?'*

At one plant where management had been seeking desperately for a solution to uneven work flows without success, one of their welders gave them the solution.

Debriefing sessions

Many progressive organisations hold regular briefing sessions. But Richard Pascale[16] believes that – even if subconsciously – too many executives are still influenced by the Frederick Taylor concept of getting ideas out of the brains of executives, and into the hands of workers. Our new approach must be to get ideas out of the brains of our team members so that, collectively, we can evolve more effective, successful strategies to gain a competitive advantage.

So, if you already hold 'briefing sessions' for reasons of psychological emphasis, can I suggest that you now call them 'debriefing sessions' and deliberately restructure them to allow time for your team members to report on progress, and on what they have learned. Wal-Mart does this weekly to ensure essential feedback from customer-facing staff.

What to communicate

Ann Ferguson, formerly Head of Group Communications at ICI, in discussion with each of the businesses within ICI, identified six key areas which it was felt important for the group to reinforce. At the time, these were:

1. The values of ICI, what it stands for.
2. The ICI Group objectives and strategies.
3. The member's role in achieving these objectives.
4. How each member contributes.
5. Business performance.
6. Policies and changes.

It is interesting to note the focus on values, objectives, strategies, goals and contribution. The topics she emphasised are equally relevant in smaller organisations.

A structure of communication

Both MBWA and AWWA are easier to handle in a small organisation. The larger we become, the more important it is to have a structure. I am grateful to Mike Judge of Peugeot for permission to reproduce the schematic of their communication processes shown in Table 11.1.

Peugeot executives believe, rightly, that nothing is worse than for their team members to receive information from the media, or from third parties, before they receive it from the company itself. They have a 'red document' which ensures that everyone is told of any newsworthy development *before* the media. When Peugeot first started, they used external experts to make videos. Now they use their own staff. They have reached a high standard and their videos have already been used.

Unipart also produces superb videos, using satellite communications to project them to every location.

Table 11.1 Peugeot Talbot Motor Co Ltd employee communications

METHOD	PURPOSE	RECIPIENTS	SPEED	FREQUENCY
COMPANY CHARTER	The Company Mission and Vision Statement outlining the broad objectives of the company.	All employees.		
COMPANY OPERATIONS NEWS	Managing Director calls monthly Operations Committee meetings. Operations Committee consists of 25 functional Directions.	All employees.	Within 72 hours of operations committee meeting.	
BRIEFING MEETINGS	Briefing document contains details of meeting subject matter, eg productivity, quality, financial information, sales figures. Every employee receives briefing document and those in manufacturing receive manufacturing bulletin as well. Line management also receive background information, and adds local working area news. Production is stopped whilst managers/supervisors give verbal presentation of the briefing document to employees. All employees are free to ask questions at briefing meeting and receive either immediate or subsequent replies.			
URGENT INFORMATION COMMUNICATIONS- IMMEDIATE DOCUMENT	To get very urgent information to all employees before the media. (Known as 'red documents').	Distributed to functional heads, line management and supervisors. Then given verbally to all other employees	Information reaches all employees same day as document preparation.	As required.
MANAGING DIRECTOR'S REVIEW	Conveys news which is less urgent than that carried by 'red document' but, which will not wait for inclusion in the next Peugeot Talbot Times (known as 'green document').	All employees either: verbally from supervisior or posted on notice boards.	Information reaches all employees within 2 – 3 days of preparation.	As required.
IN HOUSE NEWSPAPER 'TIMES' COLOUR TABLOID	Local newspaper for employees giving a blend of employee, motor industry, company news. Promotes and reports on various employee sports and social events, employee communications, retirements, appointments, etc.	Copy for each employee – circulated to company dealers.	Normally distributed to all employees within 1 – 2 days of preparation.	10 issues per year.

Table 11.1 *(contd)*

METHOD	PURPOSE	RECIPIENTS	SPEED	FREQUENCY
COMPANY OVERVIEW MANAGING DIRECTOR'S REVIEW	Often preceded by a video presentation of major topics of current interest, eg new model launch, analysis of past performance, future business plan. Managing director's presentation takes the form of either one evening meeting of all managers or a number of smaller meetings with group managers. The presentation is also made to Trade Union reps at separate meetings chaired by managing director.	Management. Senior Trade Union representatives.	2 – 3 weeks	Twice a year.
COMMUNICATION AND TRAINING VIDEOS	The company produces, entirely in-house, videos dealing with specific subjects, eg quality, facility and operating changes. Pensions Scheme administration. These are normally shown to employees as an extension of briefing meetings where there is the opportunity for questioning.	Identified groups of employees.	Within one week of filming.	As required.
ANNUAL REPORT	Report on performance of the company in the past year, including the accounts. Explanatory video and simplified explanatory documents also produced.	All employees, financiers/bankers, media, suppliers, local community.	Within 2 weeks of publication.	Annual.
LOCAL OPERATIONS NEWS MANUFACTURING SUPERVISOR'S BRIEF	Provide snap-shot of what happened 'on plant' the previous week. Production achieved in each area - quality, appointments, targets. Gives detailed information relating to all work areas.	All manufacturing supervisors.	Distributed to all manufacturing supervisors in one day.	Weekly.
MANUFACTURING FORUM	Employees meet manufacturing personnel manager and other managers to discuss issues of concern outside formal negotiating machinery. There is an open agenda, any issue can be raised.	25–30 manufacturing employees are picked at random from the payroll computer.		Weekly.
NOTICE BOARDS	Used to display up-to-date details on such matters as pay negotiations, job vacancies, fire/safety regulations, sporting and social events.	Notice boards are sited throughout plants and offices.	Distribution to all notice boards 1 – 2 days.	As required.

Table 11.1 *(contd)*

METHOD	PURPOSE	RECIPIENTS	SPEED	FREQUENCY
IN HOUSE RADIO RADIO RYTON	In-house radio station for Ryton Plant covering the track areas. Tapes prepared at Ryton Plant also played at Canterbury Street factory. Broadcasts – anything from music to sports results. Provides instant means of communication on non-contentious items.	Ryton and Canterbury Street shop floor employees.	Immediate.	Broadcast daily.
PUBLIC RELATIONS/ MARKETING PUBLICATIONS	To promote launch of new car and emphasise commitment to Coventry.	All employees.	Within one week of printing.	As required.
AGREED MINUTES	Jointly agreed minutes of negotiations on pay and conditions containing TU submissions and company offer.	Management, Trade Unions, notice boards.	Immediate.	During negotiations.
DIRECT CONTACT	The company communicates directly with the employees by mail, primarily when faced with a potential or actual dispute but also on other occasions.	Appropriate group of employees.	Distributed by mail to employees' homes or handed out.	As required.

It's also what we do

It's not only what we say, it's what we do. Jan Carlzon[15] writes that, when he travelled by plane, he made sure that all the fare paying customers were seated before he took whatever seat was available. In the plane, he asked his cabin staff to make sure that the fare paying customers were supplied with the papers or magazines they wished, before he took his selection. He believes that this was the only way that he could live the philosophy of 'putting customers first'. Yet all too often, in many businesses, executives who are saying one thing do the opposite in practice.

Communicating the vision: at every level

While it is the primary responsibility of the leader, he or she cannot do it all by themselves. Help is needed at every level of the organisation. The Body Shop have created what are known as 'Charter Working Groups', which focus on the eight important areas of communication, integration, appraisal, recruitment/induction, training/development, social events, fund raising and motivation.

Under the last topic of motivation, the aim of the working group was defined as being 'to encourage staff and develop their realisation of their importance within the workplace and their role and contribution in the success of BSI'. One of the ideas to develop from the motivation work group was the DODGI awards. DODGI stands for the 'Department of Damn Good Ideas'. The team concerned states that they intend to continually review external success stories of motivation and adapt or extend these for themselves.

'Swim better!'

It remains the responsibility of the leader to communicate his or her vision. For an organisation going through a process of change, when people may feel threatened or insecure, it is even more important. Jack Welch faced this problem during the period when he was introducing massive changes at General Electric. He explains: 'I was intellectualising the issues with a couple of hundred people at the top of the company. Quite clearly I was not reaching hundreds of thousands of other people.'

The message they heard – *'swim better!'* – wasn't much help. It took time for Jack Welch to find a way of opening a dialogue with GE's whole workforce. He began a process – still very far from complete – of winning the large mass of employees over to his way of thinking. He explains:

> It's not that I changed. We just expanded the reach of our communication. We refined it, got better at it, and it began to snowball. If you have a simple, consistent message, and you keep on repeating it, eventually that's what happens. Simplicity, consistency, and repetition – that's how you get through. It's a steady continuum that finally reaches a critical mass.

What communication is not

In one speech, Jack Welch says:

> We've learned a bit about what communication *is not*. It's not a speech .... or a video tape. It's not a Plant newspaper. Real communications is an attitude, an environment. It's the most interactive of all processes. It requires countless hours of eyeball-to-eyeball back and forth. It involves us all in more listening than talking. It is a constant, interactive process aimed at (creating) consensus.

It takes a tremendous amount of time.

Sound business decision

No organisation has the time to tell all its employees exactly what to do but like any CEO, Jack Welch needs his workers to further his goals. He needs people who not only understand GE's objectives but sincerely believe in them. Only when everyone is on the same wavelength does 'liberating' people, as Jack Welch puts it, become a sound business proposition. This is the ultimate objective. To get every member of your team so committed to your vision, your objectives, that they can use their initiative to act as independent entrepreneurs on your behalf.

To reinforce an earlier point because it is important, we need to ensure a culture in which everyone has the competence to take decisions – on a similar sound approach, with rigour and lack of emotion – which help them to help *their* company succeed.

CREATING A CULTURE OF SUCCESS

We all have to be aware that every organisation develops its own 'culture'. This is a tremendously important, even vital issue. Kotter and Heskett[4], break it down into two elements.

- **Shared values**: important concerns and goals that are shared by most of the people in a group that tend to shape group behaviour, and, that often persist over time even with changes in group membership.
- **Group behaviours**: common or pervasive ways of acting that are found in a group that persist because group members tend to behave in ways that teach these practices to new members, rewarding those who fit in and sanctioning those who do not.

They point out that group behaviours, being more visible, are easier to change. Shared values, being invisible, even subconscious, are far harder to change.

Unadaptive cultures

Like human personalities, corporate cultures result from the interaction of temperament and experience. Over time, their dictates slip from the conscious to the subconscious. People cling to once useful beliefs and patterns of behaviour as if no alternative existed. John Kotter and James Heskett, in their book *Corporate Culture and Performance*[4], explain that when organisations fail to adapt to changing circumstances, it is because they have what they describe as an *unadaptive culture*.

In their view, it is the prime reason for business failure.

Paradoxically, the wrong culture often develops from great initial success. The strong culture that such companies generate can easily become arrogant, inwardly focused, politicised and bureaucratic. Common examples are IBM and General Motors, both of whom initially achieved market dominance. But, in an increasingly competitively and rapidly changing world, they were overtaken. **Their culture unquestionably undermined their economic performance.** Jack Smith is beginning to change the culture of General Motors. IBM is back into profits.

How many companies in your own trade or industry do you know of with unsuitable unadaptive cultures?

Nothing fails like success

A section of Richard Pascale's book[16] starts with the challenging sentence that *'Nothing fails like success'*. He points out that a high proportion of companies once in the Fortune 500 Listings have now disappeared, or slipped badly. He writes that '99 per cent of managerial attention today is devoted to the techniques that squeeze more out of the existing [ways of doing things] and it's killing us. Results may be positive and profitable in the short run but ... are fatal over time.' He adds that 'What is disheartening is how slowly we are closing the gap between ourselves and our ever-improving global competitors.'

Inherent conservatism

Many other writers confirm the inherent conservatism of most organisations. Professor Zaleznik[18] says: 'Out of this conservatism, organisations provide succession to power through the development of managers rather than leaders ...... this ethic fosters a bureaucratic culture.' He continues, 'Leaders tolerate chaos and lack of structure. Managers seek order and control. In my experience, seldom do the uncertainties of potential chaos cause problems. Instead, it is the attempt to impose order on potential chaos that makes trouble for organisations.' In short, focusing on what we have always done, and the promotion of managers who seek to impose order, can result in an **Unadaptive Culture.** This can be death to an organisation.

Table 11.2 Adaptive versus unadaptive cultures

	Adaptive	Unadaptive
Core values	Most managers care deeply about customers, shareholders and employees. They also strongly value people and processes that can create useful change (eg leadership at every level).	Most managers care mainly about themselves, their immediate work group, or some product (or technology) associated with that work group. They value the orderly and risk-reducing management process much more highly than leadership initiatives.
Common behaviours	Managers pay close attention to all their stakeholders, especially customers, and initiate change where needed to serve their legitimate interests, even if that entails taking some risks.	Managers tend to behave somewhat insularly, politically, and bureaucratically. As a result, they do not change their strategies quickly to adjust to or take advantage of changes in their business environment.

Source: Kotter and Heskett, *Corporate Culture & Performance*, Free Press

Kotter and Heskett's conclusions (Table 11.2)

Paraphrasing the conclusions of John Kotter and James Heskett, they are:

1. *Unadaptive cultures are widespread and stem from initial success.* Unadaptive cultures that inhibit strong long-term financial performance are common. They develop easily, even in firms full of reasonable and intelligent people. They tend to emerge slowly and quietly over a period of years, usually when the company concerned is performing well. They can be enormously difficult to change because they are often invisible to the people involved, because they help to support the existing power structure in the firm, and for many other reasons. **The result is that they encourage inappropriate behaviour and inhibit change to more appropriate strategies.**
2. *Corporate culture will be an even more important factor in determining success or failure in the future.* In a world of increasingly dramatic change, companies that do not change their culture will face severe problems of survival.
3. *Establishing a flexibly appropriate, adaptive culture is an essential ingredient for long-term success, and for the achievement of the organisation's vision.*

Benefits of strong culture

I strongly recommend that you get a small team of your people to study Kotter and Heskett's[4] book in detail. It is invaluable, not least for its case studies. In their chapter on 'Strong Cultures', the two authors underline the importance of the twelve Pillars we have been discussing. Again, slightly paraphrasing their remarks, let me give a few examples.

> Strong cultures provide needed structure and controls without having to rely on a stifling formal bureaucracy that can dampen motivation and innovation.

They quote one CEO as saying:

> I cannot imagine trying to run a business today with a weak or non-existent culture; why, people would be going off in a hundred different directions.

Tandem Computers is said to have no formal organisation chart and few formal rules, yet workers keep off each other's toes and work productively in the same direction because of the unwritten rules and shared understanding. **This culture is maintained because top management spends considerable time in training and in communicating the management philosophy and the essence of the company,** because achievements consistent with the culture are recognised on bulletin boards as 'Our Latest Greatest' and because rituals such as the Friday afternoon 'Beer Bust' symbolise that culture. All this makes workers feel like they belong to an exclusive club. Most develop great respect for and loyalty to that 'club', a feeling which often translates into long hours of hard, productive work.

> Strong cultures help business performance because they create an unusual level of *motivation*. They make people feel good about working for their firm, have greater commitment and loyalty and feel that their work is more rewarding. Involving people in decision making and recognising their contributions are two examples quoted.

Enhancing culture

Let's look at the two authors' ideas for enhancing culture.

■ *Context:* Leader(s) are able to put across that increasing competition at a time of rapid change, requires change. This could involve lowering costs, creating higher quality, being more innovative, attracting and sustaining financial support, and being able to recruit the right calibre of people.

■ *Leadership:* The CEO and his senior colleagues provide effective leadership by communicating in words and deeds a new vision and a new set of strategies and then motivating many others, their missionaries, to provide the leadership needed to implement the vision and strategies.

Kotter and Heskett[4] make a point that leaders must distinguish between the ability to identify the *values needed* for their organisation to be adaptive, from the more specific *practices needed for day to day performance*. They must communicate endlessly about these core values and behaviours, which should change rarely. But they should ensure that 'specific practices' are changed as appropriate, and that new systems or new executives do not undermine the core *values and beliefs*.

Effective leaders will not tolerate arrogance in others, and remind people often of the need to serve the best interests of their customers, and all their other stakeholders.

They keep their own egos under control. They make room for other egos.

■ *Values:* Everyone develops a high regard for leadership at every level, particularly leadership and other processes that produce change. Everyone cares deeply about the people who have a stake in the business – suppliers, dealers, customers, shareholders, the community and competitors.

■ *Behaviours:* Because everyone is focused on meeting the needs of their customers, they are quick to recognise changes in their competitive situation. They are then willing and able to devise new strategies to continue to satisfy customers, and other stakeholders, even if changes must be made in culturally ingrained behaviours. They take part in providing the leadership needed to create and implement new strategies and practices and seek to develop and promote those who share their core values.

Collective knowledge

In the above paragraph, I am paraphrasing Kotter and Heskett. Their recommendations involve all the ingredients we have been discussing. I would like to highlight one to which they do not refer specifically. I am convinced that tapping into the collective knowledge of everyone involved with us, is likely to be the biggest and most powerful way of creating, and sustaining a performance-enhancing culture.

Consider this most telling quotation by G Hamel and C G Prahalad in their *HBR* article, 'Strategic Intent'[41]: 'The ability to absorb, process and act upon data from the environment *systematically at all levels of the firm* has been demonstrated in the most chilling fashion by Japanese companies.'

Note their comment '...at all levels of the firm'.

A culture of loyalty

Excessive loyalty to individuals holds back many organisations. As ever, Jack Welch has some highly pertinent remarks on this point.

> GE had an implicit psychological contract based on perceived lifetime employment. People were rarely dismissed except for cause or severe business downturns. This produced a paternal, feudal, fuzzy kind of loyalty. You put in your time, worked hard, and the company took care of your life. That kind of loyalty tends to focus people inward.

> But given today's environment, people's emotional energy must be focused outward on a competitive world where no business is a safe haven for employment unless it is winning in the market place. The psychological contract had to change. People at all levels have to feel the risk-reward tension.

> My concept of loyalty is not 'giving time' to some corporate entity and, in turn, being shielded and protected from the outside world. Loyalty is an affinity among people who want to grapple with the outside world and win. Their personal values, dreams and ambitions cause them to gravitate towards each other and towards a company like GE that gives them the resources and opportunities to flourish.

It comes back to the hard issue of employability. I hope you will agree that it raises very important issues of culture. Tom Farmer, Chairman of Kwik-Fit set out his views on his organisation's culture.

A CULTURE OF INTEGRITY

'The right culture will mean that an act of dishonesty becomes a betrayal of oneself and one's colleagues'

(reproduced with permission of *The Financial Times*)

I have always believed that most people are fundamentally honest and, provided they are given the proper opportunity and recognition, they will of their best. While there have been occasions when I have been disappointed, it is a view that has served me well throughout my life. With the correct recruitment policy and people it is the only approach that you can take when running a business, whatever the scale.

Honesty is an intangible quality for which it is impossible to legislate. You can have as many rules as you want but if people choose to break them then there is little that you can do to stop them. It is the responsibility of management to create an environment which reduces temptation by having adequate controls which are sound but not stifling.

The most effective deterrent is to build within the company a culture based on pride in one's job. Not only will this improve the quality of the service or product offered, and produce profit, it will mean that an act of dishonesty becomes a betrayal of oneself and one's colleagues. This culture must stem from the top down and the attitude of management towards their people is a vital element in its creation.

I have found that the best results are achieved by treating people as you would wish to be treated. People must be provided with a decent working environment and all the facilities they require to do their job. A proper pay scheme must be in place which reflects their contribution and everyone should have the opportunity to share in the profits they help to create.

Everyone should know what is expected of them and should have received sufficient training to enable them to be fully skilled in that task. There should be opportunities for everyone to develop to the best of his or her abilities; the promotion prospects and training programmes within the company should encourage ambition.

CREATING A 'PICTURE' OF YOUR ORGANISATION

Worthwhile exercise

If you organise an evening meeting of your staff, or hold regular training courses at an in-company training centre, there is another exercise you can develop for yourself. Get those present to make a random list of all the values and practices they can think of. Then, get them to express each value or practice they have listed in terms of extremely positive and extremely negative quality. Then get them to design a questionnaire along the lines of our example.

Having done so, get each individual to rank each quality out of five. Thus, a high degree of trust would rank 5, positive mistrust would rank 1, with grades of trust or mistrust in between these (see Table 11.3).

To the extent that any replies from the members of your team fall short of your idea, you have a clear indication of the areas in which you need to take action. It may be that you need to improve your communication. It may be that you have not yet put all your philosophies into place. Or it could be that some of your executives are not walking, talking and living your values in the way in which you had hoped.

Table 11.3 Creating your own culture map'

	5	4	3	2	1	
High degree of trust	5	4	3	2	1	Positive mistrust
High degree of loyalty/	5	4	3	2	1	Sense of insecurity and
security	5	4	3	2	1	disloyalty
Initiative applauded	5	4	3	2	1	Conformity essential
Learning encouraged	5	4	3	2	1	Learning discouraged
Sense of equality and respect	5	4	3	2	1	Status and 'kow-towing'
Candour and openness	5	4	3	2	1	Secrecy and dissembling
Ethics and integrity	5	4	3	2	1	Expediency, low ethics
Executive empathy	5	4	3	2	1	Executive arrogance
Total						

More detailed exercise

A more detailed exercise would be to get a small team of people to go through this book marking up each point they feel impacts on your culture. A few examples:

- Focusing on leaders rather than managers.
- Focusing on top-line rather than bottom-line.
- Being contentious rather than compliant.
- Being assertive or saying nothing.
- Building confidence or being highly critical.

In fact, this could become a regular exercise whenever you have any group of your people together. First, it would emphasise and reinforce the transformation needed, and second, it would indicate the areas needing priority attention. Most importantly, it would open up the organisation to debating the key issues confronting everyone involved with your organisation.

You may wish to investigate techniques of this type but let's look at the fourth issue, that of understanding the 'cultural web' of your organisation.

UNDERSTANDING YOUR 'CULTURAL WEB'

Gerry Johnson is Professor of Strategic Management and Director of the Centre for Strategic Management and Organisational Change at Cranfield School of Management. He writes[42] on the way in which the deeply held mindset – he uses the term 'paradigm' – of executives can inhibit change:

There is likely to exist at some level a core set of beliefs and assumptions held relatively commonly by the managers. This paradigm is essentially cultural in nature as it is the deeper level of basic assumptions of beliefs that are shared by members of an organisation that operate unconsciously and define in a basic 'taken for granted' fashion an organisation's view of itself and its environment.

At its most beneficial, it encapsulates the unique or special competencies of that organisation and therefore the bases by which the firm might expect to achieve real competitive advantage. However, it can also lead to significant strategic problems.

The examples of this are common. Executive teams who discount competitor activity or changes in buyer behaviour as aberrations; who persist with outmoded practices or dying declining markets or competitor substitution; management teams that choose to ignore or minimise the evidence of market research, the implications of which question tried and tested ways of doing things. Ask any manager who has found it frustrating to use apparently objective evidence to persuade a management team of their need to change their way of thinking or their behaviour.

He explains that this mindset, or paradigm, acts as a filter for all the information that the organisation processes, and thus defines a way it reacts to its environment.

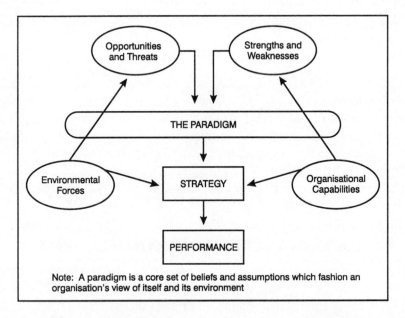

Figure 11.1 Strategy development – A cultural perspective

Reproduced courtesy of Professor Peter Johnson

The 'cultural web'

This mindset, or paradigm, lies at the centre of the cultural web of an organisation as shown in Figure 11.2. This cultural web can be used as a convenient device for a culture audit which Gerry Johnson uses frequently as an exercise to allow managers to 'discover' the nature of their organisation in cultural terms, the way it impacts on the strategy they are following, and the difficulties of changing it.

In his paper, he gives three case studies: a manswear clothing retailer, a consulting partnership, and a regional newspaper which – with the permission of him and his publishers[41] – is reproduced as an example (Figure 11.3).

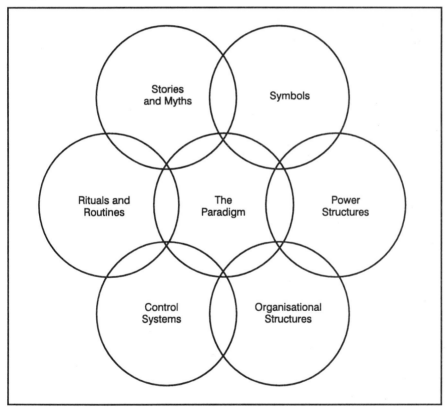

Figure 11.2   The Cultural Web of an Organisation

Figure 11.3   How Managers Define the Cultural Web – One Case Background

Company C is a regional newspaper business operating in a market in which it had enjoyed long-standing dominance with its local evening newspaper. It now faced increasingly competitor pressure from free newspapers and entry by competitors historically based elsewhere. Moreover a changing local population meant less traditional loyalty to the newspaper: and longer term developments of media alternatives for the public raised both strategic opportunities and possible threats.

The need was for a substantial short-term rethink of competitive strategy and longer term rethink of the direction of the business. Yet the culture audit undertaken by the managers revealed a taken-for-granted view that their paid-for daily newspaper 'would always be around', and that the local community somehow needed them. Moreover the technology, structure and routines of the business did little to promote strategic thinking: the business was necessarily run on short term deadlines – hours not days – the 'macho' self image of those running the business, and the vertical, hierarchical ways of doing business, prevented a free flow of ideas across management boundaries.

Suggestions by some younger managers that the prime purpose of the business was to create an effective advertising medium (the main source of revenue) were set aside given the dominant belief that 'we are a *newspaper*'; a view reinforced by the symbolic significance of the presses, the associated technical jargon, street distribution system and the stories linked to news gathering and coverage.

Table 11.4   Managers' definitions

Paradigm	Rituals and routines
We are in the newspaper business	'Slaves to time' to meet deadlines for
Our paid-for daily will always be there	publication
Readers will pay for news	'Product' developed in hours and
Advertisers need newspapers	minutes, not days and months
	Long working hours common
	Ritualised executive meetings at senior
	level

Power	Stories
The parent company – a newspaper group	Macho personalities and behaviour
The autocrat CEO	Scoops and coverage of major events
Departmental rivalry between production,	Stories of the past
commercial and editorial departments	Major errors in print
	The defeat of the unions

Table 11.4 *(contd)*

Organisation	Symbols
Vertical, hierarchical system with little lateral communication and much vertical referral	Symbols of hierarchy: the MD's Jaguar, portable phones, car-parking spaces etc
	The 'press'
Autocratic management style	Technical production jargon
	The street vendors

Control systems
Emphasis on targeting and budgeting to achieve a low cost operation

The cultural audit

Gerry Johnson makes the valid point that it is important to expose that which is taken for granted. He writes, 'One way in which this might be facilitated is to undertake the sort of culture audit which helps to make explicit that which is taken for granted and to generate managerial debate about the cultural barriers to change that exist.' One division of the fast growing Emap Group carries out a regular 'culture audit' of each of its operating units. Former Divisional Managing Director, Colin Morrison, finds it an invaluable tool. (When it acquired my company we came top or second in most of the headings).

In fact, it is the ideal complement to the type of 'Staff Attitude Survey' we discussed earlier.

Basis of communication strategy

The more you can bring to the surface these unspoken assumptions about the values and beliefs of your people, the more effective will be your debate on these issues. It can truly serve to open up your own organisation. It is the first step to truly effective communication.

CONCLUSION: COMMUNICATE ENDLESSLY

As we have seen, your culture can be your stumbling block or your launch pad. Which it is, depends upon you as the leader of your organisation. Your success depends upon your ability to articulate your vision, your values and beliefs, and your strategies. It requires you to give a significant amount of time to communication: to communicate endlessly.

You have to take the lead by initiating highly participative discussions on all twelve of the ingredients we have discussed. As Jack Welch observed, communication is not a set of techniques, but a process, an attitude, a total ambience of highly participative, assertive, contentious, challenging, two-way communication in which every individual is treated as an equal.

Clauswitz observed that, once battle is joined, Generals have little control. They have to rely on the commitment and ability of the 'lower ranks' to use their initiative in attaining their objective. One of the reasons that Montgomery was highly acclaimed was the thoroughness with which he personally briefed his troops before every battle. He drove around in a Jeep, told those he met to gather round, and spoke to them man-to-man. His belief was:

> *The leader must have infectious optimism ... the final test of a leader is the feeling you have when you leave his presence.*

While every single ingredient we have discussed to date is important, they will count for nothing unless you, and every leader at every level of your organisation, can achieve this degree of infectious optimism.

BRAINSTORMING EXERCISES OR PROJECTS

Communicating to Ensure Superior Performance

■ If you are Chief Executive, do you spend enough time on communications, bearing in mind that some successful executives reckon to spend 40 per cent of their time on this essential activity?

■ Do you and your team feel that the level of communication in your organisation is at the level needed to achieve extraordinary performance? If not, what actions do you and your team feel are necessary to reach this level? Are you happy with both your formal and informal *structure of communications,* and is this reinforced by the actions of you and your senior colleagues?

■ Do you feel that you are effective in communicating your vision: is there a sufficient level of participation and consultation: involvement in decisions: AWWA, and debriefing sessions? If not, what actions do you need to take to encourage this level of involvement?

Creating a Culture of Success

■ Do you feel that you have created a *culture of success* which is highly adaptive to the rapidly changing environment in which you operate? If not, how do you feel that you and your team need to set about creating such an adaptive culture?

■ Do you feel that your culture provides structure and controls without stifling bureaucracy which dampens motivation and innovation? If not, how do you set about creating such an empowering culture?

■ Is your culture based on the recognition that your continued existence depends on the day-to-day mobilisation of every ounce of intelligence so that you are able to absorb, process and act upon data from all levels of your organisation? If not, what actions do you need to take?

Creating a 'Picture' of your Organisation

■ Do you need to set up a series of in-company meetings, discussions and perhaps competitions to draw a 'picture' of your organisation and create your own 'culture map'? If so, how would you set about doing so?

■ Should you get a project team to study Professor Gerry Johnson's concept of a 'cultural web' and carry out the type of 'cultural audit' he recommended?

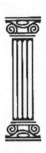
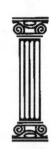

12

YOUR CHARTER FOR EXTRAORDINARY ACHIEVEMENT

WHY?

Why should you expect your suppliers not merely to deliver their goods and services, but to work in a partnership with you, making sure that you get precisely what you want when you want it and, if necessary, by helping you to resolve any emergencies you may have? Why should they have that extra commitment to use all their expertise and knowledge to help you to improve your existing products and services, or help you to be innovative in developing new products or services?

Why should your executives 'sweat blood' for you, work long hours, and lie awake at night worrying about their contribution to your success?

Why should every member of your team commit themselves to an **extraordinary** 110 per cent effort, to doing their best to achieve their goals, and thus help your organisation to achieve its goals?

Why should those, like your distributors or dealers, who help you to get your products to your end user customer, give priority to positioning and projecting them to achieve or exceed the market penetration you desire?

Why should your competitors help you, even share information with you, and generally be supportive on issues of concern to you?

Why should your shareholders invest in you, on occasions waive their dividends and, when asked, reinvest further sums?

Finally, why should the community within which you operate be supportive to you and help where appropriate?

Quality of relationship

It's not just money (though the financial relationship has to be fair and realistic). The reason why customers, suppliers, executives, team members, competitors, shareholders and your community either do or don't sustain their involvement is the 'quality' of the relationship they experience in their dealings with you.

If you think about the type of organisations with which you prefer to deal, it is likely that they project a strong sense of 'identity'. They seem to have a strength of character which is normally reflected in the sum total of all your relationships with all the members of the organisations with whom you deal, or come into contact.

The extra dimension

This almost indefinable 'extra dimension', this sense of 'identity' comes, in my view, from all the ingredients we have been discussing together. In particular, it comes from *our sense of vision*. As Warren Bennis and Burt Nanus[8] put it:

> ...a clearly articulated vision of the future that is at once simple, easily understood, clearly desirable, and energising.

So, we all face three vital challenges:

1. *Vision*: How do we establish and project?
2. *Hearts and minds*: How do we win the hearts and minds of every member of our team?
3. *Reputation*: How do we create the right perceptions of our position in our market place?

Argue through

Starting first with our philosophical base:

■ What are our philosophies and principles?
■ Most importantly, what are our values and beliefs?
■ What sense of meaning do we provide to those who work with us?
■ What is our mission?
■ Finally, what is our vision?

Turning to our strategic base, how do we define and quantify our objectives?

■ In particular how do we intend to optimise upon the *'value stream'* of our business, all our relationships with all our stakeholders?
■ What are our business goals?

- ■ What are the strategies by which we intend to achieve our goals?
- ■ How does this relate to our vision?

It's not a question of worrying too much about brilliantly crafted words. Sir John Harvey Jones[2] is right – if all you end up with is some bullet points on a flip chart or whiteboard, that's good enough initially. What matters is that you have a highly participative argument, involving as many people as possible, and start to reach an understanding and agreement. In a small company this may be enough. In larger companies, it may help to formalise the argument into a series of statements on each issue, which can then be incorporated into a charter.

ADVANTAGE OF A CHARTER

To evolve a written charter can have a number of advantages. It can help to establish more effective relationships with all your stakeholders.
    It can:

- ■ clarify your relationship with your suppliers and dealers;
- ■ become the basis of your psychological contract with every member of your team;
- ■ be shown and become part of the recruitment and induction of new colleagues, and an essential reminder to those you consider promoting;
- ■ become part of your marketing platform, being given, as appropriate, to customers, and being attached to the major quotations or tenders you may need to submit;
- ■ be the basis of your public relations activities; particularly in the community at large.

So it can be of tremendous benefit to set down in writing a succinct explanation of all the ingredients which **drive you and your team to achieve extraordinary performance.** However, several issues need to be borne in mind.

SIX CAUTIONS

1. Credibility

At a Strategic Planning Society conference, Professor Andrew Campbell of Ashridge gave a significant warning. He mentioned the example of a Commissioner of the Metropolitan Police who worked hard to produce an attractively presented, hard covered booklet, setting out what he felt to be the philosophies and principles on which policing should be based. Unfortunately, when the policemen 'on the beat' read it, he lost all credibility.

In their view, it did not relate to the realities of their experience in their day-to-day work. Thereafter his effectiveness as Commissioner was undermined.

2. Participation and ownership

As Bill Quirk of Synopsis Consulting said at the same conference:

There can be no commitment without ownership....
There can be no ownership without participation.

There has to be a high level of participation before people will accept ownership and, until they accept ownership, we cannot expect effective commitment. Sir Peter Thompson of NFC[9] went to a tremendous amount of effort to involve people in every significant decision, in the formulation of his mission statement, and even, at one point, commissioned MORI to do a survey of every shareholder/worker. I like the comments made by Richard Pascale[16] on this issue (see below). There is truly a **no pain, no gain** dimension.

Experience teaches us that an effective statement of vision, values, and guiding principles cannot be hammered out by the public relations staff or the human resources personnel department. Nor do they blossom from crash efforts of an executive task force. Values are truly a 'no pain, no gain' proportion. If top management doesn't agonise over them and regard them as a never-to-be-broken psychological contract between themselves and employees and society, such statements are little more than empty words. But if hewn from discussion and introspection, values come to be internalised as honoured precepts of behaviour. They serve like the North Star – valuable guiding lights that orient an organisation and focus its energies.

A key ingredient in this quest is choice of language. Many well intended efforts to draft statements of vision, values, and guiding principles bog down in platitudes. The same weary words appear: *leadership, superior, teamwork, excellence, highest standards, rate of return.* The challenge is to use fresh language that inspires and connects.

One of the pitfalls awaiting those who craft lofty vision and value statements is that they overreach. Swept away by rhetoric that stresses personal concerns and the company's commitment to society, they ignore the imperative to survival. So doing, they set themselves up to charges of hypocrisy when times get tough and the company's *enacted* behaviour doesn't square with its *espoused* values.

3. Realism

Richard Pascale[16] is right on his last point. There has to be realism. As Jack Welch has said, 'No company can offer security, only customers can.' In one of his Annual Reports he focused on the need for every member of his team to realise that they had to justify themselves by the quality of their contribution. **In our recruitment processes, we make it plain that we want 110 per cent effort from those who join us, and try to discourage those who demonstrate any reluctance at this stage of the processes.**

4. Language

Richard Pascale has a brilliant command of language. As a Professor, he should do. However, I once read that the intellectual age of the average TV addict is equivalent to a 14 year old. The American Army has spent vast sums applying cartoon techniques to its manuals because of the low educational levels of its recruits. Millions read *Sun* and *Mirror* type newspapers which focus on short, simple words, sentences and paragraphs. We have to do the same.

5. Presentation

In *Moments of Truth*[15] Jan Carlzon describes the way in which he revitalised the then loss making SAS airline. A key element in his strategy was to change attitudes. He distributed a little red book entitled *Let's Get In There and Fight* to every one of his executives and team members. This gave, in concise terms, the vision he was striving to achieve. He writes:

> By defusing responsibility and communicating our vision to all employees we were making more demands on them. Anyone who is not given information cannot assume responsibility. But anyone who is, cannot avoid assuming it. Once they understood our vision, our members accepted responsibility enthusiastically which sparked numerous, simultaneous and energetic developments in the company.

The entire company – from the executive suite to the most remote check-in-terminal – was focused on service. As you can see from the illustration on page 215, he used the cartoon format dramatically and effectively.

6. Vibrant

While your values and beliefs should be changed rarely, your mission statement certainly needs to be updated regularly. British Airways and NFC have both changed their statements over time.

But if you do make the effort, it's got to be an on-going activity. It should be part of every recruitment, induction and promotion process. It should be the test of every decision taken. When his colleagues ask him a question about how far they should go to satisfy customers, Mike Snowdon of Snowdon Honda in Paignton refers them to their mission statement.

Examples

Clearly, it is easier to demonstrate the concept with practical examples, so I am very grateful to the senior executives of Hewlett Packard and to Sir Peter Bonfield, when he was Chief Executive of ICL, for giving me permission to reproduce their 'Charters'. As explained, we spent some time at our monthly 'Company Meetings' arguing through our own charter, and while we feel that we can still improve this, you may find it helpful to use as a basis for your own deliberations.

HEWLETT-PACKARD

In 1957, Dave Packard and Bill Hewlett set out in writing the specific commitments they wanted to establish between their company and their employees. They called it 'The HP Way'.

PRINCIPAL OBJECTIVES OF 'THE HP WAY'

1. The commitment to help employees share in the company's success through a generous stock option programme.
2. Job security based on satisfactory performance.
3. Recognition of individual achievement.
4. Maintaining a climate that helps people gain a sense of satisfaction and accomplishment from their work.
5. Fostering initiatives and creativity by allowing individuals freedom of action.

Since then, HP has developed the following strategy:

1. Getting the highest return out of the company's most important asset, its people.
2. Getting the best output from a given technology.
3. Giving the customer the best performance for the price paid.

Members of HP are under no misconception that profit is Hewlett-Packard's number one objective. This is reinforced in a tangible way. Every six months, a proportion of the profits is distributed back to team members. The half year results for one recent year resulted in every team member receiving 7.5 per cent of his or her gross earnings for the previous six months, a significant contribution to income.

Trust, respect and personal dignity are still there, together with the concept of a 'single status' company where team members are encouraged to let management know what they think. The creation of a leaner organisation has sharpened up the Corporation to the need to be more assertive.

One night, a friend was taken into one of the Hewlett-Packard offices. Despite the fact that it had gone 11 pm, the offices were still brightly lit, and there was a fair sprinkling of people working at their consoles. He asked if it was a night shift. 'No', was the reply, 'people work whatever hours are necessary to achieve their objectives.' There can be no finer verdict on the impact which 'The HP Way' has upon the members of the organisation.

The Hewlett-Packard 'Charter' is reproduced on pages 218 to 221.

ICL

Sir Peter Bonfield took over as Chief Executive of ICL at a time of trauma in the British computer industry. It is a tribute to him that ICL remains a major player, albeit a member of the Fujitsu organisation. In giving a 'Key Note' speech to a major conference, Peter Bonfield explained that:

> To develop our organisational capability we needed more than just a structure. We also needed a statement of the type of company we wanted to be – our beliefs and behaviours. This we encapsulated in a booklet called 'The ICL Way'. It is a statement of how managers and (team members) are expected to behave. The ICL Way gave us a basis of a shared vision for what we wanted ICL to be.

In effect, though he does not use the term, it could be described as their 'Charter'. I wish I could reproduce the full text of the speech made by Peter Bonfield to which I have referred. It would make a brilliant case study. Sir Peter Bonfield's key point is that he recognised that '**Our human resources are a prime source of competitive advantage in our fight for market share.**'

ICL's 'Charter' is reproduced on pages 222 to 230.

PRINCIPAL OBJECTIVES OF ICL

Confidence: We had to instil confidence into our people. We needed to devise a system to communicate to all our people that change is part of a continuing process and that we would equip them to handle and meet the changing demands. This provided the overall rationale for our major training and education investment based on the realisation that in our business – a global business – our people must be as good as the best of our competitors world-wide. So, not only was there a heavy initial investment in bringing people up to a basic level of competence, but there is an ongoing investment to ensure that they keep pace with the best of our competitors.

Strategic vision: We need to get [our people] to see their activities in the context of our international competitors and not to compare themselves with internal standards and colleagues, not, indeed, just to guess how they had done the previous year. To achieve this strategic vision we set up a programme of intensive education and training of the top 200 executives, starting with the Board, using a team of external world class academics, the best we could find, including Rosabeth Moss Kanter.

Marketing skills: To be a market-led company, we clearly needed to understand marketing and have marketing skills widely spread throughout the company.

Core training: We developed a series of training modules for executives at different levels within the organisation designed to support the organisation we needed to be. And, specifically, ICL's business strategies.
We also have another major cultural training programme for all [colleagues] based on quality of the way of life – all our people are involved.

Managing for performance: I have placed intense focus on a 'Managing for Performance' programme. An intense focus on the objective setting, appraisal, and counselling role [plus] a much more focused linkage between individual performance and individual pay progression.

The whole system depends on the successful and comprehensive implementation of the appraisal process. To ensure implementation we had to come up with some different approaches which focused managers' minds on the fact that the appraisal system is a vital tool in managing people.

Sir Peter Bonfield, Chief Executive ICL

SEWELLS INTERNATIONAL

As explained we have been arguing through the creation of our own Company Charter (shown later). Some of the headings àre:

- We need you
- We will demonstrate our commitment to you
- You will be important
- You will be appreciated
- We will want you to stay
- You will be developed
- You will not be 'thrown in at the deep end'
- You will know where you stand
- You will be an individual

But we make it clear that, in return, we expect total commitment.

CONCLUSION

Let's go back to the opening questions. Why should you expect:

■ *extraordinary* performance from your people;
■ *extraordinary* loyalty from your customers; and
■ *extraordinary* support from all your other stakeholders?

The answer must be because you have transformed your organisation by the quality of your leadership, by optimising every ingredient we have discussed.

But, you won't reap the rewards you deserve unless you project your achievements effectively. In a small company, you may be able to do this with some bullet points on a flip chart or whiteboard, but I suggest that as you grow, you will need to formalise a 'Company Charter'.

So, as Jan Carlzon put it in his booklet:

'LET'S GET IN THERE AND FIGHT'

Figure 12.1 'Let's get in there and fight!'

You might like to use the following questionnaire as a basis for discussing your priority attention areas.

Marking	
Untrue	1
Partially True	2
True	3

'Transformational' leadership. "We have trust and confidence in your expertise and commitment. We will share information on our vision, goals and performance to enable you to gain satisfaction and recognition from making a meaningful contribution to our team's success."

	Clear 'vision' of worthwhile future.
	Relations with suppliers, 'members', dealers, customers, shareholders, community viewed as mutually inter-dependent.
	Leaders encourage everyone to contribute ideas and information including formal 'brainstorms' to benefit from collective knowledge.
	Clear objectives, strategies and goals evolved collectively, communicated clearly and cascaded down the organisation so every team and individual knows the goals which they must achieve if the organisation is to be successful.
	Organisation designed to enable teams to perform effectively in co-operation with one another with project teams from every level and activity to ensure integrated approach to all issues. Great attention given to attitudes and competencies required if organisation is to be successful.
	Tremendous time and effort devoted to all aspects of recruitment, induction, promotion and, particularly, appraisal to optimise everyone's performance with demotion or dismissal applied if necessary.
	'On the job' coaching a way of life, supported by careful analysis of training needs if organisation is to achieve its goals, to establish long term integrated approach to developing all relevant educational skills and attitude competencies based on common approach to goal achievement.
	Motivation based on setting demanding targets, providing necessary degree of support and showing genuine appreciation in recognising every effort to make worthwhile contribution to goals.
	Communication based on philosophy that those without information cannot take responsibility, those given information cannot avoid taking responsibility. Teams and individuals receiving information they need to establish and achieve their own goals by understanding the contribution this will make to the organisation's goals.
	Leadership is recognised as existing at every level of the organisation. Front-line workers expected to show leadership in achieving their goals. Middle line executives see their role as supporting, coaching, facilitating and encouraging the front-line.
	Leader gains consensus involving and sustaining superior organisation based on 'superior phliosophies' and transforms performance by communicating his or her vision of an organisation, making a meaningful contribution to society and building a culture of pride in everyone, thus contributing to the successful achievement of the vision.
	TOTAL SCORE
33	TOTAL POSSIBLE

Figure 12.2 Questionnaire

BRAINSTORMING EXERCISES OR PROJECTS: 12

Your Charter for Success

■ Do you have a formal, or informal 'Charter' which projects your vision, helps to win the hearts and minds of every member of your team, and creates the right perceptions in your market place? If not, how do you recommend that you set about establishing such a Charter?

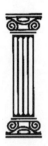
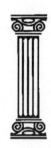

COMPANY CHARTER

Hewlett Packard: The HP Way

Organisational Values

HP's values are a set of deeply held beliefs that govern and guide our behaviour in meeting our objectives and in dealing with each other, our customers, shareholders and others.

- **We have trust and respect for individuals.** We approach each situation with the understanding that people want to do a good job and will do so, given the proper tools, and support. We attract highly capable, innovative people and recognise their efforts and contributions to the company. HP people contribute enthusiastically and share in the success that they make possible.
- **We focus on a high level of achievement and contribution.** Our customers expect HP products and services to be of the highest quality and to provide lasting value. To achieve this, all HP people, but especially managers, must be leaders who generate enthusiasm and respond with extra effort to meet customers needs. Techniques and management practices which are effective today may be outdated in the future. For us to remain at the forefront in all our activities, people should always be looking for new and better ways to do their work.

'The principles of the HP way are still the basis for how we operate.' John Young, 1988

- **We conduct our business with uncompromising integrity.** We expect HP people to be open and honest in their dealings to earn the trust and loyalty of others. People at every level are expected to adhere to the highest standards of business ethics and must understand that anything less is totally unacceptable. As a practical matter, ethical conduct cannot be assured by written HP policies and codes; it must be an integral part of the organisation, a deeply ingrained tradition that is passed from one generation of employees to another.

■ **We achieve our common objectives through teamwork.** We recognise that it is only through effective co-operation within and among organisations that we can achieve our goals. Our commitment is to work as a world-wide team to fulfil the expectations of our customers, shareholders and others who depend upon us. The benefits and obligations of doing business are shared among all HP people.

■ **We encourage flexibility and innovation.** We create a work environment which supports the diversity of our people and their ideas. We strive for overall objectives which are clearly stated and agreed upon, and allow people flexibility in working toward goals in ways which they help determine are best for the organisation. HP people should personally accept responsibility and be encouraged to upgrade their skills and capabilities through ongoing training and development. This is especially important in a technical business where the rate of progress is rapid and where people are expected to adapt to change.

Corporate Objectives

HP's corporate objectives are guiding principles for all decision-making by HP people.

Profits	To achieve sufficient profit to finance our company growth and to provide the resources we need to achieve our other corporate objectives.
Customers	To provide products and services of the highest quality and the greatest possible value to our customers, thereby gaining and holding their respect and loyalty.
Fields of Interest	To participate in those fields of interest that build upon our technology and customer base, that offer opportunities for continuing growth, and that enables us to make a needed and profitable contribution.
Growth	To let our growth be limited only by our profits and our ability to develop and produce innovative products that satisfy real customer needs.
Our People	To help HP people share in the company's success which they make possible; to provide employment security based on their performance; to ensure them a safe and pleasant work environment; to recognise their individual achievements; and to help them gain a sense of satisfaction and accomplishment from their work.

Management   To foster initiative and creativity by allowing the individual great freedom of action in attaining well-defined objectives.

Citizenship   To honour our obligations to society by being an economic, intellectual and social asset to each nation and each community in which we operate.

'Improvement is accomplished by better methods, better techniques, better machinery and equipment and by people continually finding better ways of doing their jobs and to work together as a team. I will never see the day when there is not yet room for improvement.'

Strategies and Practices

HP's values and objectives guide us in forming our strategies and practices and in managing a dynamic business in a changing world.

Management by Wandering Around: An informal HP practice which involves keeping up to date with individuals and activities around the entity through informal or structured communication. Trust and respect for individuals are apparent when MBWA is used to recognise employees' contributions and to listen to employees' concerns and ideas.

MBWA Might Look Like: A manager consistently reserving time to walk through the department or to be available for impromptu discussions.

Individuals networking across the organisation.

Coffee talks, communication lunches, hallway conversations.

"The HP way, when you really come down to it, is respecting the integrity of the individual." Bill Hewlett, 1987

Management By Objectives HP's practice of participative management. Individuals at each level contribute to company goals by developing objectives which are integrated with their manager's and those of other parts of HP.

	Flexibility and innovation in recognising that alternative approaches to meeting objectives provide effective means of meeting customer needs.
MBO is Reflected In:	Written plans which can be traced through the organisation. Co-ordinated and complementary efforts, and cross-organisational integration. Shared plans and objectives.
Open Door Policy	The assurance that no adverse consequences should result from responsibly raising issues with management or personnel. Trust and integrity are important parts of the Open Door Policy.
Open Door May be Used	To share feelings and frustrations in a constructive manner. Gain clearer understanding of alternatives. To discuss career options, business conduct, communication breakdowns.
Total Quality Control	A management philosophy and operating methodology to improve quality and achieve customer satisfaction. TQC efforts to offer the best possible products and services to our customers are supported by our value of achievement and contribution.
TQC Encourages:	Continuous process improvement using scientific methods. Universal participation in quality and customer satisfaction. Meeting or exceeding internal and external customer expectations.

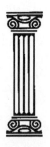

COMPANY CHARTER

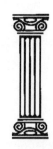

The ICL Way

What is the 'ICL WAY'?

First, it's an attitude to business. Second, it's an attitude to people.

Our attitude to business arises from our determination to succeed in the international marketplace by applying information technology to provide high-value customer solutions for improved operational and management effectiveness. Our acceptance of that challenge places certain distinct commitments on all employees and managers – commitments which are essential strands in the ICL WAY.

Our attitude to people is created by the fact that we are in a knowledge industry. Our business success will therefore be led by people first and products second. We are no longer mainly selling boxes of computer equipment. We are mainly selling creative solutions to business problems. If we are to be successful, to excel in all we do, to win rather than merely compete, then the full capabilities of all ICL people must be realised and released into action. That is the business of our managers, who are expected to cultivate employees' skills continuously and systematically.

The ICL WAY therefore consists of:

- **Seven basic commitments** expected of every man and woman in the company.
- **Ten Management obligations** laid equally upon every manager for the full development and application of our business strategies and personal skills.

The following spells out these commitments and obligations as simple and practically as possible for the guidance of everyone in the company.

By following them with consistency and determination we shall create and 'everybody wins' pattern of growth and success, providing good results for the company and a rewarding and satisfying working life for everyone in it.

Commitment to Change

Every part of our business has changed, is changing and will continue to change.

We no longer sell just boxes and products. Instead, we sell business solutions, consultancy services, knowledge and creative thought.

We must be able to manufacture flexibility, providing systems which reflect the constantly changing needs of our customers.

In these and many other ways our business has been fundamentally affected by change in the last few years.

Success in our company now depends on each individual's willingness to accept change as something valuable, something to be welcomed, something to be responded to with energy and resourcefulness.

Our business is change. Our opportunities arise from change. To succeed in today's markets, we have to predict, manage and exploit changes in technology, in software, in manufacturing techniques, in marketing and selling. Therefore ICL managers and employees have to be able to respond fast and effectively to all the risks and challenges of change, and to adopt new attitudes and practices willingly and creatively whenever the situation demands.

'Adapt to Succeed'. That's not just an empty catch-phrase. For our company and everyone in it, it's now an everyday fact of business life; the ability and willingness to adapt is now essential to us all, simply because no risk plus no change equals no business.

Commitment to Customers

Our business objective is to apply information technology to provide high-value, high volume solutions to customer problems. That is now the driving aim of the entire company and everyone in it.

We cannot begin to achieve that aim until all our thinking is directed towards the marketplace, towards developments that are taking place in the marketplace, and towards the evolving business needs of our customers. Only by concentrating on these can we anticipate and plan the integration of future technology and future market needs. And only then can we set in motion our own programmes to meet those needs with brilliantly conceived solutions and the finest possible service.

The overriding importance of the needs and expectations of our customers should condition all our thinking and govern all our planning. We are now a company driven by the business needs of our market. We all have to become steeped in the concept that 'there is nothing too good for our customers'.

We owe them 100 per cent quality, 100 per cent reliability and 100 per cent service. Our 'zero defects' standards illustrate this commitment to our customers. We cannot be satisfied with less.

All work units within the company also have to adopt the same attitude towards their in-house 'customers'. Staff people towards their field customers; development divisions towards the sales force that will market intelligence; these too should adopt an attitude of 100 per cent service.

The customer matters most, and comes first in everything we do. We must never allow our own problems to distract us from understanding and solving his.

Commitment to Excellence

ICL's sights are now set on world success. That demands excellence in everything we undertake. And excellence will be achieved only by adopting 'can do' attitudes and the highest levels of co-operation and team-work right through the company.

Yes, we can build systems that are outstandingly reliable, easy to use and economical to service; systems that can plug in and perform with minimum start-up time.

Yes, we can enable our customers to eliminate unnecessary computing complexities and to treat their ICL systems as a solid, hard-working, non-temperamental piece of office equipment.

Yes, we can deliver business results which are not just better than we as a company achieved last year, but which are better than the best in the market.

Excellence is an attitude which never accepts second best, never overlooks a need, never allows an opportunity to slip. It is also an attitude which recognises the complex nature of our business and the need for team-work and integration. 'Can help' is as important as 'Can do' , and our commitment to each other is an essential part of our commitment to excellence.

Every new task demands that we set and agree standards of excellence, define the ways in which those standards are to be met, and then go on to achieve them without compromise.

Only by doing that day in, day out, can we expect to make real progress as individuals or as a company in the highly competitive world markets of the future.

Commitment to Team-Work

Team-work is vital to ICL, simply because it improves our performance in two crucial ways.

First, we are under constant pressure to raise the levels of skill and resourcefulness that we offer our customers. Team-work helps us to raise our individual standards by sharing talent and by improving each other's creative performance.

Second, our business is now so integrated that no individual can look after every aspect of a major task unaided. We have to work closely with others in order to harness all the skills the job requires.

Even when formal team structures are absent, we have to get into the way of talking to each other and working together whenever it would improve individual performance to do so.

Effective team-work produces results which are far superior to anything the individuals concerned could achieve working in isolation. To secure this 1 + 1 = 3 return, our team-work must be based on the need to heighten the capabilities, competence and contribution of each individual. ICL wants all its employees to express their opinions, to challenge the illogical, to suggest better ways of doing things – and we expect managers to respond positively when they do.

ICL accepts its obligations as a company to provide individuals with a high degree of freedom to do their job and to develop their own individuality and contribution to the full, within the context of real achievement through team-work and co-operation.

Commitment to Achievement

ICL is an achievement company. Recognition, rewards, promotion and opportunities for career and job development depend absolutely on results delivered.

Performance is the way forward – for every individual and for the company as a whole. It is therefore vitally important that every individual has a clear understanding of his or her work objectives and responsibilities, because performance will be measured against them. It's down to managers to make sure that those objectives and responsibilities provide maximum opportunity for the development of individual talent and to operate the company's recognition and reward systems on their achievement.

Achievement in ICL does not merely mean crude numbers. It isn't just volume of sales, for example, or manufacturing through-puts. We care just as much about the quality of the sales, the standard of the manufactured products.

All employees are asked to find ways of adding value by eliminating low-value tasks. Qualitative objectives help us to ensure that the time spent on a task is consistent with the value that will result; for we can no longer afford to spend excessive time on low-value activities.

We therefore have to define the criteria for the success of any new task before starting work, and also define the steps which will enable us to meet those criteria as time efficiently as possible.

Outstanding performance on a low-value task is a waste of talent and represents poor achievement. Outstanding performance on a high-value task is high achievement and contributes to real progress for all concerned. That's the difference.

Commitment to People Development

Our commitment to achievement demands a commitment to develop our skills and abilities in every possible way.

We are a people company. Our main strength lies in the quality and skill of the people who work here. So real progress will come about only by constantly developing and improving our skills. Development of this kind – people development – is one of the basic requirements for business success.

The company will constantly aim to provide you with responsibilities and objectives which measure up to your abilities and ambitions – and ideally stretch them a little too. The company is determined to satisfy your need for personal growth and job satisfaction, and to create the supportive environment which enables you to achieve them.

However, individuals have to make a good deal of the running. The most rewarding development is self-development and employees are expected to help themselves by pushing their managers for guidance, for opportunities, for appropriate formal training and for new kinds of work experience.

The opportunities are all there within the company, but it's up to individuals to seize them and to respond flexibly when new demands are made on them. Real growth will come to those who are willing to adapt, to learn, to enlarge their horizons and to tackle new challenges. We have to think for ourselves, find our own chances and set clear objectives for our own personal development.

Managers carry a corresponding obligation to respond to and encourage employees in every possible way, for the company's success in the future is closely bound up with the success and personal growth of everyone working in it.

Commitment to Creating a Productivity Showcase

Would you be proud to invite prospective customers in to see how you do things in your job? Do you have demonstrations there of leading-edge applications of our own information technology? Is your department a productivity showcase for the company's skills and products?

Another fundamental part of our business policy is to make ourselves a showcase for the latest and best applications of information technology. We must be seen as the kind of profitable, efficient, high productivity company that our customers would like to become themselves. We must be able to offer practical, working demonstrations of the finest equipment, systems and business solutions, so that we can more easily go on to sell those solutions in the market place.

Everyone is encouraged to accept innovation, seek improvements, and find ways of applying ICL technology to the problems of their own departments.

All our systems and all aspects of our performance should be of 'showcase' standard – a standard which gives customers something to strive for. It will also keep us constantly on our toes as we strive to improve our own use of information technology solutions.

The showcase attitude means that we should always be ready to open our doors and say to the world: 'Come in; look; see how it should be done; this is how technology and talent can work together to create the finest business solutions; this is the ICL WAY, the way of excellence, the way of innovation, the only way we know.'

Once this attitude has taken root and found practical expression in every division and every department of the company, we shall have something solid and truly valuable to show and sell to the world at large.

The Ten Obligations of the ICL Manager

The commitments of the ICL way will happen only if we make them happen. As we said in the introduction, their implementation rests to a large degree on ten management obligations.

The ICL manager is accountable for creating and maintaining a business environment which supports and translates into practice the attitudes expressed in the seven commitments.

These ten obligations are an integral part of every manager's job. They will play a major part in the assessment of successful management performance in ICL.

1. Business Manager: People Manager

ICL managers must meet the challenge of being effective business (operations) managers and effective people managers.

Management success in ICL is about optimising results not just achieving targets. It is an ICL belief that unless a manager is an effective people manager, his business results must fall short of the maximum attainable.

In our industry in particular managers must understand that profits are made by people, not by products. Consequently they must effectively manage, invest in and develop their people if they and ICL are to enjoy long-term success.

2. Direction

Managers must have detailed knowledge of ICL's objectives and strategies. They must understand them in relation to the Information Processing industry, to our competitors, customers and products.

These objectives and strategies must be effectively communicated to all employees. They must provide the basis for determining sub-unit objectives and work priorities. All employees must clearly understand their individual responsibilities and the standards required for the successful completion of tasks.

The performance of all staff must be regularly assessed by way of reviews, formal performance appraisals and informal one-on-one discussions. These two-way assessment processes help to maintain standards and to encourage adaptability in our ever changing business environment.

3. Strategic Thinking

The greatest challenge facing managers arises from their responsibility for identifying changing long-term business needs and for planning effectively to meet them. In our industry in particular, predicting, managing and exploiting change are key demands calling for foresight, judgement and leadership of the highest order.

Managers are expected continually to identify future opportunities, to monitor and communicate risks, and to take corrective action to avoid excessive exposure.

By analysing the critical long-term issues which confront the business, a manager can establish for his team a clear vision of the future. He can also develop the strategies upon which that future will be secured.

4. High-Value Outputs

Achievement in ICL is about output, not input or effort. More specifically it means high-value output . . . output that creates a demonstrable inpact on our business results.

ICL managers must ensure that the work tasks and actions of their staff reflect this basic principle. Managers are obliged to identify and eliminate sub-standard performance and ineffective work situations. High performance of a low-value job provides a poor return for the individual and the company.

5. Team-Work

Success in a knowledge industry such as ours depends upon an effective sharing of the talent we have in the company.

Through their leadership, ICL's managers must stimulate team-work as a means of obtaining better results. Team-work is achieved by developing individual talents, building on the ideas and know how of the team and gaining commitment by way of listening, involving and communicating.

Leading by example, being seen, being involved, providing common understanding and direction are essential elements of a manager's role in developing the co-operative team-work attitudes which are essential to obtaining the best results.

6. Development

The achievements of a manager are dependent on the achievements of those for whom he is responsible.

ICL is committed to developing its employees to the full extent of their potential. Managers must first ensure that optimum use is being made of current skills and that individuals are given tasks which 'stretch' them in their existing jobs. They must then agree development and career progression plans with their staff and rigorously monitor the implementation of those plans to make sure they are effective. International and inter-divisional opportunities must be considered as a way of accelerating career and personal development.

ICL can offer almost unlimited job opportunities. It is the manager's task to match the needs of the business with those of the employee in order to stimulate the fastest possible growth for both.

7. 'Can do' Attitude

ICL managers are required to set the pace and lead by example. Their 'Can do' attitude to tackling tasks must be infectious, influencing others to adopt the same willingness and positive approach.

The successful manager thinks in terms of opportunities rather than problems, uses his initiative to pick up 'loose balls' and willingly volunteers relevant skills to help others to achieve their objectives. When a commitment is made it is invariably carried through.

Such an attitude is essential if we are to meet the challenging, constantly changing demands of our industry.

8. Innovation

Innovation is the key to managing change and to meeting our commitment to excellence, Managers must consciously strive for improvements in their personal and work unit performance

They must exploit modern management techniques and information technology as ways of eliminating low-value tasks and increasing output of high-value activities.

It is the manager's obligation to set the framework for creativity . . . a clear understanding of the need; freedom to challenge the traditional and try out new ideas; and encouragement provided by a supportive team-work environment.

9. Difficult Issues

Recognising difficult issues and facing up to them quickly is a basic obligation, essential to every effective manager. By openly and constructively discussing problems as soon as they arise a manager can dramatically reduce the risk of negative impact and more severe long-term effects.

To ignore or hide problems is poor management; the ICL WAY is to confront and resolve them.

The effective manager walks his office and workshops, talks frankly with his people, listens, counsels, communicates, understands; he is able to eliminate problems before they can do us harm.

Positive action of this kind creates the atmosphere of openness and trust necessary for an enjoyable and productive work environment.

10. Self Measurement

High performance objectives will be realised only if accompanied by an equally strong commitment to self-assessment. Managers must continually challenge and appraise their own management actions and the way they as individuals, and their work units, contribute to the business results.

A manager must measure his own effectiveness as a people manager, for his ability to provide leadership is particularly important. Time must be allocated to people management in order to create the balance of attitudes, commitments and business effectiveness which constitutes the ICL WAY.

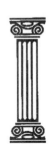

SEWELL'S COLLEAGUES' CHARTER

OUR CULTURE

Our culture relates to the way in which we will deal with everyone who comes into contact with our company; recognising that these relationships depend on the reactions of every member of our team.

Customers

Every colleague is expected to appreciate that 'customers really do come first'.

Every customer, or their representative, will be treated in a friendly, courteous manner and with the utmost of integrity, and – should we fall down in any way – the justified complaints of customers will be resolved expeditiously and honourably. We will always put ourselves out for our customers. We will make it simple for them to deal with us. We will ensure that we respond immediately to any request and no customer should ever need to ask us a second time for our help.

Confidentiality: Where clients and subscribers give us confidential information, we will honour the basis on which the information is given to us.

Our Company has only one purpose, one objective. It is to identify, attract, satisfy and retain an increasing number of customers profitably.

Colleagues in our marketing and database activities are helping to identify customers.

Colleagues in our sales activities are helping to attract and retain customers.

Colleagues in our research and library activities are helping to satisfy customers by the quality of the information that they receive. But equally, colleagues in accounting, administration, mailing and despatch activities are helping to satisfy customers by ensuring that they receive their services promptly, with hassle-free administration.

Finally, the quality of the information produced and the level of pleasantness which we can achieve in all our relationships with all our customers, will help not only to retain them, but to ensure they recommend our services to their friends.

We recognise that some of our colleagues may have chosen to work in an administrative role because they are shy. However, all that we require is for colleagues to be pleasant and friendly and, where appropriate, to ensure that a customer's needs are met by a qualified colleague. We are prepared to arrange for individual training, while relationships with customers will be discussed at our regular monthly colleagues' meeting.

Suppliers

Vital 'partners': We cannot sell right, unless we buy right, therefore suppliers are equally important 'partners' in the success of our company.

In particular, we already make extensive use of information technology, so it is vital that we build relationships which ensure that we keep abreast of any technology which can help us to enhance the quality of the services we provide to our customers.

So, every colleague will go out of their way to establish friendly relationships with suppliers and deal with them in a courteous and ethical manner.

Any problem between the company and its suppliers will be raised immediately, in a positive, constructive manner, and resolved to the mutual benefit of both parties. Credit terms and other trading relationships will be honoured and any variations in the agreement which become necessary, will be resolved by discussion.

All relationships

Every colleague should recognise that all relationships are important, including, the community in which we are based, and the industry in which we operate. Everyone can make a real contribution to our success by being open, friendly, helpful and courteous to everyone with whom they come into contact.

COLLEAGUES' CHARTER

Our commitment to you

We need you: Our Company will not succeed unless it has the right, dedicated team of colleagues. It is the sum total of the contributions from each individual in every department which will make our company successful.

Two-way commitment: We recognise that this involves a two-way commitment. If you are going to give our customers, your colleagues, and thus our company a 110 per cent commitment, then we have to be equally committed to you.

You will be important: You will be an important member of our team doing a worthwhile, vital job. Your colleagues, and our company will depend on the commitment with which you apply yourself to the 'key tasks' assigned to you.

You will be appreciated: You will be appreciated, and thanked whenever you do a good job, make an extra effort, or come up with an idea. You may even get the occasional present of a bottle of wine, a box of chocolates, or a drink at the pub to show our appreciation of that little extra effort.

We feel that as the person carrying out the particular duties under your control, you are the expert. We shall consult if any other activity infringes upon you, and – as the expert concerned – we will look to you to make recommendations about how the tasks for which you are responsible could be simplified or improved.

You will be an individual: We use first names throughout our company. On your birthday, you will receive a card signed by all your colleagues and we will have a small get-together to present you with a birthday present.

At Christmas, we will have a party to which you, and your partner, will be invited.

If you have any personal problems, we will do our best to help and support you.

You will be a colleague: As a colleague you will be treated as an 'equal' with the quality of your contribution the only basis on which you will be assessed. Your 'status' will depend on the level of responsibility you accept.

You will be developed: We will do our best to develop your confidence and self-esteem and, also, to help you to improve your competence.

In addition to our in-company discussions and development activities, we will consider seriously any request, from any colleague, for any training which they feel will either help them to carry out their existing duties more effectively, or to assume greater responsibilities. We will consider, for example:

■ Paying for one subscription to an appropriate professional or vocational association.

■ Paying for a subscription to an appropriate trade or professional magazine (in which case, we will expect the colleague concerned to draw our attention to any interesting articles which we might be able to quote in our own publications).

- Making a loan to pay for a correspondence course or set of evening classes, aiming at a particular examination on a basis that the loan will be written-off by us once the programme of study has been completed.
- Sending colleagues to trade and similar exhibitions which will extend their awareness of products and services which may be of benefit to them in their work.
- Giving serious consideration to sending a colleague on an appropriate external training course or courses.
- Sponsoring a colleague for an appropriate long-term programme of study leading to a recognised qualification on the basis that, while the bulk of the study will be carried out in the colleague's own time, the company will be helpful in making allowances for the time being spent in this way.

You will not be 'thrown in at the deep end': The fact that you are reading this company manual is an indication of our commitment to making sure that you understand what is expected of you, and the environment within which you will be expected to work.

You will be given every assistance to ensure that you understand what we expect from you, and how we expect you to contribute.

Your 'key tasks': In particular, your job will be explained fully to you, and you will be given, in writing, the two or three 'key tasks' together with the performance standards relating to these tasks on which your contribution to our company will be judged.

You will know where you stand: We feel it important that every colleague should have the opportunity of knowing, on a regular basis, where they stand with our company. It is important for you to have a regular opportunity of a frank, open, and undisturbed discussion with your immediate superior. Therefore, once every four months an appraisal meeting will be held between you and your immediate superior. This discussion will be based on the following points.

- What were your three main achievements in the previous four months?
- What successes, or difficulties, did you experience in seeking to achieve your key tasks?
- Do you feel that your superior was as helpful as possible in assisting you to achieve your key task, or did he or she inadvertently fail to provide you with all the help you needed?
- Have you introduced any improvements in the way in which you achieve your key tasks, or do you have any ideas for improvements which you would like your superior to support?
- Where relevant, how would you rate the performance of those reporting to you, and how far have you been able to help all those reporting to you to progress and develop? How many are now ready for promotion?
- What do you regard as being your three most important tasks in the next four months?

- How will you measure your success in achieving these tasks?
- What aspect of your work interests you the most (because you feel more confident and competent), or the least (perhaps because you feel a lack of confidence or competence)?
- Are there any areas of your job in which you could improve your performance? If so, what action do you need to take to achieve these improvements, or what help or additional resources do you need from your superior, or the company?
- Do you feel that your present job fully utilises your abilities, training and interests? If not, which of your abilities could be used more fully? Would your job have to be changed; and what benefits would result from such a change?
- Looking to the future, what kind of work would you like to be doing within the next few years. Perhaps with a more responsible position, or something entirely different such as ...?
- If you would like a more responsible job, or something different, what steps have you or could you take to equip yourself for such a job, and what additional training and help do you feel you would require?

The intention is to provide you with a regular opportunity for a frank, two-way discussion with your immediate superior with a few simple objectives:

- To praise you, and to thank you for the things you have done well.
- To help resolve any areas where we can be more effective in the support we give you.
- To help you derive greater satisfaction from feeling that you are going to be helped to make progress and thus enhance your contribution to your team's success.

We will want you to stay: If you are doing a good job on our behalf, we will want you to stay. If for any reason there are issues which you feel that you cannot raise with your immediate superior, you can talk in confidence to his or her immediate superior.

However, we recognise that, as a small company, we may not be able to offer you the longer term career progression which your talents deserve.

This will probably emerge at your regular Appraisal Interview. In this event, we will work with you to agree upon your future career, and do our utmost to help you with introductions and recommendations to find a posting which will give you the prospects you wish.

Salary: We undertake to do our best to pay you a fair and realistic salary which, as far as possible, will be equal to, if not above, the 'going rate' for the job in the area, or in your profession.

This will be transferred by credit transfer into your own bank account not later than the last Thursday of every month.

Your salary will be reviewed on 1 July each year.

We hope that, on the basis of your three appraisal interviews, the commitment you have demonstrated, and the extent to which you have achieved or exceeded your key tasks, we will be able to show our appreciation by an appropriate increase.

Merit reviews: In addition to your annual review, if you are seen to be putting in an above-average effort, resulting in above-average results, you will be eligible for a 'merit' review to show our appreciation for your efforts which could result in an increase in salary, or an appropriate bonus or present.

Profit scheme: You will be eligible to join our Profit Scheme which is based on the extent to which we achieve or exceed our monthly income targets. These figures will be discussed at our monthly company meetings, so that every colleague can understand how gaining and retaining customers impacts on our profitability.

Additional benefits: In addition to the foregoing, after one year of committed service, your total remuneration package will be reviewed with you. Depending on your personal circumstances, and your level of contribution to our company, consideration will be given to:

- A contribution, on your behalf, into a pension fund of 2 per cent of your salary.
- Inclusion into our private medical, BUPA scheme.
- Inclusion in a permanent sickness scheme, and 'death on service' policy.

Holidays: In addition to statutory holidays, every full-time colleague has a holiday entitlement running at the rate of one and two-thirds day's holiday for every completed month of service, making an annual total of 20 days.

Your commitment to our company

110 per cent effort: We need your contribution to the success of our company, and your contribution is only going to be fully effective, if you make a 110 per cent effort.

Quality of contribution: As mentioned earlier, we operate on the basis of being a team of equals (with varying levels of responsibility), where the quality of the contribution being made by our colleagues is all that matters.

Stressful responsibility: We accept that our approach may have a certain level of extra stress. We expect every colleague to accept total responsibility to think through every implication of what they are doing and, most importantly, to accept 'ownership' of any problems or potential problems, and comment constructively on how you can improve your contribution.

It will be particularly for you to liaise with all the other departments in our company upon whom your work may have any impact by communicating any information which would help them carry out their work more effectively.

Open style: To provide the support needed by colleagues, a totally open style of management will be adopted throughout the company and – in particular – by everyone in a supervisory or management position.

A weekly senior management meeting will be held to resolve day-to-day tactical issues and the senior managers present at this meeting will then report back to their own departments to keep them fully informed.

A monthly meeting will be held with every colleague present. (We will employ a 'temp' to man the switchboard.) At these monthly meetings, all colleagues will be briefed fully on how far we are succeeding in achieving our objectives; particular on key issues such as customer retention and new business conversions.

These monthly meetings will also be devoted to training sessions on subjects of interest to every colleague.

Responsibility for development: We expect you to accept total responsibility for seeking to develop your confidence and competence in the way you carry out your work, and thus be able to improve the quality of your contribution to our success to gain promotion.

We expect everyone in a supervisory position to recognise that their 'key task' is to develop those colleagues for whom they are responsible. Everyone in a supervisory position will be judged on how well they develop people, and thus prove themselves worthy of further promotion.

Assertiveness: We expect you and every colleague to be assertive. We expect you and every colleague to have enough confidence in yourself to be positive, while at the same time understanding other people's points of view. It means being able to behave in a rational and adult way. It means being able to negotiate and reach workable compromises. Above all, it means having self respect for oneself, plus respect for your colleagues.

As one example, if overloaded with work, don't build up resentment and eventually 'blow a fuse'. Discuss the problem openly and honestly with your immediate superior, ideally coming up with positive and constructive ideas on how the problem might best be minimised.

(Note: one meeting of all our colleagues was devoted to a training session on assertiveness, and the subject will be covered again in future meetings.)

Admitting mistakes: In many organisations there is a 'conspiracy of silence' so that mistakes are hidden from more senior management. It is said that we all 'learn from experience' but this experience is gained by making mistakes.

You *are* likely to make mistakes from time to time. You will not be criticised for making a genuine mistake, or misunderstanding a particular issue, but it will be regarded as a serious breach of contract for you, or any other colleague, not to immediately own up to the mistake or understanding and to ensure that the consequences are minimised as quickly as possible.

It will be regarded as a breach of your contract if, at any time, you deliberately withhold any information from management which is relevant to exploiting opportunities, resolving threats, or is in any way relevant to the smooth, successful running of our company.

Vigorous debate: Nobody has a monopoly of good ideas. As indicated earlier, you are likely to have the most expert understanding of what is involved in your own special contribution to our company. We expect you to take responsibility for striving to take advantage of every possible area of improvement which will improve the quality of your contribution, or to draw attention to anything which could be done by others which would help you to improve the quality of your contribution.

In short, you and every colleague has a responsibility to put forward any idea which you feel can help our company, and equally, has the responsibility to criticise constructively anything which you deem to be hindering company progress.

Provided these constructive criticisms are put forward with sensitivity to the feelings of others, they should be made without fear, since everyone must accept that they are being made in the best interests of our company.

There is seldom 'one right solution' to the increasingly complex problems facing businesses. We need to be able to argue vigorously about the options open to us, and to select the most favourable after debate, with everyone feeling free to be passionate about the opportunities and threats they may see from different courses of action.

Team spirit: We intend to do our best to encourage an enjoyable working atmosphere proven to encourage a good 'team spirit'.

The most pernicious habit which does most to destroy team morale and spirit is where one colleague fosters animosity, or seeks to create problems for another colleague by criticisms behind that colleague's back. It is your responsibility to sustain team morale and team spirit and to 'shoot down' or report to a senior colleague, anyone creating a 'bad atmosphere'.

(In the unfortunate event that we find a colleague back-biting, gossiping and 'stirring' this will be regarded as a breach of their condition of employment.)

Flexibility: In any team game, everyone has a position. In a football team, there are those who primarily attack and others who defend, but – on occasions – everyone will get involved in defending, and at other times, virtually everyone may be thrown forward into an attack.

Similarly, while you have a defined position, we expect you and every other member of our team to be totally flexible. For example, even if your work does not normally involve answering the telephone and dealing with customer queries, if you hear the phone being unanswered, it will be your responsibility to answer the phone and deal with the caller or, if you can't, to ensure that you get all the information needed so that you can brief one of your colleagues to return the call.

If we have a particular problem, we expect you and everyone else to rally round and, if necessary, adjust your own working arrangements to help to resolve the problem.

We are a small, highly reactive company. While we have done our best to define the organisation we need to be effective, and the role you must play in this organisation, we need to grow, to react to the market place, and to take advantage of advances in technology. We may therefore need to change your role in our company as you progress with us.

We accept the responsibility to ensure that you are fully aware of, and are trained for any new position. However, we expect you to respond positively when such changes become necessary.

Positive attitude: We expect you, as one of our colleagues, to be totally positive in your attitude to your work, to your colleagues, and to our company. We will regard your approach, your attitude, as of critical importance.

We are seeking to take a totally positive approach by striving to ensure that you can enjoy and derive satisfaction from the contribution you make to the success of our company. However, we must make it plain that every point raised is, in effect, an implied term of your contract of employment with our company.

Evaluating your contribution

Knowing what you are expected to achieve: The only way in which you can make an effective contribution to the success of our company is by understanding what you are expected to achieve. It is therefore our responsibility to agree with you, in writing, your key tasks. It is your responsibility to ensure that you understand these key tasks. Prior to your appraisal interview, you should review thoroughly these key tasks.

Because we are a fast-moving company, it is your responsibility to go to the appraisal meeting with a clear understanding of precisely what may have changed for the better or for the worse, so that you can discuss with your superior the impact of these changes, and agree on any changes needed to your key tasks.

Evaluating your performance: As explained, to help you to improve your contribution, your performance will be evaluated three times a year. This will be done under two headings:

■ Your attitude to customers and colleagues.
■ The competence with which you carry out your duties.

Of the two, we regard attitude as more important, since lack of competence can be improved by training.

Attitude: Your attitude, and the attitude of colleagues, will be marked under the following ten headings:

1. *Customers*: That you handle all customer contacts in a friendly, helpful manner, and that you follow through to ensure that any requests made by the customer, or promises you make to the customers, are honoured, if not by yourself, then by the appropriate colleague.

2. *Colleagues*: That you make a positive contribution to good 'vibes' in our offices by being cheerful, friendly, cooperative and constructive in all relationships with all your colleagues.

3. *Creative*: That you think creatively about your work and show initiative in seeking to improve every aspect of your own duties, particularly where they interreact with those of other colleagues in other departments. In particular, that you are 'forward thinking' seeking to anticipate opportunities which can be exploited, or potential threats which can be minimised.

4. *Assertive*: That you are prepared to contribute in a positive, constructive manner to all discussions with colleagues and at departmental and company meetings and thus demonstrate your commitment to the company and its success. And, above all, to do so on an enthusiastic basis which adds to the enjoyment of those attending the meeting, or working with you.

5. *Responsible*: That you are prepared to act responsibly by accepting 'ownership' of any problems which arise; to admit any mistakes you make and to be conscientious in caring for what is good and in the best interests of our company.

6. *Profitability*: That you are concerned about the profitability of our company and seek every opportunity to gain extra income, or to control costs, even down to the basics of switching off unnecessary lights and not wasting supplies.

7. *Time Management*: That you manage your time effectively, by arriving for work, and returning from lunch on time, do not waste time, are prepared – if necessary – to put in an extra effort, including working late to finish an urgent project: and while communicating effectively with colleagues, do not waste time unnecessarily, nor accept or make personal phone calls in office hours (unless of an emergency nature).

8. *Pride*: That you take pride both in your own personal appearance and in the appearance of your work area, and the furniture, equipment and furnishings of your work area.

9. *Self-improvement*: That you are committed to improving yourself so that you can better carry out your current duties, and also qualify yourself for enhanced responsibilities in the future.

10. *Reliability*: That you are consistent in displaying a positive attitude and approach to all the preceding points so that you are an honest, trustworthy and valued member both on your own immediate team and our company.

Grading for attitude: Your attitude in these ten important areas will be graded as under:

Above expectations 1   Acceptable ½   Unacceptable 0

We expect you and your colleagues to gain full marks under every heading since we are working hard to establish a team with total commitment.

In theory, a mark of five or above would indicate a generally acceptable level of behaviour but, in practice, any point on which only half a mark is given would suggest that your attitude needed boosting.

It will be, frankly, unacceptable if you were to receive a nil mark against any one of these ten points and we would ensure that you received appropriate counselling to establish whether or not there are any personal circumstances giving rise to the unacceptable attitude or attitudes.

(If after investigations, counselling and coaching, attitude were not to improve, then it is unlikely that the person concerned would continue to be a colleague.)

Technical competence: You and every colleague will be given three or four 'key tasks' to achieve. As explained earlier, a key element of your regular appraisal discussion will be:

What have been your three key tasks, and how well have you achieved them?

and

What will be your key tasks in future, and how will you judge whether or not you succeed in achieving them?

Prior to your appraisal, you will be responsible for revising your own 'key tasks'; discussing them with your superior at the meeting; and agreeing with him your revised key tasks.

Grading for competence: It follows that you will be rated primarily on your performance in achieving your 'key tasks'. You will be given one of the following ratings:

Transforms nature of job by total mastery so consistently exceeds in performance of 'key tasks'.	5
Well on top of job, and always achieve key tasks.	4
Reasonably confident, and normally achieves key tasks, but needs further training and support in specific areas.	3
Lacks full confidence/competence and therefore does not always achieve key tasks.	2

Were you to gain only two points, we would need to discuss whether you can come up to standard by further training, coaching and counselling in the hope that you would be able to come up to performance within the next four month appraisal period.

Team membership: No cricket team can afford to include a player whose consistent failures in batting, bowling or fielding lose the team its matches. Similarly, no business team can continue to employ someone who lets down their colleagues.

Even if you were to achieve high scores on your attitude, because you are a 'nice' person, like any other team, we have to achieve results. So, we would not be able to retain any colleague who – by failing to achieve their personal key tasks – was letting down the overall performance of our company.

But, we do accept the responsibility, in such instances, to make sure that we do our utmost to provide training or other support (or even, if it can be done without disrupting the team, a reallocation of duties) before discontinuing team membership for the person concerned.

Collective responsibilities

Individual and collective responsibilities: Within these broad guidelines, it is important that every member of our team is aware of his or her personal contribution. These we will consider shortly.

However, every colleague within our company must accept responsibility to do everything within his or her power to help every activity within the company. The following are merely indicative of the ways in which everyone is expected to exercise their collective responsibility.

Editorial: Anyone who sees an interesting article, or hears an interesting radio or TV item should ensure that their editorial colleagues are aware of it, or give them the relevant information for them to follow through.

Library: Similarly, it would be appreciated greatly if anyone coming across any books, reports or other information likely to be relevant to the library, brings them to the attention of the librarian.

Marketing: Every colleague has the responsibility for helping to identify, attract, satisfy or retain customers, so anyone coming across any form of market intelligence which will better help us to understand our market place should bring it to the attention of their marketing colleagues.

Sales: Every colleague, however introverted, or involved in administrative work, must accept that our company will only succeed if every enquiry is converted into a sale. So, the telephone must be answered promptly, customers must be assured of our interest in meeting their needs, and full details of their query, name, address and telephone number, must be taken down and passed through to the sales department. No colleague must abdicate his or her responsibilities at that point. They must follow through to make sure that the customer does get what he or she wants.

Accounts: Every colleague must ensure that where they supply any product or service, that they inform their accounting colleagues immediately and ensure that they are provided with all the information they need to invoice both promptly and accurately.

Administration: Finally, every colleague has to ensure that they play their part in the smooth administration of our company. By ensuring, for example, that:

■ messages are recorded accurately and received by the person for whom they are intended;

■ inter-departmental paperwork is processed promptly and received by the person responsible for taking further action;

■ all relevant information is punched and filed neatly in clearly labelled files so that another colleague can find the information easily whenever necessary; and

■ all desks, drawers and cupboards are kept equally neatly, again for ease of reference and retrieval of information by colleagues.

Environment: Most of us work hard to keep our homes attractively presented, and spend both time and money on home improvement. Equally, we want to provide an attractive environment within which our colleagues can work, and which our customers can enjoy visiting.

We therefore expect every colleague to treat their work areas, desks, chairs, carpeting and other facilities with the same degree of care as they would extend to their own furniture at home. Where accidents happen they will be reported immediately, so that appropriate action can be taken to clean or repair the resource concerned.

Similarly, every colleague is on trust to ensure that all equipment is always in effective working order, that it is maintained regularly as appropriate, and that failure in the equipment is promptly drawn to the attention of a more senior colleague so that it may be repaired or replaced as appropriate.

Strategic issues: Finally, every colleague who has even the germ of an idea on how our company might be more successful should draw it to the attention of a more senior colleague, or raise it at our monthly colleague meeting, and thus help senior management to devise more effective tactics and strategies to secure overall success.

Collective success: But, we must return to the point that it is the ability of each individual to achieve their key objectives which constitutes to the success of their team, and, by the teams cooperating together to achieve their objectives, our company can be successful.

BUILDING OUR ORGANISATION

Introduction: If we are to build the best organisation, every colleague must be aware of the importance of:

- ■ *Recruiting* new members of our team;
- ■ *Inducting* new colleagues properly;
- ■ *Appraising* existing members of our team;
- ■ *Promoting* from within in a manner which is fair to the person being promoted; and
- ■ *Dismissing* those who after being given every opportunity fail to make the grade.

Recruitment

Important task: Building a successful organisation depends very much on the skill and care with which new colleagues are recruited. Colleagues entrusted with recruitment must recognise that they are being given a very responsible task and they must ensure that they receive enough support and training to carry out the task effectively.

Organisational review: Prior to any new appointment, or to the replacement of an existing colleague, both the department concerned and the senior management team will review the organisational implications, particularly if there is an opportunity of redesigning our organisation so that it is more effective.

Key tasks: Prior to any appointment, key tasks will be prepared (or existing ones revised). This will be discussed thoroughly at both a departmental and a senior management meeting.

Advertisement: If necessary, professional help will be obtained to drawing up an advertisement which sells our company to attract the right applicant, and explains fully the key tasks which the successful applicant will be expected to achieve.

As far as possible, those responding should be set some simple task along the lines of asking them to indicate, in their application, how their previous experience would enable them to contribute effectively to our team.

Preliminary interview: Every application will be acknowledged as a matter of courtesy.

As far as possible, any applicant with potential will be given the courtesy of a preliminary interview. The aim will be to determine their attitude and general suitability against the job description.

Letter from Chairman: Any applicant deemed worthy of being shortlisted will receive a letter from our Chairman. They will be loaned an abridged copy of this company manual for them to decide whether they wish to take their application further.

Shortlist interviews: Anyone who then wishes to proceed will be given a copy of their key tasks.

The interview will then be a mutual discussion on the extent to which each applicant feels qualified to achieve the contribution expected from them.

Only when both the applicant and the interviewer, on our behalf, are satisfied that the applicant has a reasonable probability of being able to achieve the tasks set out, will the process be taken any further.

Staff introduction: Every applicant who reaches the final shortlist will be given a conducted tour of our company, and be introduced to every colleague throughout our company. They will spend some time talking to the colleagues in the department for which they are being recruited. The views of these potential colleagues in the department concerned will be sought as to the likelihood of any applicant settling in well in their department.

Psychological test: Every 'approved' shortlist applicant will be given an appropriate psychological test. The results of the psychological test will be discussed thoroughly before any decision is made on which applicant is to be successful.

Criteria: Those interviewing on behalf of our company must appreciate that to build our company we must recruit high quality staff. Those in a supervisory role must not be deterred from recruiting an applicant they deem to be as good, if not better, than themselves for fear of losing their job. It is only when they recruit somebody able to take over their job, that we will be able to consider that supervisor as available for promotion.

(This does not mean that we should seek to recruit people who do not meet our predetermined 'personality profile'.)

Induction

Vital, first impression: We all appreciate the importance of 'first impressions', so it is vital that new colleagues gain the right first impressions of our company.

Every colleague is therefore expected to play their part in communicating our vision, mission, values and objectives, though we hope that the recruitment process – described above – will have set the scene effectively.

Welcome: It is the responsibility of the new colleague's immediate superior to ensure that they are on hand to greet their new colleague on their first morning. If necessary, they should arrange to arrive earlier than usual to make sure that the new colleague is not kept waiting.

On arrival, they should have an initial chat with their new colleague over a cup of coffee, and familiarise them with the layout of the building and other information which may be deemed helpful.

Company manual: As noted above, each new colleague will be sent their personal copy of our 'Commitment' binder and asked to read this prior to their arrival.

The next stage for the supervisor is to spend as much time as may be necessary in talking the new colleague through the contents of the binder, stressing our vision, mission, goals and culture and making sure that the new colleague appreciates thoroughly all that we are striving to do.

Contribution: Particular attention will be given to that section of our manual which describes the contribution expected from the post which he or she will be occupying, and a thorough discussion will take place on the 'key results' section of his or her job description.

Departmental welcome and introductions: By this time, it would be appropriate to take a coffee break. This is an opportunity for every member of the department to join in a general discussion on the department's mission, followed by each member of the department explaining how they personally contribute towards achieving departmental objectives.

Senior executive welcome: A new colleague will then be taken to meet the most senior executive present on that day. Ideally, he or she should meet the Chairman and Managing Director, but if they are absent, he or she should meet the most senior director present. (The Chairman and Managing Director will always make a point of greeting the new colleague as soon as they return to the office.)

Mentor: Prior to the arrival of any new recruit, and based on the knowledge gained during the interviewing process, a mentor will be appointed for the new colleague concerned. As far as possible, an existing colleague will be chosen who is most likely to be able to form a rapport with the new colleague.

On the first day, it will be the responsibility of the mentor to take the new colleague out for lunch (at the company's expense), and thereafter to continue to help in every way possible to ensure that he or she settles down well in our company.

Initial training: After lunch on the first day, the new colleague will be told how we intend to 'play them in' to their work, by being introduced to each phase of the work in turn, and should any formal training sessions be needed, the programme for such training will be discussed and agreed.

Progress meetings: During the first month of employment, the superior will have a short weekly meeting with the new colleague to 'touch base' with them, review their progress, and assess any additional training needed.

Review meeting: After ten weeks of employment, a thorough review meeting will be held for the new colleague to assess whether or not they wish to continue with our company, and for the superior to review whether or not we feel that he or she will be able to make a worthwhile contribution to our company's success. If necessary, a more senior director, if not the Managing Director, will join this review meeting so that in both the interests of the colleague concerned, and our company, the correct decision can be made.

Appraisal

Company procedures: A report setting out the procedures we adopt in carrying out appraisal interviews will be given to every colleague, and be kept by them in their personal 'Commitment' binder.

Training: Prior to the first appraisal interview, this appraisal procedure will be explained thoroughly to every new colleague.

We have already devoted a number of colleagues' monthly meetings to the question of appraisal. Where appropriate, some of the training questionnaires and other aids we have used in these earlier training sessions will be explained to a new colleague also.

Promotion

Self-development: No company can stand still; it has to get better in quality and quantity. So, growth is inevitable and will give you the opportunity for self-development and enhance your contribution to our success. You will certainly grow in stature and you may become eligible for promotion to a more demanding and challenging position.

A really thorough appraisal interview will then take place between you and your immediate superior where your competence and confidence to handle every aspect of the job will be discussed thoroughly.

At the end of this meeting, you will be joined by an appropriate senior director so that both you, and your immediate superior, can test the conclusions you have jointly reached with the director concerned.

It is very important that great care is taken over any promotion, and we will be particularly interested in discussing with you (when your time comes to be considered for promotion) the extent to which you need further training.

Management review: Any recommendations for promotion will be considered thoroughly at the weekly meeting of the senior management team, and be confirmed or otherwise by the monthly meeting of directors.

Trial period: Any promotion will be for an initial trial period of six months. An appraisal of performance will be held after the first two months, and a further appraisal meeting will be held after the first five months.

Where deemed appropriate, these post-promotion appraisals will be reviewed by a more senior director.

Demotion

Relinquishing position: Your superior and your directors will be keen to provide coaching and counselling to ensure that you can handle your promotion effectively and successfully.

It would be unfair to you, your team, and to our company, to allow you to retain a position if, in the event, you found that you lacked either the confidence or the competence to handle the work effectively on our behalf.

In this event, you would be expected to voluntarily relinquish your appointment until such time as you had gained the further experience and training needed to be considered for any vacancy.

Dismissal

Letting down the team: No cricket team can afford to include a player whose consistent failures in batting, bowling or fielding lose the team its matches. Similarly, our team cannot continue to employ someone who consistently lets down their colleagues and thus hinders our company's growth.

Attitude: We regard a positive, constructive attitude as the most important quality, since if you have this attitude, we can help you by coaching, counselling and training. But in our judgement, should you develop the wrong attitude and be unwilling to respond to the efforts we will undoubtedly make to help you adopt the right attitudes, we would be unable to allow you to continue to be a member of our team.

Competence: However, no matter how good your attitude may be, we, like any other teams, would not be able to continue your employment if you were consistently unable to achieve your personal key tasks.

We would do our best to help you find alternative employment more suited to your own talents and circumstances.

Developing our organisation

Strategic objectives: It is the responsibility of the Board of Directors, aided by everyone, to evolve the strategic objectives of our company and to set out, in writing, realistic marketing and business plans.

Every colleague will attend a company meeting at which our strategic objectives will be debated. You can be sure that you will understand what we are trying to do, and therefore how you need to contribute to our success.

Key tasks: Once the strategic objectives have been agreed and explained, the key tasks, or key contributions expected from you and each of your colleagues will be redefined in consultation with you.

Key performance indicators: We will not be able to assess whether or not we are achieving our objectives unless we measure our progress regularly. It is possible to measure our selling effort both weekly and monthly, and to produce accurate monthly management accounts.

You, in common with all your other colleagues, will receive any management information you need to assess your progress towards achieving your key results.

If you are, or become a member of our senior management team, the weekly and monthly sales information will be discussed at the weekly management meeting.

If you become a director, you will be involved in a thorough discussion of our monthly management accounts.

In short, you may be assured that if you need any information to help you to be more effective to measure your contribution, we will provide it, in addition to providing you with the general background as to the progress arising from our monthly management accounts.

Job improvement plan: Your four-monthly appraisal interview will, as explained, be based on a discussion on how successfully you have achieved your key results in the previous period, and how you intend to achieve your revised key results in the next period. The results of this discussion will be communicated to you in writing.

Where appropriate, you and your immediate superior may decide that you need a formal 'job improvement plan'. This sets out the:

- key tasks to be achieved;
- next review date;
- appropriate 'key performance indicators' which will help you to see whether or not you are achieving the improvement needed;
- ideas, agreed by you with your superior, as to how best you might achieve the improvement on which you have both agreed.

Company development: We hold a monthly meeting involving every colleague of our company. You and your colleagues are free to put forward any topics to be discussed, or training to be undertaken at these monthly meetings.

We accept responsibility for ensuring that these meetings are worthwhile and that you, in common with your colleagues, have the responsibility of contributing to the success of these meetings by joining in wholeheartedly, taking part in any team exercises, and participating in the open discussion session.

From time to time you, as an individual or in partnership with your departmental colleagues, may be asked to give a presentation to the meeting on some aspect of the work you do, and the systems or equipment you use to achieve your objectives.

Self development: As indicated, the purpose of your regular appraisal meeting is to help draw up any programme of support or training you need to be more effective in developing yourself, and thus enhancing your contribution to the company.

Achieving success: We can only be successful if every member of our team understands all our objectives – particularly our marketing objectives —and the strategies by which they will be achieved; given all the changes taking place in our industry. You will be involved fully in discussions on the way we wish to position ourselves, our strategies and business plans. This will enable you to both understand and play your part in achieving our objectives.

You, in partnership with all your other colleagues, will be expected to participate in discussions on these issues at our monthly meetings.

Redesign of organisation: Revising and refining our strategies may mean that we then have to redesign our organisation, so the growth of our company is a constant process of:

- striving to set realistic strategic objectives;
- defining the organisation we need to achieve these objectives;
- building the organisation on which we have decided; and
- developing our organisation so that, by achieving our original objectives, we have a platform for growing and expanding our company to better serve its customers, and to provide better opportunities for you and all our colleagues.

In a nutshell: We can only succeed if you and every other member of the team is fully committed. You can be sure we will do everything we can to help you succeed.

REFERENCES

1. Stayer, Ralph (1990) 'How I let my workers lead', *Harvard Business Review*, Nov.
2. Harvey Jones, Sir John (1988, Collins, 1989, Fontana Paperback, 1994, Harper Collins), *Making it Happen*.
3. Kotter, John P (1990), *A Force for Change*, Freepress, New York.
4. Kotter, John P and Heskett, James (1992), *Corporate Culture & Performance*, Freepress, New York.
5. Champy, James and Hammer, Michael (1993), *Re-engineering the Corporation*, Nicholas Brearley Pub, London.
6. Barlett, Christopher and Ghoshal, Sumantra (1994, 1995), 'Changing the role of top management', *Harvard Business Review*.
7. Collins, James and Porras, Jerry, *Built to Last,* Century, London.
8. Warren, Bennis and Nanus, Burt (1985), *Leaders*, Harper Row, New York.
9. Thompson, Peter (1990), *Sharing the Success*, Harper Collins, London.
10. DTI (1994), *Winning*, DTI, London.
11. Womack, James, Jones, Daniel and Roos, Daniel (1990), *The Machine that Changed the World*, Maxwell Macmillan Int.
12. Sparkes (1995), *The Ethical Investor*, Fount.
13. Carling, Will and Heller, Robert (1995, Little Brown, 1996, Warner), *The Way to Win – Strategies for success in business and sport*.
14. Levitt, Theodore (1962), *Innovation In Marketing*, McGraw Hill, Maidenhead.
15. Carlzon, Jan (1987, 1995), *Moments of Truth*, Harper Row, New York.
16. Pascale, Richard (1991, 1996), *Managing on the Edge*, Penguin, London.
17. Pettigrew, Andrew and Whipp, Richard (1991), *Managing Change for Competitive Success*, Blackwell Publishers, Oxford.
18. Zaleznik, Abraham (1992), 'Learning leadership', *Harvard Business Review*.
19. Heller, Robert (1995), *The Naked Manager for the Nineties*, Little, Brown and Company, London.

20. Drucker, Peter (1954), *The Practice of Management*, Harper Row, New York.
21. Chandler, Alfred (1962), *Strategy and Structure*, The MIT Press, London.
22. Womack, James and Jones, Daniel (1994), 'From lean production to the lean enterprise', *Harvard Business Review*, Mar/Apr.
23. Garrett, Echo Montgomery (1994), 'Innovation and outsourcing = big success', *Management Review*, Sep.
24. Handy, Charles (1995), 'Trust in the virtual organisation', *Harvard Business Review*, May/Jun.
25. Hirschhorn, Larry and Gilmore, Tom (1992), 'New boundaries in the boundaryless company', *Harvard Business Review*, May/Jun.
26. Katzenbach, John and Smith, Douglas (1993), *The Wisdom of Teams*, Harvard Business Press.
27. Schumacher, E. F. (1973), *Small is Beautiful*, Blond & Briggs.
28. Jones, Daniel and Womack, James (1996), *Lean Thinking*, Simon & Schuster, London.
29. Wickens, Peter (1987), *The Road to Nissan*, Macmillan Press, Basingstoke.
30. Peale, Norman Vincent (1963), *The Power of Positive Thinking*, World's Work.
31. Buzan, Tony, *Mindmapping*, BBC, London.
32. De Bono, Edward, *Six Thinking Hats*, Penguin, London.
33. Case, John (1995), *Open Book Management*, Harper Business Books, London.
34. McGregor, Douglas (1960, 1995), *The Human Side of Enterprise*, McGraw Hill, Maidenhead.
35. Herzberg, Friederich (1966), *Work and the Nature of Man*, World Publishing.
36. Kennedy, Carol (1993), *Guide to the Management Gurus – Shortcuts to the ideas of leading management thinkers*, Century Business, London.
37. Tichy, Noel and Sherman (1995, 1996), *Control Your Destiny or Someone Else Will*, Harper Collins, London.
38. Schaeffer, Robert (1991), 'Demand better results and get them', *Harvard Business Review*, Mar/Apr.
39. Hamper, Arthur (1992), *Rivethead – Tales from the assembly line*, Fourth Estate, London.
40. Locke, Edwin and Latham, Gary (1984), *Goal Setting, a Motivational Technique that Works*, Prentice Hall, London.
41. Hamel, G and Prahalad, C. K. (1989), 'Strategic intent', *Harvard Business Review*.
42. Johnson, Gerry (1992), 'Managing strategic change – strategy culture and action', *Long Range Planning*, Vol 25, No.1, Elsevier Science Ltd.

INDEX